BAYOCEAN

Bayocean and vicinity today. Map data ©2023 Google. *Bayocean* and *Bayocean Road* added by the author.

Bayocean

Atlantis of Oregon

JERRY SUTHERLAND

Beaver State Press Portland, Oregon

Cover: Photo looking south at Bayocean Natatorium ruins taken by the Army Corps of Engineers in 1939. Image 4189, SB Box 13, RG77, National Archives and Records Administration, College Park, MD.

Library of Congress Control Number: 2023930441

Publisher's Cataloging-in-Publication
(Provided by Cassidy Cataloguing Services, Inc.).

Names: Sutherland, Jerry, author.
Title: Bayocean : Atlantis of Oregon / Jerry Sutherland.
Description: Portland, Oregon : Beaver State Press, [2023] | Includes bibliographical references and index.
Identifiers: ISBN: 979-8-9873463-0-3 (paperback) | LCCN: 2023930441
Subjects: LCSH: Bayocean (Or.)--History. | Seaside resorts--Oregon--Bayocean--History--20th century. | Beach erosion--Oregon--Bayocean--History--20th century. | Coast changes--Oregon-- History--20th century. | Tillamook County (Or.)--History--20th century. | Oregon--History--20th century. | Historical geography. | LCGFT: Local histories. | BISAC: HISTORY / United States / State & Local / Pacific Northwest (OR, WA) | HISTORY / Historical Geography.
Classification: LCC: F882.T5 S88 2023 | DDC: 979.544--dc23

First published in 2023 by Beaver State Press
Printed in the United States

Dedicated to my parents,
Art (1931-2020) and Vi Sutherland.

Aerial photo of Bayocean taken by the Army Corps of Engineers in 1939. Image O-382, RH-Box 170, RG 77, National Archives and Records Administration (NARA), College Park, MD.

CONTENTS

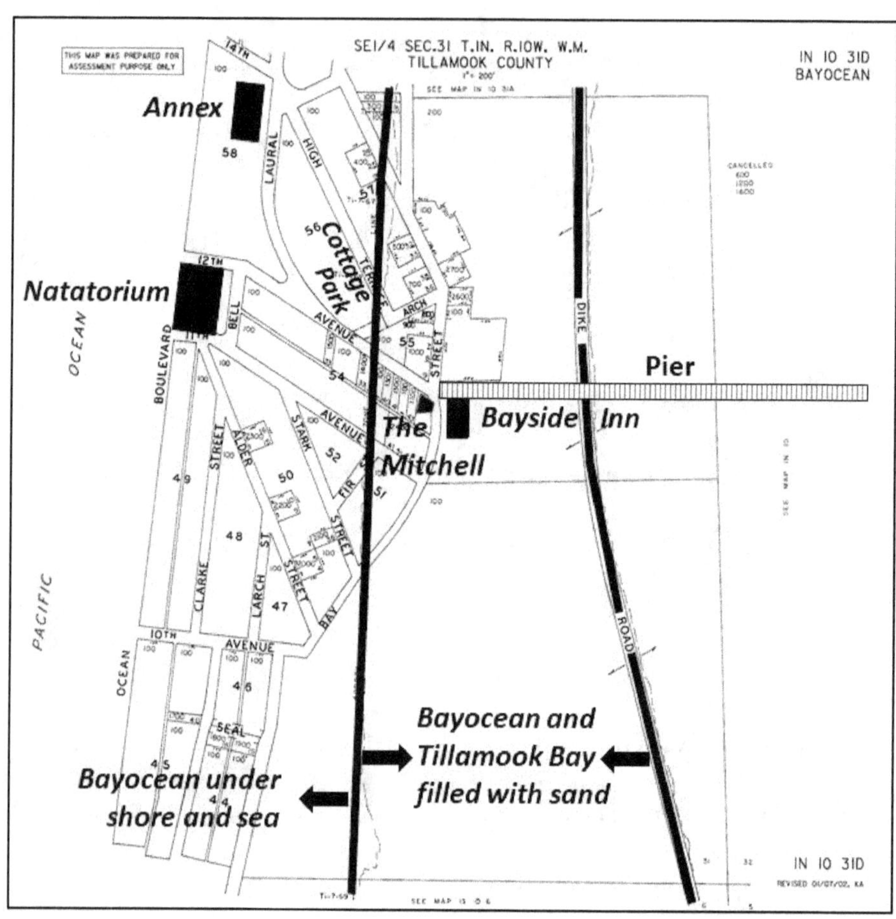

Tillamook County Assessor map 1N 10 31D, with Bayocean boundaries (high water on the ocean side; breakwater on the bay side) emboldened and resort structures no longer extant added by the author. See more at https://www.bayocean.net/2015/02/bayocean- then-and-now.html.

INTRODUCTION

Why the Bayocean Story Matters

On Sunday, December 14, 1941, Betty Coats woke to high winds and rain battering her home, which was perched a hundred feet above Bayocean's shoreline. She had designed it to withstand such forces, and it had done so for nearly a decade, so Betty was not concerned—until she noticed her backyard missing and waves crashing directly below her feet.[1]

The $10,000 ($218,000 in 2022) Betty and her husband Bill had spent on their Fo'c'sle went farther than most because he managed A. F. Coats Lumber Mill in Tillamook, Oregon. The town was on the east side of the bay protected by the four-mile-long sandspit upon which Bayocean had been built a couple of decades earlier. When it was finished in May 1932, the *Oregonian* deemed the "New England-style home…one of the most attractive on the Tillamook coast." The Tillamook County Assessor

Bird's-eye sketch of Bill and Betty Coats's Fo'c'sle, as viewed from the northeast, looking southwest towards Cape Meares. *Oregonian*, May 22, 1932, sec. 2, 2.

confirmed that by appraising it at three times the value of any other home in Bayocean Park in 1933. None finer would ever be built.[2]

Dorthea (Hahn) Mills, who served as the Coatses' live-in domestic between July 1936 and July 1937, later recalled the Fo'c'sle having a full basement with four bedrooms and a bath. On the main floor, a master suite took up the entire south wing and a garage the north wing, with the main living area spanning the distance between them. Windows and a deck spanned its west side, creating a magnificent view that Dorthea loved. "Through a large telescope mounted on the deck I watched whales, seals, and an occasional sea lion. Every hour of the day brought changes—the phosphorescent glow of the waves on a clear moonlit night, the seagoing vessels on the horizon."[3]

When the Coatses began building their Fo'c'sle in 1931, the dune's edge was 120 feet away. By the time Dorthea left six years later, erosion had cut the distance in half. They and other locals blamed the erosion on a jetty built by the Army Corps of Engineers on the north side of the inlet to Tillamook Bay, but the Corps insisted it was natural. The pace of erosion was sporadic, with no dune lost during milder winters and large chunks coming off like ice from the end of a glacier during stormy ones. Quiet summers in between stretches of mild winters allowed Bill and Betty to hope the Corps was right and that the problem was just temporary.[4]

On Sunday morning, December 14, 1941, those hopes were dashed. The Coatses roused their two young daughters and called their church to ask for help salvaging what they could before it fell to the shore. Seventeen parishioners spent most of the day packing personal belongings, moving furniture, and removing doors and windows. Trucks hauled everything down crumbling concrete streets to the center of the thirty-year-old resort town where Francis and Ida Mitchell stored it temporarily in their shuttered mercantile. On Monday and Tuesday, neighbor Swan Hawkinson ripped out fixtures, plumbing pipes, and exposed timbers until he returned from a lunch break to find all but the east end of the master suite lying on the beach. The rest fell the next day. Beachcombers scavenged Fo'c'sle remains for a few days until waves swept them away.[5]

Betty and Bill Coats were not the first or last to lose a cherished Bayocean home, for none of the fifty-nine dwellings built on the spit remain.[6] Nor do any of the facilities resort guests once enjoyed. A huge natatorium, three hotels, forty-two bungalows, a two-story mercantile, two restaurants, three dance halls, and an amusement pavilion have all disappeared.

If the resort town of Bayocean still graced Tillamook Spit, its history would be more interesting than most. Tillamook Indians lived, hunted, and gathered bounty on the spit and its shores long before European sailors first engaged them in the late seventeenth century. By the time Americans homesteaded it two hundred years later, Tillamook lodges lay rotting, their inhabitants having died from diseases brought by sailors.[7]

In 1907, Bayocean Park was promoted as the grandest resort on the Pacific Northwest Coast. One of the first steps towards that end involved a massive earthmoving operation, using sand dredged for a harbor to expand the east side of the spit into Tillamook Bay. A quarter-mile-long pier running along the south edge of the harbor served ocean-going ships that delivered construction equipment and materials. Tillamook bustled with Bayocean Park activity and excitement over the economic growth anticipated. Rail lines running to Tillamook enabled lot owners and resort guests to travel there from across the United States.

Unfortunately, economic downturns, its remote location, and litigation slowed construction, resulting in a resort less grand than promise and struggles to survive financially. Two men went insane watching their Bayocean dream die. Students from Portland's Reed College tried to make a go of it one summer, as did the Bayocean Military Academy another. Neither succeeded nor returned, and the resort continued to deteriorate. During the Great Depression, a commune livened things up for a couple of years before leaving.

World War II brought some degree of prosperity as working-class families moved to Bayocean and converted the once exclusive resort into a community. War dogs patrolled the shoreline, and machine gun practice by their Coast Guard handlers provided some excitement. Boys put fresh sand exposed by slides to use by sliding down them on cardboard. All that ended in November 1952, when a storm surge blew out the entire south end of the spit. In 1956, the Army Corps of Engineers destroyed all but three of the resort's remaining buildings in the process of reconnecting Bayocean Island to the mainland and raising minimum elevations to prevent the same calamity from recurring.

As interesting as Bayocean's history would be otherwise, the fact that nothing remains is why telling it matters—now more than ever, while some of its last residents are still alive. Unlike others with fond memories of their hometown, those who lived in Bayocean were not able to return to buy picnic supplies at The Mitchell, chat with old neighbors, or meet the new inhabitants of their old homes. These folks deserve a more comprehensive explanation of what happened to their hometown than they have received in the past.[8] And everyone who lost a home on Bayocean deserves at least a footnote in history. Others can take what lessons they might from this chronicle of a resort town destroyed by the sea.

CHAPTER 1

A Grand Notion Set in Motion

(1906 – 1911)

Bayocean Park was first imagined by nineteen-year-old Thomas Irving Potter when he visited Tillamook during the summer of 1906. Six years later, Portland's business weekly, the *Spectator*, told his story with flair:

> T. Irving, [who] was boating in Tillamook Bay with his revolver in his lap, discovered a gold goose about a half mile away toward the peninsula which separates the bay from the ocean. He aimed, fired, and the report so astonished the bird that it fell on a high promontory. The pioneer resident of Tillamook, who was piloting the boat, insisted on getting the goose which had been felled by such masterly skill with a toy gun. The view from the spot where the goose fell determined the development of Bayocean.[1]

T. Benton Potter Develops a Midas Touch

By 1912, T. Irving had gained wealth and social standing among Portland's elite, but in 1900 he lived with his father, Thomas Benton, his mother, Mary Frances (Fannie), and two sisters in a Los Angeles boarding house. The family's situation improved when they moved to Portland the following year and T. Benton began selling real estate on the east side of the Willamette River, where housing had escalated in anticipation of the Lewis and Clark Exposition. He joined forces with Harkness Lucius Chapin, a civil engineer who had moved there from Duluth, Minnesota for the same reason with his wife Ina and children.[2]

Potter and Chapin developed a system of working with homesteaders to subdivide their land and sell lots, bringing quick profits with little capital or risk. The first four developments bore the name Arleta Park, in honor of T. Benton's youngest daughter, Arleta. A neighborhood in Southeast Portland grew up around one of them. T. Benton, the more gregarious of the two men, joined social organizations and hung out with men like railroad

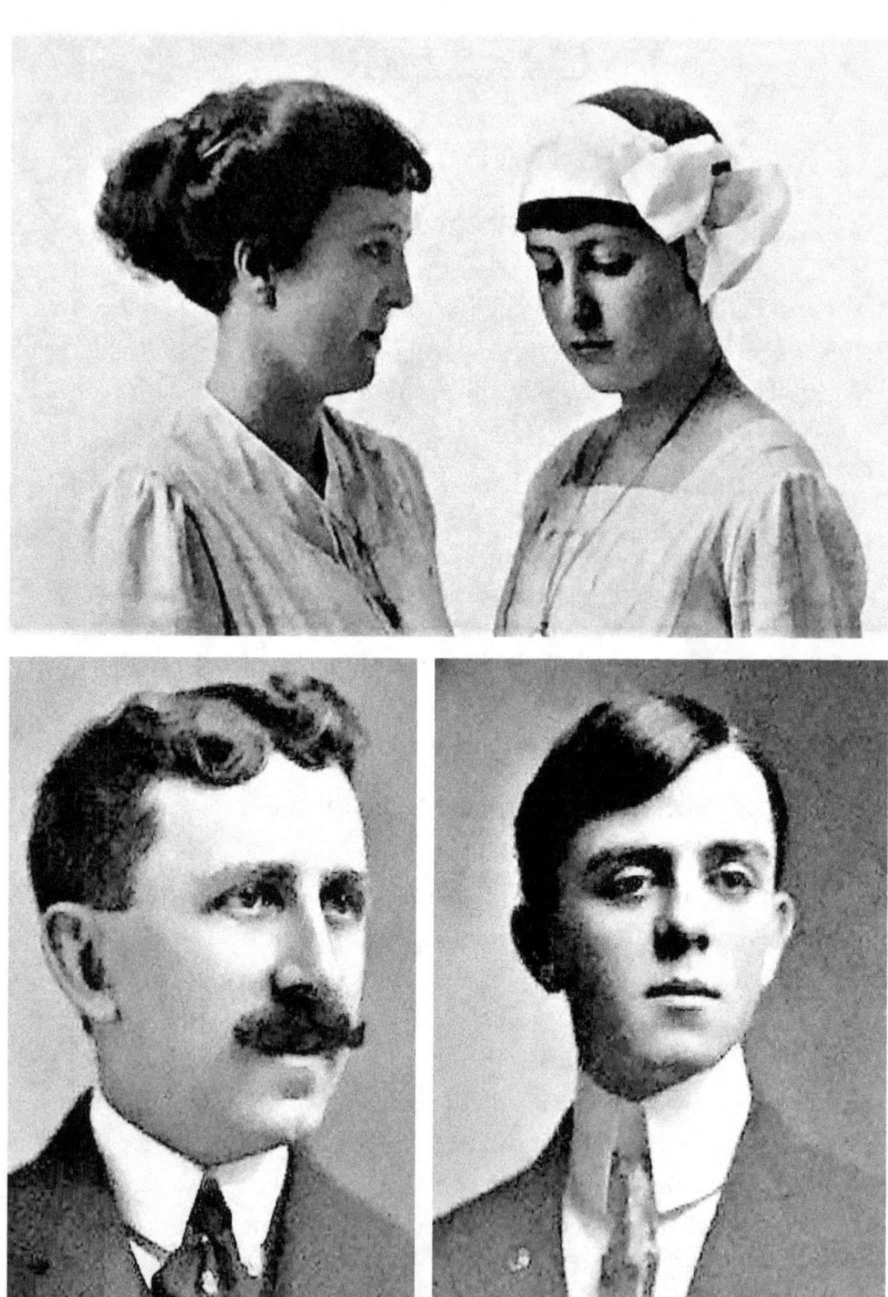

The Potters involved with Bayocean Park, clockwise from top left: Fannie, Arleta, T. Benton, and T. Irving. Potter Family Archives.

magnate E. E. (Elmer) Lytle, who would later play a critical role in developing Bayocean Park.[3]

Harkness Chapin. *Oregonian*, June 29, 1907, 10.

In February 1904, T. Benton left Harkness behind to develop Lester Park, Ina Park, Elberta Park, and Vernon in North Portland and moved his family back to the Bay Area to develop the Reis Tract in South San Francisco. Selling all 3,350 lots by the end of September pleased local partners so much that they decided to change their corporate name to T. B. Potter Realty Company.[4]

From 1905 through 1908, Potter developed the Rose Lawn subdivision in San Jose, California, another Arleta Park in Half Moon Bay, California, and Marlborough Heights in Kansas City.[5] His son T. Irving joined him at Half Moon Bay during the summer of 1906. Something about selling lots with a view of the ocean must have impressed the younger Thomas because, as reported to a Tillamook audience five years later,

> He studied the map for about two weeks for the purpose of satisfying himself which was the most suitable and logical location for a summer resort on the coast. He marked the peninsula on Tillamook Bay as the spot, after which he made a personal inspection along the coast for the purpose of making a selection, and as a result his company decided to purchase the peninsula on Tillamook Bay.[6]

The gold goose motif used by the *Spectator* a year later suggests that T. Irving believed that any project his father touched was bound to succeed, that he had the Midas touch. And who could blame him? T. Benton had risen from retail clerk to real estate magnate in just six years. All he needed was the right piece of ocean property to turn into gold.

Why Tillamook Spit? Because it was the beach closest to Portland, the largest metropolis north of San Francisco, and the only competition in the vicinity was a tourist hotel in Ocean Park (renamed Pacific City in 1909), twenty-one miles to the south at the mouth of the Nestucca River. The breathtaking view of bay and ocean T. Irving enjoyed while retrieving his gold goose from its ridgeline was aesthetic icing on a strategic cake. Prosperity brought by the Lewis and Clark Exposition had increased the percentage of Portland's 160,000 residents who could afford to vacation on the Oregon Coast—if they could get there. Today, it takes an hour and a half to drive from Portland to Tillamook on the Wilson River Highway (OR 6), but in 1907 only horses and wagons could navigate the toll road that preceded it. And downed trees and bridge washouts often precluded that. Ship passage risked seasickness, injury, and drowning on the treacherous Columbia River and Tillamook Bay bars. Both bad choices took at least two days.[7] Tillamook needed a railroad, which is where Elmer Lytle came into the picture.

In October 1905, Hillsboro residents had convinced Lytle that hauling timber cut from Tillamook County forests would generate more than enough profit to justify the cost of extending railroad lines from Hillsboro through the Coast Range and along the Pacific Coast. He established the Pacific Railway and Navigation Company (PRNC) that November and contractors were soon laying tracks, building bridges, and blasting tunnels. In September 1906, after T. Irving shot his gold goose, Elmer negotiated a deal with Tillamook leaders to speed things up. They granted him land for terminals and rights of way so men could start laying tracks from their end in return for his guarantee that Tillamook would have rail service by the end of 1908.[8]

That was just what the Potters needed to act. They quickly located Tillamook Spit homesteaders, only to find out partnering with them would not work. But by then, T. Benton had enough saved to pay cash. He offered them top dollar, which eliminated potential competition and haggling.

Homesteaders Paid Top Dollar

Webley and Mary Hauxhurst had been the first to claim land on the spit. In 1867, they paid an unnamed squatter to leave and then built a house on the north side of Cape Meares, where the view of the spit reminded Webley of his childhood home on Long Island, New York. He had left as a young man to seek adventure and ended up in Oregon Country, where he fell in love with Wat Tiet, daughter of Yamhill Chief Staywich. She changed her name when they both converted to Christianity and married in 1837. Twenty years later, wagon train pioneers from the South and Midwest pressured Webley to divorce Mary, leave his métis family behind, and start a white one. Instead, he found refuge in the lee of Cape Meares.[9]

Tillamook pioneers were no less racist than those in the Willamette Valley. However, they tolerated Indians and métis families living on the periphery of their settlements because Tillamook Indians had been critical to their survival upon first arriving in the 1850s. That gratitude did not stop them from taking the Tillamooks' land, and by the time the Hauxhursts showed up, most of them had been "influenced to move" (no treaty had been signed) to the Grande Ronde Reservation or the Salmon River encampment near Lincoln City. The few who stayed set up camps like "squaw town" just north of Hobsonville Point. They were left to themselves, "largely out of neglect by the Bureau of Indian Affairs and acceptance by local residents, who didn't demand their removal."[10]

In 1870, the Hauxhursts filed a claim for 156.8 acres, including land grazed by their cattle on the south end of Tillamook Spit. Mary received their land patent in 1877, because Webley had died three years earlier. Thirty years later, on March 18, 1907, T. Benton Potter paid her $5,000 for all but ten acres at the eastern edge of the homestead which she and Webley had given their son Joseph. The dollar being worth more than thirty times then as in 2022, it was a windfall for Mary. It passed on to her children after she died that November.[11]

The first to settle out on the spit were William Lattie and his wife Sarah, one of the Hauxhursts' daughters. In 1876, they built a cabin on the bay, just north of what was later known as Jackson Gap. A. B. (Absalom) Hallock bought it from them in August 1880, moved there that December, and filed a claim on 125.85 acres—everything between the Hauxhursts and the hills in the center of the spit.[12]

As one of Portland's first inhabitants, Absalom had made a name for himself surveying many of its earliest subdivisions and designing, engineering, or supervising the construction of sixty commercial, public, and residential buildings. He served as Portland's first official surveyor, the chief engineer of its fire department, a police commissioner, and a city council member. But in the 1870s, Hallock struggled to compete with younger, better-trained architects arriving. This led to an embarrassing foreclosure suit made public by the city's involvement.[13]

Like the Hauxhursts, but for different reasons, Absalom decided to start over in Tillamook, where his skills were in demand. The Tillamook County Board of Commissioners hired him to design and supervise the construction of its first courthouse and survey a new road to Nestucca. Hallock also served as a Justice of the Peace and Deputy US Marshall when the need arose. With the help of his son Edward—who would become Astoria's Chief of Police—Absalom built a wharf and hired neighbors to can fish, clams, and crabs for the retail market. Friends from Portland occasionally visited, as did the son of his informally adopted daughter, Annette (Buffomeir) Cotter. Absalom's ever-present keg of beer and readiness to hold a party when more than one person showed up made his cabin a popular destination for locals, especially Frank Elliott, the homesteader just north of him, and his son George.[14]

In June 1891, Hallock set up a post office in his cabin to serve "about 20 voters including light keepers." He named it Barnegat, after a famous lighthouse on the New Jersey Coast. When Absalom died in October 1892, Elizabeth Biggs (another Hauxhurst daughter) took over as postmaster. She and her husband John Albert Sr. (Bert) lived at Pitcher Point. Webley had named the point for a prominent rock shaped like a milk jug hanging out over the bay. After Elizabeth died in 1898, locals started calling it Biggs Point and the cove west of it, Biggs Cove. The name reverted to Pitcher Point after Bert died despite its namesake having been destroyed during the construction of Bayocean Road.[15]

Local settlers embraced Barnegat as the name of their growing community. They applied it to their census, voting, and school districts, and the *Tillamook Headlight* started running a regular community column. Barnegat earned the attention of Portland's metropolitan press in May 1899 when a north slope on Cape Meares began sliding into the sea. A civil engineer traveled there to survey the slide as well as the new location of residences and trail up to the Cape Meares Lighthouse.[16] Media attention drew summer vacationers who rented rooms from residents or camped on the spit, an apparent confirmation of the Potters' assumption that if they built a resort, people would come.

Edward Hallock died the December following T. Irving Potter's first visit to the spit in 1906, leaving no heirs to his father's homestead other than Annette Cotter. Then an unemployed widow, the $5,500 T. Benton offered her would have come in handy. She received a $500 down payment in Portland on March 4, 1907; the rest had to wait until Edward's estate settled.[17] Absalom Hallock's homestead would become the heart of Bayocean Park.

Scott and Elizabeth Bozorth signed a contract in Portland the same day as Annette Cotter for $12,500. $6,000 was for Frank Elliott's 145.52-acre homestead. $6,500 was for Bay City property directly across from Bayocean's pier where Potter and Chapin would build a pier to ferry resort guests from an adjacent railroad station. T. Benton gave the Bozorths half as much down as he did Cotter because George Elliott was suing them to reclaim the homestead he had inherited but lost through foreclosure on a loan. Elliott won an initial decision in Tillamook County Circuit Court two months later, but the Oregon Supreme Court reversed it in October 1908. Scott Bozorth testified he and his brother John bought the land because they, too, considered the spit an excellent resort location. But they were satisfied to let the Potters take all the risk, invest their quick profit in Bay City subdivisions, and use Bayocean Park publicity to sell lots near the train station.[18]

The last piece of the puzzle was the northeast corner of the spit, where the first recorded battle between an Oregon Indian tribe and white men occurred on August 16, 1788. Tillamook warriors had traded peacefully with Captain Robert Gray's sailors for a couple of days before his black servant Markus Lopeus lost his life while he and fellow sailors fought with them over his cutlass. This part of the spit was later named Kincheloe Point to honor Julius Kincheloe, who drowned while sounding the Tillamook Bar in 1867 to create the first hydrological chart of the bay. Olivia and Lee Alley got $4,500 for their 167.4 acres.[19] Why they or T. Benton thought it was worth anything is puzzling since, at the time, it was bare sand with a couple of hillocks and a few clumps of grass.

The only land on Tillamook Spit not for sale was 125.09 acres at its northwest corner. In 1901, the Army Corps of Engineers withdrew it from public entry "for use by the United States in constructing jetties at the entrance to Tillamook Bay." In 1886, local lumbermen had recommended jetties as a way to deepen the channel and allow larger ships to reach their mills. The Corps concluded that "small coasters, drawing from 7 to 10 feet and by lumber vessels drawing 12 and 13 feet" were sufficient to fill the need then, but it secured the land in case that changed.[20]

In just two weeks, T. Benton Potter had secured all 585.57 acres—467.80 on Tillamook Spit and 117.71 on the mainland below Cape Meares—that would become Bayocean Park. Including the Bay City property, he had spent $27,500, equivalent to $900,000 in 2022.

Designing and Selling a Grand Resort

After he was done writing checks, Potter headed to Kansas City. Since rails would soon enable people to reach Tillamook from anywhere in the United States, he needed to prepare salesmen there to sell wealthier prospects the idea of owning a summer cottage on the Pacific Coast—after selling them a Marlborough Heights lot, of course. Given that Potter had sales offices in five cities by then—San Francisco, San Jose, Half Moon Bay, Kansas City, and Portland—he would travel those rails more than most.[21]

Harkness Chapin had remained in Tillamook. Lytle's railroad was critical to getting Bayocean Park built because transporting people, machinery, and materials any other way would be prohibitively expensive. The Bay City pier needed to go up quickly so the railroad construction crew fast approaching could run a spur line onto it. That would make it easier for Bayocean Park guests and their luggage to transfer from the train station to bay launches. After laying out the pier, Harkness put George Jones (who had been selling lots in his Portland subdivisions) in charge of building it. Harkness then surveyed the spit and mainland to gather information needed to design the subdivision and lay out its water system. Chapin used one of the monuments placed during a government survey in 1857 as the Initial Point from which everything in the subdivision would be measured.[22]

When he returned to Portland, Harkness plotted 148 blocks and 4,031 lots on a subdivision plat map. Most lots were fifty by one hundred feet, the same as a standard city lot, but some were larger. Harkness labeled seventy-eight oddly shaped lots at angled intersections with the letter A instead of a number. He deemed them inferior, not to be sold, but many were. Meanwhile, T. Irving moved to Portland, set up the office, hired salesmen, and found an advertising agent. He found enough free time to date socialite Sarah Elizabeth (Bess) Kern, whom he married in September. On June 19th, after returning to Portland, T. Benton and Harkness incorporated the Potter-Chapin Realty Company (PCRC). They signed the Bayocean Park Deed of Dedication ten days later and mailed it to the Tillamook County Clerk. It would be T. Benton Potter's last subdivision and the first with nothing bearing Arleta's name.[23]

On June 29, 1907, the *Oregonian* introduced Bayocean Park to the world in a full-page article, with images of a resort beyond anything seen previously in the Pacific Northwest. Its success was guaranteed by "unlimited resources…If a million dollars is needed it is forthcoming." T. Benton was introduced as a successful California developer who had "enabled more people to make more money in suburban realty than any other individual in the United States." Harkness was referred to simply as a local realtor; but Elmer Lytle, being the best known of the three to Oregonians, received as many column inches as Potter. He said the only reason Tillamook Spit was not already a resort was lack of access and reiterated his promise to resolve that by the end of 1908. Bayocean Park was then sure to become a coastal destination "eclipsing all the resorts for tourist travel in Europe, excelling anything on the Atlantic Coast and outstripping the best on the Pacific shore."[24]

On July 28th, a full-page "Management Letter" announced the start of Bayocean Park lot sales the following day. It was the first installment of a four-year-long, $27,000 marketing blitz. Ads ran every week in the *Oregonian* and *Oregon Journal* through October 1907. Some were full-page, and most were illustrated. Photos of Tillamook Spit by Portland's top nature photographer, Fred Kiser, were featured in many of the dozen brochures readers could have delivered by mail or salesmen.[25]

The Grand Hotel Bayocean promised. *Oregonian*, October 4, 1909, 10.

Hotel Bayocean would be the main attraction. It would cost $250,000 and be ready for the 1908 season. Portland architect John Wrenn designed the six-story, 300-room structure to be the grandest north of the Hotel Del Monte in Monterey, California. It would sit in the middle of a six-acre site a hundred feet above the sea below where a bathhouse would serve guests. Full-time staff would live in a three-story, forty-seven-room annex. A tent city set up along the bay would enable others to experience a more primitive experience. The central pier would deliver boaters to the heart of the resort. Two others would access commercial zones to the north and south. A baseball diamond, amusement pavilion, roller skating rink, and golf links would assure everyone a fun time. Paved streets would accommodate automobile enthusiasts after Bayocean Road was built along the south side of the bay.[26]

The bay shore, just a 350-foot hike from the ocean in one spot, "slopes so gradually that the tide, when out, uncovers it for over half a mile. This sand, being warmed by the sun, in turn warms the water as the tide comes in, making it fifteen to twenty degrees warmer than the water on the ocean side." Other natural attractions—nearby if not on the spit—were bird watching, fishing, clamming, crabbing, canoeing, boating, hiking, rock climbing, and hunting. This combination of amusements and recreation was available nowhere else on the Pacific Coast. Those wishing to invest or build summer cottages could choose between $450 lots on the ridge or $60 lots in the dunes of Kincheloe Point, with assurances that "the lots you can now purchase for $60 will be worth $5,000."[27]

PCRC had to sell every lot on a contract until Edward Hallock's estate and George Elliott's lawsuit was settled, but salesmen would have produced a better-sounding reason. Most buyers chose to make payments even after cash became an option. The Tillamook County Clerk recorded Bayocean Park's first deed on April 8, 1908, just eight more that year, thirty-three in 1909, and forty-nine in 1910. T. Irving would have sold every lot on a contract if he could because the 6% interest charged doubled the lot price over the eight-year term. Salesmen felt the same because they could pitch buyers on owning one of the best lots for just $1.50 per week, with no down payment. No consumer laws required them to disclose total interest paid or the time it would take to receive a title. Nor would they have highlighted the clause saying PCRC could repossess a lot thirty days after a missed payment and keep the money invested.[28]

Despite the expensive marketing campaign, sales got off to a slow start. One reason was a reluctance to buy sight unseen. To resolve that, Harkness Chapin built a six-foot-long scale model so salesmen could invite prospects to "put your finger on the lot you want." Buyers must have also expressed doubt that PCRC could honor all its grand promises because the company ran an ad inviting readers to contact its banks in Kansas City, San Francisco, and Portland to confirm their success, reliability, and honesty. Another one offered $1,000 to "anyone proving that the descriptions by us are not correct." An ad one week later said that no one claiming the reward proved their honesty.[29]

The aggressive marketing worked, at least according to PCRC. On November 3, 1907, it announced having sold "practically 1,000" lots and reaching the milestone "faster than we thought possible—sanguine as we were." The company warned readers to buy soon because "we positively guarantee that values will advance $50 a lot the instant 1,400 lots are sold." Bayocean Park lots were not selling as fast as the Reis Tract, but if they continued selling fifteen lots per day, all 4,031 would be gone within a year.[30]

Panic of 1907 Hinders Progress

Unfortunately, the Panic of 1907—a global economic crisis that began with New York City trust companies—reached Oregon the second week of November, after which it became "almost impossible to sell said lots and collect the installments due on the lots already sold." Then Elmer Lytle's short-term financing gave out, forcing him to halt construction.[31]

PCRC responded by suspending advertising and sending salesmen out to pitch lots door-to-door, including one who solicited teachers in the halls of Chemawa (an Indian boarding school in Salem) between classes. In February 1908, the company moved into the Couch Building and raised lot prices—earlier and more than projected—by $75 to $150. After the crisis had passed that October, net lot sales had grown to 1,500. So, it appeared Bayocean Park had weathered the storm. But the increase had come entirely from Christian Lauritzen's efforts in the Inland Empire—his Willamette Valley cohorts had just barely kept pace with foreclosures.[32]

Lauritzen had arrived in Spokane, Washington at the end of January 1908 and sold thirty-seven lots in the first three days. His pitch was, "People living in Spokane and Butte will no longer spend four days going to Long Beach [California] when there is a better one within 18 hours ride." Two months later, Lauritzen led three "prominent citizens and Spokane boosters representing one hundred lot owners" to Tillamook. Their enthusiastic report sold more lots, as did the stereopticon Christian used to project the grandeur of Bayocean Park on theater screens. That summer, he branched out to Anaconda and Helena in Montana and Pendleton in Oregon, riding the rails as much as T. Benton.[33]

In August 1908, Elmer Lytle secured new financing and put contractors back to work; but the ten-month delay meant he would not get trains to Tillamook by the end of that year. He could not have done so anyway. The Pacific Coast Range presented more significant challenges to laying rails than the Willamette Valley. Old-growth forests were harder to cut paths through, tunnels had to be dynamited through mountains, and expansive trestles were required for steep gorges and estuarial wetlands along the coast. Winter storms destroyed completed work, and men unhappy with the wages and working in miserable conditions frequently walked off the job.[34]

In any case, PCRC returned to aggressive advertising once Lytle's railroad was under construction again. To reassure potential lot buyers of rail service if Lytle failed, a brochure published ahead of the 1909 resort season included a map showing three other railroads progressing towards Tillamook. Oregon Electric's route followed the Wilson River to Tillamook, then around the south end of the bay to the southern pier at the foot of Cockle Street. United's line took a southern route. Northern Pacific planned an extension south from Seaside, where its line from Astoria ended.[35]

On May 30, 1909, an ad listing every buyer and their lots invited acquaintances to ask them about Bayocean Park. It touted the collective value of $742,840 rather than the number of lots sold, probably because it had decreased by 492 to 1,108. The most expensive lots at the time were $600, so the $670.34 average meant salesmen were reselling foreclosed lots at higher prices, but PCRC was losing ground.[36]

Competition explains why more Bayocean lots were being foreclosed than sold, the best example being Gearhart Park, which opened in May 1909. Just forty miles north of Bayocean Park, it featured a charming hotel and lots selling for $125, also with easy payment terms. A rail line from Portland, which had just been extended from Astoria to Seaside, ran past it. Bayocean Park promised to be more spectacular, but nothing had been finished. To make things worse, in October 1909, George Higgins started selling lots in a small subdivision upslope, along the south edge of

Bayocean Park called Oceanview for $40 to $150. He promoted it as "the better Bay-Ocean resort on Tillamook Bay."[37]

Potter and Chapin responded by making even grander promises. They would spend another $100,000 on the Hotel Bayocean. Thirteen rooms would be added to its annex to house more staff. A six-acre park would be added to the hotel grounds, doubling its size. A large natatorium on the beach would feature a fifty-by-one-hundred-foot pool filled with warm seawater, a grandstand, and three hundred dressing rooms. Natatoriums were already operating inland, but this would be the first along the Oregon Coast.[38]

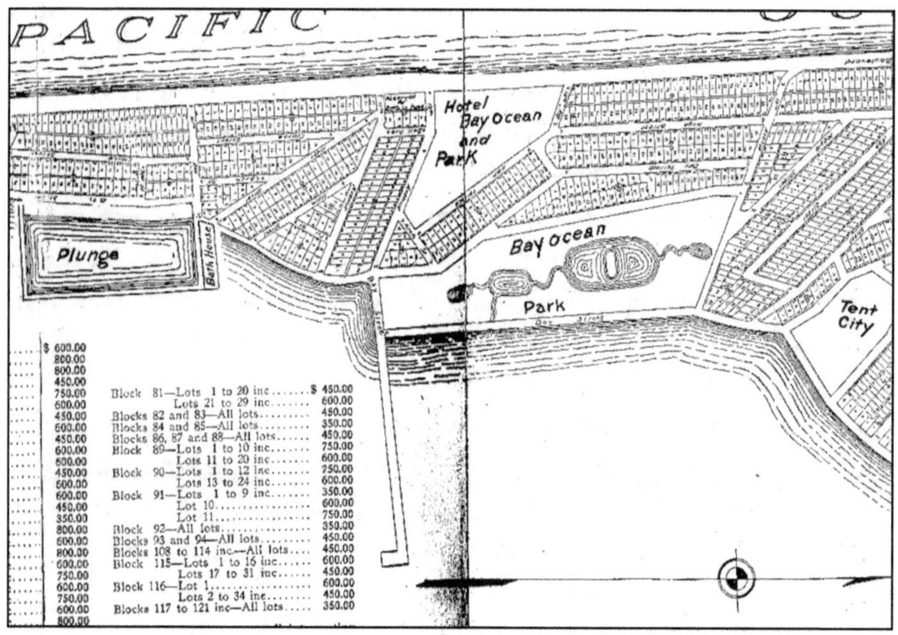

The plunge, bathhouse, worker's camp (first Tent City), expanded hotel grounds, and Coney Island-style amusement park proposed, cropped from *Views of Bayocean at Tillamook Bay* (PCRC, 1909). Author's collection.

Upgrades to the bayside recreation park were more spectacular. Twenty-three acres would become "a regular Coney Island," with a theater, restaurant, amusement halls, and three artificial lakes. The largest lake would include an island with a bandstand and a one-hundred-foot "shoot the chutes" twice the height of the one in Portland's Oaks Amusement

Park. A fountain in the smallest lake would deliver water to the others and fill the channel connecting them. Seals and other aquatic species would inhabit the middle lake.[39]

In addition to paid advertising, PCRC entered a float in Portland's 1909 Rose Festival. Festival organizers acclaimed it "one of the most beautiful in the entire parade... [It was] the first time...the beaches of Oregon, now recognized as one of the state's most valuable assets, have been represented in any of the parades." The *Tillamook Herald* credited the Bayocean Park float with raising resort business expectations for the upcoming summer to the extent that three stages would operate on the Wilson River Road. It also informed Portlanders that they could book a two-day passage on one of two steamers or ride one of "six stages from North Yamhill, Forest Grove or Sheridan, most with overnight stays en route."[40]

Another public relations tactic was the sponsorship of trips by the Portland Automobile Club, of which T. Irving was a member. They drove to Tillamook for the first time a month after sales started in 1907, heading southwest from Portland to McMinnville, west across the Cascade Range to Grand Ronde, and northwest through Dolph to Tillamook. In 1908, they stayed home, but in 1909, Portland insurance man W. J. (William) Clemens led three trips, giving the metropolitan newspapers updates before, during, and after each. News that seventy-five autoists on the Fourth of July trip stayed in Tillamook for a week because of rain and that several got stuck on the way home was not the kind of publicity PCRC was after. Clemens was a member of the Oregon House of Representatives, so he lobbied county and state officials to deal with the muck and misery of driving to Tillamook.[41]

A variety of creative ads ran during the summer and fall of 1909. One suggested people buy two lots and sell one after prices doubled so that they would have paid nothing for the one kept. Another had mothers testifying that Bayocean Park was the best possible place for families to escape the summer heat. Despite the aggressive marketing and creative public relations events, all geared to Willamette Valley prospects, Christian Lauritzen continued outperforming his cohorts.[42]

Tillamook Bustles with Bayocean Construction Activity

William Clemens's lobbying for better roads did no good, for the same reason PCRC did no marketing in Tillamook: less than a thousand people lived there, and farmers, loggers, and dairymen had neither the money nor the time to lounge on the beach during the summer.

Despite its sparse population, Tillamook boasted two weekly newspapers—the *Headlight* and the *Herald*. Both promoted Bayocean Park despite receiving no ad revenue because its construction and patronage would put their town on the map, bring economic growth, increase newspaper subscriptions, and prompt advertising by those riding on Bayocean Park's coattails. Elmer Allen, whose parents owned the Allen House, later recalled Tillamook bustling and the hotel rarely having a vacancy during the resort's construction. He described Harkness Chapin as "a kindly man who made the Allen House his home whenever his business called him to town." Harkness sold Elmer's mother, Nellie, two lots near Hauxhurst's dock during one stay.[43]

The first men working on the spit lived in tents, some with their families, along the bay. As their number increased, it made no sense for a lighthouse keeper to be postmaster, as had been the case since 1900. So, George Jones's wife Mary took on the role in September 1907 and continued serving when the Postal Service changed the name of her post office tent from Barnegat to Bayocean on February 24, 1909.[44]

When the Panic of 1907 hit in November 1907, PCRC crews were busy clearing the Hotel Bayocean site, grading streets, and setting posts for the central pier. T. Benton Potter was so pleased with their progress that he assured *Oregonian* readers "no tightening of the money market, temporary as it may be, will affect their work or the original plans." The telegram he sent from Kansas City spun the financial downturn as an opportunity to hire more men at lower wages when others laid them off.[45] That was before Potter learned Elmer Lytle was one of the others.

Portland newspapers said nothing when all but one of the PCRC crews went home. Bayocean Park had no direct impact on the metropolitan area, so embarrassing T. Benton would have risked future ad revenue for no reason. Tillamook newspapers were in the opposite position. Still, the

Herald handled the news delicately when it let readers know, "the company is not working in large force at present as they are keeping tabs on the railroad and will rush things next spring as soon as the weather settles" in October 1908.[46]

In fact, the only men working for George Jones in April 1908 were Barnegat homesteaders Joseph Hauxhurst, Bert Biggs, and Sam Grabel. They were building the central pier, which had to be ready for boats carrying equipment and materials when the fiscal crisis passed. The pier began three hundred feet east of the resort's main intersection at 12th Avenue and Bay Street. A wide boardwalk would span the gap between them. Pilings raised the deck to match the ocean-going ships that would arrive after a channel was dug from the bay inlet. Until then, shallow draft launches would bring materials across from Bay City. The pier was 1,400 feet long to get past the tide flats at high tide. The problem with the preliminary arrangement became apparent when 7,700 board feet of pilings were lost after a tow rope snapped during a fast, outgoing tide.[47]

After the pier was finished, the crew drove pilings 250 to 600 feet from the spit's eastern high-water line along three of its four miles. Boards nailed to the posts created bulkheads behind which a dredge would pump a million cubic yards of sand seven feet deep. The purchase of tideland rights made this 119-acre land expansion possible. It also covered up the sun-warmed sands Potter and Chapin touted in their ads. Bertha (Weaver) Morgan, whose family had arrived early that summer, explained why in a memoir written decades later: it was actually "quicksand, not fit to walk on [that they] needed to make safe."[48]

In the fall of 1908, ten-year-old Bertha—who had no playmates her age on the spit—looked forward to hiking a mile and a half each day to attend classes with nine Hauxhurst children and two from the lighthouse in the one-room Barnegat School built on federal land at the base of Cape Meares in April 1894. Their favorite recess activity was swinging over the ocean on a rope hung from a tree limb twenty feet above the rocky shore—until workmen sawed it off to prevent a disaster. The children then spent their time watching the Grabel house slide down the slope just north of the schoolhouse.

When it landed upright on the beach, they explored the ruins until waves swept them away.[49]

After the recession ended and more workers started arriving at the end of 1908, George Jones got them back to clearing the hotel grounds and grading streets. Others started framing PCRC's two-story Administration Building at the southeast corner of 12th Avenue and Bay Street. During the winter, it "blew down in a violent storm that whipped through the gap one day killing one man and sending several others to a doctor, a big wave and wind just simply took out the whole structure in one whish," recalled Bertha (Weaver) Morgan.[50] This is the only record of any Bayocean Park construction casualties. It is also the earliest mention of waves rushing down 11th Avenue, later known as Natatorium Gap. No newspaper mentioned either event, so they were lost to history until now.

In November 1908, construction of the dredge *Tillamook Bayocean* began on the east side of Tillamook Bay. Harkness Chapin was there to place it in service on August 2, 1909. His family had joined him on the spit that summer, making it easier to keep an eye on construction activity as it ramped up. Whatever Harkness saw led him to replace George Jones with M. J. (Jim) O'Donnell as superintendent.[51]

O'Donnell's first assignment for the dredge crew was excavating a 3,000,000-square-foot harbor from the tide flats north of the pier. They pumped the dredged sediment behind the bulkheads built earlier to fill the twenty-three acres where Bayocean's Coney Island would rise. Next, they dug a channel 12 feet deep, 100 feet wide, and 4,300 feet long out to Sturgeon Channel, which was deep enough for ships to sail down from the bay inlet. That material filled a twelve-acre alcove in the hilly section north of the harbor, where an organized camp was set up for workers. By the time Bertha's family left in the summer of 1910, it included a company store, post office, "two or three bunkhouses, the superintendent's house, and tents for the married couples." Her mother supervised "two dishwashers, a baker, two cooks, and a fry cook, two helpers, and one man to peel, and one to scrub and clean, five or six girls to wait tables."[52]

On August 14, 1909, a schooner cruised into Tillamook Bay loaded with equipment needed for Bayocean Park. A "dinky locomotive" and thirty-seven dump cars sat on the forward deck. The large, oil-fired boiler next to the locomotive would provide electricity to run the rock crusher that crews were building at the foot of 7th Avenue. Also on board were the components of a machine shop and a blacksmith shop. In September 1909, PCRC reported forty men operating $100,000 in equipment.[53] The problem was that getting all the equipment and materials to Bay City by sea had cost more than they had budgeted to ship it by rail. Hotel Bayocean would require more of the same, and Lytle's railroad was nowhere near completion. So, PCRC put the hotel on hold and repurposed its annex to serve guests.[54]

Guests socializing on bay infill in front of the worker's camp. Bayocean Image 352, TCPM.

The dinky engine had three miles of narrow-gauge rails light enough for workers to move them wherever things needed hauling. Its first target was the hotel grounds, where a crew was setting forms to pour concrete for the first floor of the Bayocean Annex. They had cut a 110-foot-high knoll level with its 100-foot-high surroundings. Another team ran three miles of water pipe from a reservoir on the north side of Cape Meares down the spit and back up to the hotel site for mixing concrete.[55]

Figuring out the volume of water Bayocean Park would require had been a challenge. Harkness Chapin filed five water rights appropriations with the Tillamook County Clerk between May 7, 1907, and February 3, 1909, all involving Coleman Creek. Water flow rates varied from 240 to 1,000 cubic feet per minute (the latter would have required fourteen-inch diameter pipes). Fearing that one creek could not provide that much, Harkness added an extension to another creek higher on Cape Meares that ran west into the ocean. When a landslide moved Coleman Creek 250 feet eastward early in 1909, Harkness relocated both reservoirs and rerouted the pipes.[56]

T. Benton Takes Charge Before Going Insane

In January 1910, T. Benton moved his family back to Portland and took control of Bayocean Park construction. He had more time on his hands after muddying waters—literally—in the Reis Tract.

Potter had set up a water company in 1904 to serve the Reis Tract's two thousand residents. It lost money every year and city regulations prohibited a rate increase. So, he created a new water company at the end of 1907, transferred all the previous company's facilities to it, and doubled the rates. When homeowners refused to pay, he emptied the reservoir, forcing everyone to haul drinking water from a couple of private wells and leaving them with no fire protection. The *San Francisco Call* took T. Benton to task regularly during the next couple of years.[57]

In May 1908, two hundred Reis Tract residents filed suit, claiming salesmen had promised them free water. T. Benton's attorneys argued the contracts promised the water delivery system would be free, not the water flowing through it. That was enough for the judge to dismiss the case, so the homeowners paid but then pleaded with San Francisco officials to bring them into its municipal water system. The city relented in November 1909 and offered Potter $30,000. He accepted $20,000 after a city inspector found bacteria in the system.[58]

The *Oregonian* welcomed Potter back with open arms. Rather than ignore the water fiasco, he proactively portrayed San Francisco as the villain and himself as the savior of Reis Tract residents. Had a reporter checked with a San Francisco counterpart and published an accurate accounting of the affair, Bayocean Park might have come to a premature end. But so would have PCRC's future ad revenue and the *Oregonian* editor's chance to brag about a San Francisco developer returning to Portland because he found "the outlook for business here to be better than anywhere else on the Pacific Coast." And who was going to question the integrity of a man with the means to rent a prominent city mansion and staff it with three servants?[59]

T. Benton also told the *Oregonian* he had sent experienced staff from other projects to "rush the development of Bayocean." He came closer to blaming Harkness in a letter to a lot owner: "The progress made was not as great as I had expected, considering the amount of money expended." Potter told no one that on January 1st, he had bought Chapin out with a $107,000 contract and sent engineer E. C. (Edwin) Lockwood to replace him at the spit. On February 16th, T. Benton incorporated an Oregon version of the T. B. Potter Realty Company (TBPRC) and, after transferring all its assets, dissolved PCRC on May 17th.[60] Harkness left quietly and set up a new real estate business, but no Potters attended an open house he and Ina hosted at their new Irvington mansion in June.[61]

When T. Benton ousted Harkness, 922 lots remained available for sale. That meant 1,878 net lots had sold because they had reduced the number available from 4,031 to 2,800 in 1909. After conceding the dunes of Kincheloe Point would never sell, they vacated all streets north of 27th Avenue. They merged those 842 lots into one tract to lower property taxes, leaving 3,189 lots on the county assessment roll. A park added to the hotel grounds had taken up the north half of Block 56. Moving the tent city to the south half of that block removed thirty-one lots. They temporarily withdrew all the lots between 22nd and 27th Avenues and planted them with beach grass, hoping to sell them when demand picked up after the resort was operating. Unsold lots in that area and a few elsewhere removed for other reasons accounted for the remaining 358.[62]

By the summer of 1910, Potter was desperate to sell the remaining lots, so on June 26th, he announced an end to sales on July 15th and informed "the great many people who want to buy lots…the time to act is now" by way of an advertisement. T. Benton also announced the opening of Bayocean Park on July 1st and said he had recruited a manager from Atlantic City, an obvious response to ads proclaiming Pacific City the

"Atlantic City of the West." Too late, Potter realized metropolitan residents of the Pacific Northwest were not as familiar with Hotel Del Monte as were those in San Francisco. His tactics worked to the extent of pushing lots sold to "about 2,200 lots at the aggregate of over $1,000,000," but six hundred remained available when he shuttered the sales office.[63] Some of the salesmen laid off would cause problems for the company in the future.

On Saturday, July 2nd, 102 members of the Portland Automobile Club, family members, journalists, and a medical team left Portland with great fanfare. McMinnville leaders treated them to lunch. Tillamook leaders hosted a banquet that evening before giving the group a noisy sendoff at the Bay City pier. Once on the spit, the entourage danced to live music in an open-air dance hall just uphill from the fifty-four tents they all would sleep in afterward because the Annex was not ready for them.[64]

Bayocean Annex, as viewed from the east. BOB-67, TCPM.

The next day, T. Irving gave everyone a tour, showing off the electrical, water, and sewer lines and eighty-five workers and equipment installing them. On July 4th, a couple of thousand people—the most ever to that point—boated over to join the autoists. They were all treated to lunch in the dining room of the Annex. Later, some went deep-sea fishing while others played baseball and other games on the beach. A fireworks display capped off the day. $3,000 had been spent to make the first of Bayocean Park's many grand openings memorable.[65]

The media praised T. Irving for his handling of affairs. The journalists present may have been giving him the benefit of the doubt after hearing or learning that his father went "violently insane" the night of July 3rd. Fannie reported the incident to at least A. G. (Arthur) Beals, a Tillamook businessman, but the press said nothing for more than three years. Had the stress from the Reis Tract debacle, struggles to get the resort built, failure to sell lots and keep them sold, and declining revenues been too much for T. Benton to handle psychologically? The Potters must have believed his condition was biological because, after returning to Portland, putting T. Irving in charge, and moving back to California, they sailed the world looking for a cure—without success. [66] It would be up to the younger Thomas to bring his idea to fruition.

William Clemens set a record time in his new Ford returning to Portland on Tuesday, July 5th, making the 112-mile southern loop in five hours and forty-five minutes. His publicity stunt was meant to show how close Bayocean Park was to Portland. But the few Portlanders who owned automobiles did not drive like Clemens. Others were reluctant to spend two days riding a steamship or horse-drawn stagecoach to get to Bayocean Park, and no railroads were running yet. So, T. Irving set up an auto stage leaving Portland every morning at seven o'clock. Ads promised arrival in Tillamook at about five o'clock in the afternoon—weather permitting.[67]

On the first of December 1910, TBPRC announced the completion of the Bayocean Annex and promised to complete the other facilities within two years. The concrete first floor of the 50-by-120-foot structure housed mechanical rooms, the staff toilet, and the laundry. The lobby, parlor, kitchen, barbershop, guest toilet, and 135-seat dining room were on the second floor. Guest rooms and bathrooms for each sex were on the top floor. Half of the rooms offered a view of the ocean or the bay. But half of them were interior rooms with no window. John Wrenn had designed the Annex for servants, not guests, and to pack as many as possible into the allotted space. Two aisles served four rows of rooms, with the back walls of the middle rows abutting each other rather than the outdoors. The only adjustment T. Benton made after repurposing the Annex was an increase in room size, which decreased their number from forty-seven to thirty-eight.[68]

Custom Yacht Delivers Guests in Record Time

T. Irving focused on transportation in 1911. TBPRC's auto stage had not worked out, Lytle seemed to be taking forever getting his railroad built, and the other three railroads had given up entirely. Since Oregon Electric would not be laying trestles from Tillamook to Bayocean Park, T. Irving incorporated a Tillamook Bay Railroad and Navigation Company to raise $350,000 in stock sales for a rail line around the bay.[69] Then he had a better idea—building a passenger yacht faster than any then plying the waters of the Pacific Northwest.

In late February, Potter hired Fred Ballin to design the "handsome yacht Bay Ocean with clipper bow and raked stacks" capable of transporting a hundred passengers to Bayocean Park in less than twelve hours. Joseph Supple's shipwrights finished the 150-ton ship three months later for $33,518. It was 130.1 feet long, 18.7 feet wide, and 7.9 feet deep. Three gas-powered engines producing 475 horsepower moved it along at 18 knots. A lounge, galley, and owner's cabin were on the main deck. Berths for forty-four passengers and fourteen crew members were below deck.[70]

On May 27, 1911, "the largest crowd to view a launching in the history of local marine affairs" watched the *Bayocean* splash into the Willamette River after T. Irving's five-year-old daughter Elizabeth christened it. Local dignitaries gave speeches touting Portland's shipyard and waterways being capable of handling "some of the largest ships afloat." It then failed a federal marine inspection. Supple's mechanics got it certified, but with the capacity reduced to fifty-four. T. Irving put the delay to good marketing use by offering the *Bayocean* to officials to manage swimming competitions. With its float participating again that year, Bayocean Park received attention on land and water during the 1911 Rose Festival.[71]

The *Bayocean* made its inaugural voyage on Saturday, June 18th. T. Irving took twenty-seven guests, including Supple, Ballin, several Portland business leaders, and a journalist on a trip to the spit in just under twelve hours, including a publicity stop at Astoria. TBPRC's dredge crew had finished the channel, so the yacht motored up to the cheers of a crowd waiting at the central pier.[72] Finally, it seemed, TBPRC had solved its transportation problem; the *Bayocean* could deliver guests quickly and with publicity in its wake.

Guests boarding the *Bayocean*. BOS-4, TCPM.

On Sunday the 19th, Potter took his guests on a tour of the spit. That evening, he hosted a banquet for Tillamook dignitaries and his Portland entourage in the Bayocean Annex. The night before, the Portlanders had stayed in rooms opened to the public for the first time a day earlier, after the final utility was connected.[73] At the banquet, T. Irving announced that he and his father had given up plans to make a quick profit from lot sales in favor of building a resort grand enough to attract people from across the United States. They were confident that resort operations would eventually give them a return on their investment. Referring to his father in the present tense, despite his having gone insane and having left Portland a year earlier, meant T. Irving was still riding his father's coattails. Finances were clearly going downhill by this point because he hedged the recommitment to spend $350,000 on Hotel Bayocean with, "it would take several years to bring this about…persons should not judge too hastily and be a little more patient."[74]

Oregonian reporter E. C. Sammons later wrote, "Oregon's latest summer refuge bids fair this year to usurp much of the popularity of past years enjoyed by Seaside, Gearhart, Newport, Elk Creek, and Long Beach [Washington]," listing all of Bayocean Park's competitors in the process. He reported TBPRC's plans to spend $650,000 by the end of 1911 and "more than $1,500,000" eventually. Sammons did not mention the Coney Island-style amusement park, explain why the Annex had shrunk to thirty-eight rooms, or say what it was like sleeping in a room with no exterior windows.[75] As far as his newspaper was concerned, Bayocean Park was enough of a resort to begin including it in its weekly society page resort coverage. Other metropolitan newspapers followed suit. Publishing the doings of prominent citizens was powerful publicity, making 1911's grand opening the most important of them all.

Bayocean's first paying passengers left Supple's dock at the end of Belmont Street at 7 PM on Tuesday, June 27th, after additional problems discovered by federal inspectors were resolved. The roundtrip fare was $10, with staterooms adding $1.00 to $1.50. Midweek, passengers boarded after work and had dinner on board. Those who slept while descending the Columbia River were aroused in time to experience crossing the bar at sunrise. In contrast, Saturday morning departures sped guests to Bayocean Park quickly so they could enjoy as much of the weekend as possible. Return trips left every Monday and Thursday morning, arriving in Portland before dinner. Hot bearings in the main engine delayed the July 1st departure by a day, but its passengers, including T. Irving and his wife Bess, arrived in time for that year's Fourth of July festivities.[76]

A fifteen-piece orchestra from Portland accompanied dancers that week. Others from across Oregon would do the same the rest of the summer.

Champion swimmer Arthur Cavill provided paying guests with free swimming lessons and entertained everyone with daredevil stunts like swimming with his hands tied behind his back. The price of rooms and tents included meals at the Annex. Day guests from Tillamook could buy meals there or in the worker's dining room in the Administration Building.[77]

PCRC Administration Building. Later converted to a guest hotel called the Bayocean Inn, and other names through the years. BOB-51, TCPM.

The structure that replaced the one Bertha (Weaver) Morgan saw destroyed stretched 150 feet along the east side of Bay Street and 40 feet along the south side of the boardwalk leading to the pier. The first floor included sales and administrative offices, a kitchen, a bakery, a lounge, a lavatory, and a dining room. Workers lived in twenty-six rooms upstairs. Across from it, on the north side of the boardwalk leading out to the pier, was the Bayocean Amusement Pavilion. It was "constructed around three sides of a square, one wing containing a general store and post office, an ice-cream and confectionery parlor; the other wing contains a curio shop; and the main portion of the building contains a bowling alley and pool room." During off-hours in the summer, workers played games alongside guests.[78] That was as good as it would get because Bayocean Park never got its Coney Island.

CHAPTER 2

Completing Bayocean Park

(1911 – 1914)

T. Irving had reason to congratulate himself at how Bayocean Park was progressing as he returned to Portland on July 6th, 1911. But news greeted him there that ten lot owners had asked a judge to place the resort into receivership because they did not trust him to get it done.[1]

Attorney General Challenges T. Irving's Competence

The plaintiffs, led by William Eastman, were prominent Salem professionals and politicians concerned by accusations made in a letter from Oregon State Attorney General Andrew Crawford. He said T. Benton Potter was searching the world for a cure to his unnamed illness while continuing to draw his $1,200 monthly salary. Despite physicians earning $165 at the time, Crawford seemed most concerned that T. Irving's salary was just $250, saying it proved he did not have what it took to get Bayocean Park built though he was now in charge of doing so. Construction of the *Bayocean* was an example of the younger Thomas having "wasted money in useless entertaining and advertising." T. Irving refuted each accusation in the press but said, "I welcome the opportunity of presenting to the courts of this state a careful analysis of our books."[2]

Sixty contract holders learned TBPRC's ex-super-salesman Christian Lauritzen was Attorney General Crawford's source when they attended a meeting held in Portland on July 8th. He had been promoted to sales manager before the sales office was shuttered a year earlier. Lauritzen must have absconded with company information, including sales tallies and contract holder names and addresses. Rather than accuse T. Irving of fraud, he wanted to set up a fact-finding committee. Harkness Chapin and other company defenders who were there nixed that idea. Chapin portrayed Lauritzen as a disgruntled ex-employee making false accusations to gain control of Bayocean Park. Carl Jackson argued that a receivership would decrease lot values. William Clemens wanted to run Christian out of town.[3]

T. Irving told the press none of the plaintiffs had visited the spit in over a year, so they had not seen the considerable progress made. He offered to give three of them a two-night, three-day trip, expenses paid, beginning Saturday, July 15th. W. F. Staley, T. J. Cronise, and Dr. W. S. Mott volunteered.[4] Potter hired a thirty-piece military band to greet them as the *Bayocean* entered Tillamook Bay. After disembarking at the pier, they were taken to "every nook and corner of Bayocean, shown the water plant, electric plant, street grading, [and] cement walks that had been laid." Despite a twenty-seven-room bathhouse rather than a natatorium at the ocean end of 12th Avenue, Staley, Cronise, and Mott returned home Monday night sufficiently impressed to convince fellow plaintiffs to drop the suit.[5]

Potter took a more aggressive approach with Attorney General Crawford. Having learned that he was buying a lot, T. Irving accused him of using state time and money to serve personal interests. After reading the plaintiff trio's glowing report, court papers filed by TBPRC's attorneys, and T. Irving's public rebuke, Crawford wrote a second letter apologizing for causing such a fuss. He did not admit to making false statements nor accuse Lauritzen of lying. The ex-sales manager had simply withheld details like T. Benton's cash contributions exceeding his salary by several multiples.[6] No one asked why he would subsidize Bayocean Park's construction and then ask that some of it be paid back to him as a salary.

T. Irving had shown savvy beyond his years in thwarting Christian's attempt to put his company into receivership. However, he could no longer pretend T. Benton was still in charge of Bayocean Park. Documents TBPRC submitted to the court showed $312,980.17 spent between January 1, 1909, and July 1, 1911, to prove the company had met its contractual obligation to expend more than $100,000 annually. But they also divulged net lot sales had dropped by 432 to 1,868 and that another 195 were ready to be repossessed. Lauritzen and fellow ex-salesmen stood to lose $7,565 in commissions tied to those contracts with no ability to resell them. That seems the most likely reason he contacted Attorney General Crawford.[7]

Cabins Start Rising

As the plaintiff trio was hiking up High Terrace to the Annex, T. Irving would have pointed to the first cabin rising about two-thirds of the way up. When finished later that summer, his mother Fannie moved into it, sans T. Benton. She stayed there most of that winter, gathering seashells, agates, and stones along the beach to entertain herself.[8]

Fannie and T. Benton Potter's cabin. Author's collection.

Houses could not be built on the spit until 1911 because streets had to be surveyed and graded before lot boundaries could be determined and construction materials delivered. 12th Avenue and High Terrace were paved first because they led from the pier over to the ocean and up to the hotel grounds. Sidewalks ran along each side of them. No other streets would ever be so honored.[9] TBPRC launches had no room for house construction materials, so lot owners had to wait for ocean-going ships to deliver them after the dredge crew dug a deep enough channel.

In March, a crew boss predicted forty cottages would go up that summer, but only four did. Charles Blazer, a TBPRC employee, worked around the lumber shortage by using driftwood to build a thirty-square-foot house on three lots his wife Sarah purchased on the mainland section of Bayocean Park. After adding tents and a concrete swimming pool, they printed a brochure advertising their Driftwood Lodge. Despite their best efforts, the Blazers' little resort did not last long enough to be noticed and taxed by the Tillamook County Assessor. A. J. Jones, an onsite salesman, had a two-story house put up on the ocean side of Clarke Street. The paved section of it ran for half a mile down the center of the narrow, unforested dune ridge south of Natatorium Gap. The elevation at the north end was that of the Annex, providing more homeowners better views than anywhere else on the spit. E. M. (Mortimer) Fouch, owner of Portland's Western Electric Works, was the only lot owner not affiliated with TBPRC to construct a home in 1911, a six-room bungalow just south of Jackson Gap.[10]

TBPRC started publishing a monthly newsletter called the *Surf* on November 1, 1911.[11] They sent lot owners copies for free. Others could buy them for $.05 per issue or $.25 annually. It would have been easier and less expensive to mail the *Surf* from Portland, but the Bayocean Post Office postmarked it for effect. The newsletter gave TBPRC a direct connection to lot owners. Tillamook's newspapers had staunchly defended T. Irving during the *Eastman v. PCRC* trial but the metropolitan media had objectively reported both sides of the story. They had not been as accommodating to him as they had to T. Benton. Bayocean Park also needed to draw businesses to be successful. Giving them a place to advertise might help.

Each *Surf* gave detailed reports on construction, including photos of men and equipment remodeling the landscape with roads, bayside infill, commercial buildings, and private cottages. Ads provided railroad and bay shuttle schedules and rates for tents and rooms in the Annex. Stories about rich and famous guests implied contract holders were investing wisely and that Bayocean Park offered the type of customers professionals and retailers wanted. By July 1912, the newsletter had grown from four to eight pages. Bayocean businesses and Portland entrepreneurs who knew most readers lived in their city took up most of the additional space.

Port Squabbles Result in One Jetty Built Rather than Two

The front page of the December 1911 issue of the *Surf* featured the creation of a Port of Bayocean by popular vote. It was the last of three bay area votes taking advantage of an Oregon law passed in 1909. Before then, ports could only be created or expanded by the state legislature.

The existing Port of Tillamook had acted first, with voters approving its expansion in July 1909. Bay City residents approved a new port in April 1910. The two ports' taxing authority would enable them to issue bonds of $500,000 and $200,000, respectively. And a new rock quarry on the Miami River (east of Garibaldi) would reduce the cost of jetty construction. So, the two ports asked the Corps of Engineers to reconsider the decision made twenty-five years earlier against jetties. Generals at the national level agreed to do so. They appointed Major Jay Morrow, Portland District Engineer, another major, and their superior, Pacific Coast Division Engineer Lt. Colonel John Biddle, to lay out a plan.[12]

By the end of 1910, the three men had done so. They designed a north jetty 5,700 feet long and a south jetty 7,300 feet long, with 1,200 feet separating them at the terminus. Costs were estimated at $670,000 and $930,000, respectively. The channel from Garibaldi to Bay City needed to be deepened also, which would cost $144,000. If the ports contributed one quarter of the $1,744,000 ($56,201,000 in 2022) total, the net cost to the federal government would be less than the estimated benefit to local commerce. The $436,000 required was doable, but the Port of Tillamook balked at the Corps' demand that they deepen and take over maintenance of the channel from Bay City to Tillamook.[13]

To break the impasse, Bay City port commissioners came up with an idea: perhaps one jetty would do as good a job as two in deepening the bay inlet and keeping it clear. Building the north jetty and deepening the channel from Garibaldi to Bay City would cost just $814,000. If the ports contributed half of that instead of one quarter, the Corps would see an increased benefit to cost ratio. Bay City's offer to contribute all of their $200,000 got the Port of Tillamook on board because that meant it only had to contribute $207,000, leaving money left over to deepen and maintain the channel from Bay City to Tillamook.[14]

The Port of Bay City sent its revised plan to Major Morrow in May 1911. He approved it in June, concluding that one jetty would do the job as well as two, "give quick results and to some extent lasting results on the bar, and that after its completion, the necessity for the south jetty will not appear for some considerable period." Lt. Colonel Biddle disagreed: "While the action of a single jetty on Tillamook Bar cannot be foretold and may have the effect stated by the district engineer officer, the general experience of this coast is that two jetties are necessary." Despite that, he approved the plan because, even if it were temporary, any improvement justified the reduced cost, it was all the Port of Bay City could afford, and the Port of Tillamook was willing to go along.[15]

The Corps' national Board of Engineers concurred after the Port of Tillamook formally agreed to take over maintenance of the channel between Bay City and Tillamook. Chief of Engineers General William Bixby told Secretary of War Henry Stimson the project was "deemed advisable." His packet included a letter from Port of Bay City President John Bozorth confirming that he and the other newly elected commissioners were as committed to the plan as their predecessors. Bozorth must have read Biddle's comments because his support was conditional: "The object of this action is to give our consent to the United States engineers building the north jetty, only, if they think it advisable, instead of both north and south jetties, as first contemplated by the department."[16]

If there was to be one jetty, T. Irving Potter preferred that it be on the south side of the inlet, but he had no say in the matter without his own port. He also needed the tax revenue to pay for regular dredging of Bayocean's harbor and channel. On August 31, 1911, the Barnegat School hosted a Port of Bayocean vote. When it failed by thirteen votes, another was scheduled for October 26th. It succeeded the second time, which is not surprising given the affirmative votes cast precisely matched the number of TBPRC employees. Jim O'Donnell had given his fifty-nine men paid leave to vote and made sure every one of them got up to the cape. None of them had reason to vote against the port because they would not be there long enough to pay any taxes.[17]

People who would pay taxes voted overwhelmingly against the Port of Bayocean. Its boundary map looked like one gerrymandered for political purposes, with a boundary reaching thirteen miles southeast of Tillamook Bay. Folks out in the Carnahan District were farmers who lived in the watersheds of Netarts Bay and Nestucca Bay. They gained nothing from a port in Tillamook Bay and immediately put up a fuss, but commissioners were appointed, and on December 22, 1911, they authorized a ten mil (1%) tax. The $6,000 collected annually would pay six percent interest on $100,000 in bonds.[18]

In the end, neither Bayocean nor Tillamook's port would take part in jetty construction or decision-making. In June 1911, farmers in the expanded Port of Tillamook convinced state officials the vote authorizing it was illegitimate. They lost in Tillamook County Circuit Court but won upon appeal to the Oregon Supreme Court a year later.[19] Carnahan voters used the same approach when they filed suit in March 1912. On September 25th, Tillamook County Circuit Court declared the Port of Bayocean invalid because the boundary description in the election notice was incorrect, and state law prohibited ports from serving more than one bay. The port appealed the decision. In June 1913, Oregon's Supreme Court confirmed the circuit court's ruling and said that TBPRC's use of non-resident witnesses to vouch for each voter having lived within the port boundary for at least six months was also fraudulent behavior.[20]

Meanwhile, jetty funding had moved through Congress. In July 1912, it funded the Corps' share. With the Ports of Tillamook and Bayocean sidelined, the Port of Bay City had to raise $407,000 instead of $200,000. It managed to do that on August 31st when it won annexation approval from voters in territory the Supreme Court took from the Port of Tillamook. Taking issue with that, the Port of Tillamook challenged the vote that had created the Port of Bay City in 1910. Oregon's Supreme Court decided in favor of Bay City in April 1913. Commissioners of the last port standing quickly sold bonds, and in June 1914, construction of the north jetty began.[21]

Elmer Lytle Completes His Railroad

On November 10, 1911, a Pacific Railroad and Navigation passenger train finally arrived in Tillamook, loaded with freight and 125 paying passengers. Most of the town was there to greet them. It was a ninety-one-mile journey through thirteen tunnels and across sixty bridges, thirty-five of which were over a hundred feet long, and the tallest 104 feet high. On its return trip to Portland, the train "carried fully 50 persons, some of whom never had been outside their home county."[22]

Two photos by H. R. Gregg of the railroad spur run onto the Bay City pier to serve Bayocean passengers. BCL-193 above, BCL-216 below, TCPM.

Elmer Lytle closed his office and retired a month later. In the end, he was managing the PRNC for Southern Pacific Railroad, which had taken majority ownership after he defaulted on the $2,000,000 loan taken out in 1908. After Lytle sold his remaining interest in 1915, SP replaced PRN on the sides of rail cars. Despite that, passengers continued calling it the Punk, Rotten, and Nasty. Construction workers had first misappropriated the company's initials in response to working conditions that injured and killed many of their comrades. Those who rode the train continued the practice because of their riding experience.[23]

Ahead of the 1912 season, Southern Pacific cooperated with TBPRC to print twenty thousand booklets depicting Bayocean Park's wonders and distributed them nationally. A pamphlet produced later that year included every Tillamook County resort.[24] All except Bayocean Park had risen in the wake of the Punk, Rotten, and Nasty as it worked its way south along the Oregon Coast from Wheeler starting in 1910. Taking three years longer than expected cost TBPRC the revenue that would have come from being first and additional charges for shipping equipment and materials by sea. But things were going well as far as the media was concerned.

The *Surf's* January 1912 issue touted completion of the "largest outdoor swimming pool in the world." In fact, the plunge shown on the plat map ended up being nothing more than a pit five hundred feet long, a thousand feet wide, and fourteen feet deep, dug by the *Tillamook Bayocean* while expanding the southern end of the spit. Bay water flowed in and out of a channel cut into its east end with each tide. What Jim O'Donnell, his wife, and a few others were celebrating when they took a quick dip in it was the completion of a twenty-five-room bathhouse his men had built on its north edge. Manpower was near its peak of ninety at that point, making TBPRC Tillamook County's largest employer.[25]

The April 1912 *Surf* declared that ten miles of Bayocean Park streets had been surveyed and graded. That made it possible for every lot owner to build a cabin, and to encourage their construction, TBPRC offered to pay half the cost. That attracted the attention of brothers P. D. and William Hance, who built homes in Portland. They placed ads in the *Surf* that offered small cabins for $1,000 to $1,200. At the time, an average American home cost $3,500, so the Hances soon had eighteen projects lined up. They moved to the spit and put up a warehouse that could hold seventy-five thousand feet of lumber and other materials shipped at—now—affordable rates on PRNC.[26]

In September 1912, TBPRC hired Warren Brothers Company to pave Bayocean Park streets with their newly patented Warrenite-Bitulithic asphalt for $200,000 because the road from Tillamook to Bayocean was "practically assured" to start the following spring. TBPRC would have to wait for Warren Brothers to finish paving Tillamook streets. Before they had, in early 1913, city residents began complaining about quality. That led to a lawsuit and controversy exacerbated by the *Herald* and *Headlight* taking opposite sides. Warren Brothers later paved the Columbia River Highway using the same process, but doubts cast in 1913 led TBPRC to cancel their contract and use its workers to pave the resort's streets with concrete.[27]

Francis and Ida Mitchell Appear on the Scene

The only other advertisement in the April 1912 *Surf* was for "the Mitchell Building: one, two, and three-room suites." Though this was the first time they had been mentioned, the couple that would become Bayocean's most famous and enduring residents had been there for nearly four years.

Francis Drake Mitchell was born on a farm near DeKalb, Missouri, on January 18, 1870. His mother raised him and his siblings alone after a drunk killed his father. Upon graduating from eighth grade, Francis traveled to Bonanza, Oregon, to work on a farm for a year before attending Oregon State University from 1888 to 1892. There, he took preparatory classes for two years, freshman classes for two more, and then quit. After returning to Missouri, he worked as an accountant before entering the Kansas City College of Pharmacy. He graduated in 1895 and set up a pharmacy of his own.[28]

Ida J. Smith was born in West Lynn, Missouri, on August 11, 1868. She was managing the dressmaking department of a Kansas City store when she met Francis. They married on December 29, 1897, after which Ida worked in Francis's drug store and moved into his apartment above it.[29]

Peers respected Francis enough to elect him treasurer of the Kansas City Retail Druggist Association in 1904. But in April 1905, a customer publicly accused him of "substituting drugs in filling his prescription." Mitchell sued for libel, but the case ruined his reputation. So, he sold the business and the building in 1906 and began looking for a place to start over.[30]

The Mitchells had visited the Lewis and Clark Exposition and the Oregon Coast in 1905 and liked what they saw. So, when Bayocean Park ads started running, Francis headed over to the Marlborough Heights sales office and bought a lot on July 30, 1907, a day after they first went on sale.[31] The Panic of 1907 followed Francis on his train to Oregon, forcing him to linger for several months in Portland. He must have stopped by the PCRC office regularly, because in March 1908, he hired the company's architect, John Wrenn, to design a two-story Spanish Renaissance building with a mercantile on the ground floor and apartments upstairs. Francis headed for Bayocean Park as soon as the central pier was finished that spring.[32]

Ida joined Francis in November 1908. Forty years later, she told the story of her arrival to Jack Medcalf. Anxious to see Francis and find out what "their fortune had been spent for," she took a stagecoach across the mountains from Portland rather than wait two days for the next ship to Tillamook. Ida stayed at the Allen House before hitching a ride with a group that had chartered a boat to look for a dead whale beached at Kincheloe Point. The captain gallantly carried her across the mudflats to solid ground, but she stumbled while hiking south and was looking forward to a warm bath in her new home. But all Francis had ready for her was a hug. He was living in a tent just like everyone else. Ida told Jack, "I can still feel the disgust that I had on coming for the first time to Bayocean."[33]

Medcalf did not say what the Mitchells did for the next two years, but Francis's bookkeeping and Ida's tailoring were marketable skills they could put to use. In 1910, Francis started selling lots to visitors in an office on the first floor of the Administration Building, and he and Ida moved into a room on the second floor.[34]

TBPRC's relocation of the tent city had forced the Mitchells to change their store's location because there would no longer be any customers across from the lot purchased while in Kansas City. So, they bought a lot at the southwest corner of 12th Avenue and Bay Street. They suffered another setback when, after construction of their mercantile began, Harkness Chapin (prior to Lockwood taking over) forced them to move it because he had made an error in surveying The Mitchell's property line.[35]

Bayocean's town center—12th Avenue and Bay Street—as viewed from the boardwalk leading out to the pier in the bay to the east, with the Amusement Pavilion, Administration Building, and The Mitchell at the northeast, southeast, and southwest corners, respectively. All but The Mitchell stand on infill. The Annex is barely visible in the upper right corner. Culp 111, Lorraine Eckhardt's collection.

The Mitchell that opened for business in June 1912 was a simple, two-story polygon with a flat roof and straight sides filling every part of the lot. Resort layout changes, Chapin's survey error, and business income starting five years later than anticipated had reduced the Mitchells' reserves, forcing them to abandon John Wrenn's Spanish Renaissance design. Perhaps to apologize for the additional costs TBPRC had inflicted upon the Mitchells, the July *Surf* included photos of The Mitchell in progressive stages of construction. Or perhaps it was in exchange for the Bay Drug Company ad featuring prescriptions, toiletries, and cigars and others listing offices downstairs and apartments upstairs for lease.[36] In any case, the Mitchells had finally begun the Bayocean Park life they had first imagined back in Kansas City five years earlier.

Harkness Chapin Returns

As The Mitchell neared completion, the *Surf* announced plans for a Hotel Sea Crest, "a modern family hotel catering to those seeking rest throughout the year…and recreation, rather than to the formal, social guests" of the Hotel Bayocean. Mortimer Fouch planned to place his hotel on six-and-a-half lots at the south end of the spit. He got them and $2,850 for his house at Jackson Gap from Bess and T. Irving Potter.[37]

During the summer of 1912 and the three that followed, Charles Carson rented space on the pier, put up a small hut, and sold crabs caught in the bay. The Baker brothers (prize-winning Portland taxidermists) sold gems, wildlife paintings, furs, stuffed animals, and Bayocean banners out of the Amusement Pavilion during the same period. Other lessees operated a bowling alley, a billiard parlor, a game room, and an ice cream parlor.[38]

The Bayocean Commercial Club (sponsored by TBPRC) built an office just south of the Administration Building. They offered to manage cabin rentals for owners not using them and added a fireplace and canvas wall coverings to the dance hall to keep dancers warm on chilly nights. A gun club arranged shooting matches. On June 15th, the Tillamook County School District awarded Bayocean a district (No. 58) of its own. The spot chosen for Bayocean's first schoolhouse was just south of a clearing at the base of the spit where a Tillamook Indian village had once stood.[39]

The July 1912 *Surf* announced Fourth of July activities and depicted guests enjoying many resort features. A field hockey team played games on the Hotel Bayocean grounds. The Bayocean Commercial Club said they would build a tennis court north of the Amusement Pavilion, where Bayocean's Coney Island was to have been. The entire length of 12th Avenue, from the bay pier to the ocean shore, had been paved in concrete. The yacht *Bayocean* ran ocean excursions. The Wagonette Saddle Horse Burros advertised day-long rides along the beach to Cape Meares. Camping outfits were sold by the Hance brothers and H. L. (Henry) King, who had moved from Spokane where he had sold Bayocean lots after Christian Lauritzen returned to Portland. The Mitchell signboard listed D. C. (David) Baker and Francis Mitchell as real estate partners. Sunday School classes were held each week at unspecified locations.[40]

Bayocean Park was bustling in July 1912, according to the *Surf*, but it was the last issue. Perhaps T. Irving thought the newsletter had served its purpose. A more likely reason was a change in his priorities. At the end of June 1910, Potter had set up a Coin Machine Manufacturing Company to make and market an automatic coin-changing machine he had been working on for several years. That endeavor had been put on hold when his father went insane, and his mother placed Bayocean Park on his shoulders. T. Irving had hired George Don Lee to promote both companies, and the *Surf* had appeared soon after that. At the end of July 1912, Potter convinced Harkness Chapin to return, and Lee dropped the resort account to work exclusively on the coin company. T. Irving continued serving as Bayocean Park's public face and handling administrative functions, but once again it would be Chapin's job—now as an employee paid $450 a month—to get it built. Harkness bought A. J. Jones's cabin and headed for the spit.[41]

Society page columns typically featured doings of the rich and famous. Yet William Reynolds's construction of a treehouse in the summer of 1912 garnered an entire paragraph in the *Oregonian.* The thirty-three-year-old mail clerk from Spokane chose a remote location in the hills north of the harbor near the old Elliott homestead for his eyrie. He cut tree branches level fifty to sixty feet off the ground and nailed a platform to them with one end dug securely in the steep hillside. William was sure his "was the only tree dwelling that has ever been equipped with electric light, gas and hot and cold running water."[42]

Twenty-six years later, the *Tillamook Headlight-Herald* reported Reynolds and his wife staying with the Mitchells. Though identified as property owners, their treehouse was not mentioned.[43] The county assessor never recorded an improvement on the lot. And there are no extant photographs of what would have been an irresistible image to anyone passing in a boat. All of which suggests Reynolds's treehouse sailed off its perch during the first significant storm of 1912. Regardless, it was the most northerly home ever built in Bayocean Park.

At the other end of the housing spectrum, three cabins were built and furnished at the cost of $45,000 for Portland lumber baron Johan Poulsen, his wife Dora, and the families of their five daughters to enjoy. Two went up in 1912 and the third in 1913. Spread across ten lots at the curved apex of Laurel Street, 14th Avenue, High Street, High Terrace, and Bay Terrace, the Poulsen complex left no room for others to have a clear view of both bay and ocean in the vicinity (like most who built summer cottages on the spit, the Poulsens wanted more space between themselves and neighbors than a single lot would afford). The Bayocean Annex sat caddy-corner to the three houses, blocking their southwest view and facilitating photos by guests. Captions on photos now archived often speak of the Poulsen cabins being the finest in Bayocean Park, but others would later be built on Clarke Street, which was less accessible to resort guests.[44]

Three Poulsen cottages, as viewed from the northeast corner of the Annex. BOB-18. TCPM.

George Hyland, President of the Mount Hood Railway Company, and his wife Clare had an eight-room cabin built overlooking the ocean on the west side of High Street, a thousand feet north of the Poulsens. Views of the ocean from it were grand, but trees blocked the bay. William Clemens spent $6,000 to $8,000 for a house a short distance north of Jackson Gap, where he could see both the bay and the ocean from a lower angle. Engineer Lockwood chose Clarke Street. Fritz Hirsch, captain of the yacht *Bayocean,* hired the Hance brothers to put up a "land-ship" on Bay Terrace, just downhill from the Poulsens on the bay side of the spit. He sold it to Superintendent O'Donnell the following year. Portland machinist Elmer Burns erected a tiny cottage with two windows facing the sea on a lot purchased by his wife Alberta close to the shore 1,100 feet north of 12th Avenue.[45] The variety among the homes and socioeconomic status of their owners would continue in the years ahead. Though initially envisioned as a luxury retreat for wealthy urbanites, circumstances had forced the Potters to accept all comers.

The Bayocean Annex offered those without cabins an exterior room for $6 a night in 1913. Interior rooms were $5, the same price as a 9½-by-12-foot tent, meals included. Canvas walls and rough wooden floors were rustic, but the tents were about the same size as the interior rooms and had heat, electricity, and windows. Families could rent one of eight 16-by-20-foot tents for $10 per night or $60 per week.[46]

Ahead of the 1913 season, the Administration Building was repurposed as the Bayside Inn.[47] On June 13th, the *Herald* reported, "The new fireplace in the living room of the Hotel Bayocean has been completed and together with the addition of space to the dining room will add to the comfort of the season's guests." The article was speaking of the Bayocean Annex, not its grander counterpart. TBPRC had not planned a fireplace for employees, but it needed the Annex to become the "first-class hotel" promised in contracts since 1909. Guests who remembered the Hotel Bayocean depicted in ads two years earlier may not have complained, but they probably did not return because better choices were available elsewhere. All the rooms at the Outlook Inn (later renamed Lake Lytle Hotel), north of Barview at Rockaway Beach, had exterior windows. So did others, and they were all easier to get to than Bayocean Park.[48]

Seven cabins went up in 1913. In addition to the third Poulsen house, another cabin was built north of it, on the west side of High Street, for Oregon's Supreme Court Reporter Frank Turner and his wife Iva. Swan Hawkinson built Cypress Crest midway along Clarke Street. He and Othelia decided to make Bayocean their permanent home after arriving in May 1913, when Swan went to work on a street gang. Arthur C. Smith's place was at the southern extreme of the paved section of Clarke Street. And three small cottages were erected north of the Burns place along the shore for Enrique and May Mallory, May's mother, Georgia DeWitt, and B. E. and Laura Hughson.[49]

In January 1913, T. Irving put the *Bayocean* up for sale. It had provided a few passengers some exciting trips during the summer of 1911, but by August 1911, the ship was stationed in Astoria, where it took rail and steamship passengers to the spit three days a week and made occasional excursion runs. Once PRNC began delivering passengers to Tillamook in November, the ship stayed tied to the pier at Bayocean. It could not compete with seven-hour rail trips costing four dollars. Lytle's railroad may have been punk, rotten, and nasty, but it was better than getting seasick or waiting for mechanics to repair the ship.[50]

Supple's mechanics overhauled the yacht's engines in May 1912, for they were as unreliable as they were powerful. T. Irving put the downtime to practical use by letting Rose Festival officials use his ship again. It took Bayocean Park guests on ocean excursions that summer, though it "was top-heavy and considered dangerous."[51] What *Bayocean* needed was a vast expanse of quiet waters surrounded by a large population to operate profitably—a place like San Francisco Bay.

On March 21st, the yacht was sold for $17,600 at a public auction. It left for San Francisco Bay on April 6th to become the Bayocean Excursion Company's flagship. The Navy bought it for $52,500 in June 1918 and refitted it for coastal patrol service just in time for World War I to end. Mr. L. Parker of Oakland bought the *Bayocean* in August 1921 and renamed it the *Shark*. It was wrecked near Crescent City in a storm on October 29, 1924.[52]

Wave Generator Enhances the Bayocean Natatorium

Though first advertised in 1909, plans for the Bayocean Natatorium lay dormant until 1913, when T. Irving invented a wave generating machine. Gearhart Park's natatorium had opened in May 1910, so he needed something to make up for—again—having lost the competitive advantage of being first. In June, he and a few others set up the Bayocean Natatorium Company (BNC) to pay for its construction. Two months later, salesmen began offering shares in "the best investment ever presented in the history of Portland, from the viewpoint of large returns and absolute safety…to three hundred and seventy-five people, no more and no less [with] one or two hundred dollars." Selling T. Irving's Artificial Surf Mechanism across the nation would assure even greater profits.[53]

Natatorium and second (indoor) dance hall facing each other on the south and north sides, respectively, of 12th Avenue, as viewed from the hotel grounds. Lindsey 53-0, Lorraine Eckhardt's collection.

Natatorium with Bayocean Annex in the background, as viewed from the sea to its west. Miscellaneous Bayocean Images, TCPM.

BNC had sold enough stock by January 1914 to start work on the structure and hire Tillamook's Feeney and Bremer Foundry to build the key components. Six months and $60,000 later, Fourth of July festivities featured the Bayocean Natatorium in what would be the resort's last grand opening. Hoping that making its opening part of an extravaganza would make up for Seaside's natatorium having opened a month earlier, families of the Portland Progressive Businessmen's Club initiated Bayocean's natatorium on July 5th, accompanied by the two songs its "Rube band" knew. Unfortunately, the boiler and wave-generator were not functioning, so bathers endured a chilly, placid dip before dressing warmly and heading out to the beach.[54]

The Natatorium was the largest structure ever built on the spit. It stood as tall as the Annex and had a much larger footprint—88 by 250 feet. Oriented north and south, it took up most of five lots right on the beach, with a north-side entrance facing 12th Avenue. The concrete pool was 50 by 160 feet, with depths ranging from 1 to 11.5 feet. Attendants offered "sterilized bathing suits" to folks using one of a hundred dressing rooms. Lifeguards provided free swimming lessons for the price of admission.[55]

By July 21st, the boiler was operating, heating seawater to seventy-six degrees before it cascaded across colored lights into the pool. Waves magically appeared ten minutes of each half-hour. Five hundred seats in the wrap-around balcony enabled daytime spectators. A large screen was pulled down from the rafters to show movies accompanied by an orchestra at night. Patrons brought canoes and inflatable rafts shaped like animals to paddle around on, which must have made it difficult to swim laps. The Bayocean Natatorium quickly became the resort's most popular attraction, despite tickets costing $.25, at a time when regular theaters charged $.07.[56]

Men not working on the Natatorium in 1914 converted forty-two tents to "bungalows," replacing Tent City with Bungalow City. Swan and Othelia Hawkinson were its first managers. Though only fourteen feet square, each bungalow included two beds, a kitchen, a table and chairs, electric lights, and a propane heater. Initially, the lower half of each wall was wood, and the upper half was canvas so guests could roll them up for ventilation. Wood and windows replaced the canvas a few years later. And a four-foot-square outhouse was tacked onto the end. Because they had kitchenettes, meals were no longer included, so rates dropped to $2.50 per day, $12.00 per week, and $35.00 per month. That made bungalows so affordable that middle-class families booked their favorites years in advance.[57]

Concrete workers laid a tennis court where Hotel Bayocean would no longer rise, and they paved the streets and sidewalks leading up to the Annex and inside Bungalow City. Harkness and T. Irving were on the spit most of that summer, commonly greeting guests entering the dining room. There, musicians played, and "beautiful young ladies glide[d] like fairies as they serve[d] you with the luxuries of the table, unequaled in Oregon." Three nights a week, the musicians would move down the hill after dinner to play in a new indoor dance hall across from the Natatorium that had displaced its earlier, rustic version. During the day, beachcombers warmed up after frolicking in the surf at the tea house inside it. Those not interested in dancing could see a movie in the Natatorium or build a bonfire on the beach and roast marshmallows.[58]

Swan Hawkinson bought a launch to ferry train passengers from Bay City to supplement the income he and Othelia earned managing Bungalow City. The Potters enjoyed motoring about the bay in their new *Dorothy May* while Carl Shagren provided other guests bay cruises on the *Henrietta No. 2*. Others provided deep-sea fishing excursions during the day, including one on which Francis Mitchell caught a 124-pound halibut. Ship passengers watched north jetty construction as they entered and exited Tillamook Bay. Geibisch and Joplin Company of Portland had driven the first piling on April 22, 1914. By mid-August, dump cars running on rails laid on 1,500 feet of trestle extending seaward from Barview had dumped four to five hundred tons of rock between the pilings.[59]

Landlubbers picked berries and explored the woods. Some hiked north to the abandoned Elliott homestead hoping to witness "the spirit that walks there at midnight." Tillamook groups boated over during the day to enjoy resort facilities and hike up to the caves at the base of Cape Meares or visit its lighthouse. In May, they watched a twenty-acre landslide moving down its northern slope an average of six feet per day and turning waves yellow for a hundred feet out to sea. A high school group lost their way for several hours because the old trail had disappeared.[60]

Cottages rose along the bay side of the spit for the first time in 1914. TBPRC's tinner, George Burckhard, started things out by building one for himself along Bay Street in the spring. Fred and Helen Clack put up a two-story house two blocks north of Burckhard, on the north side of Seal Street. A few blocks northwest of the Clacks but higher on the dune, P. D. Hance built two cottages on adjacent lots, one for himself, the other for E. M. (Ella) Hutchinson. Hance also put up at least one of Henry King's two cottages. J. A. Dick had one built just uphill from The Mitchell. T. Irving would not have included some of these when he wrote ex-plaintiff Cronise that "over $100,000 has been invested in high-grade dwellings" at the end of June.[61]

Johan and Dora Poulsen sold two houses to their daughters that year. Thora Trommald bought the one closest to the Annex. Agnete Bates bought the one facing the ocean on High Street, and she and her husband Paul dubbed Villa Tettrazzina. The Poulsens kept the bayside cabin for themselves. O. H. (Otto) Schwerdtmann, who owned Oregon Box and Manufacturing in Portland, had a place built out past the Hylands and Turners on High Street, near the end of its paving. Harry and Minnie Woodhouse's cabin rose from the beach, two-thirds of a mile north of the Natatorium, out past the Burns cabin.[62]

Only one house went up on Clarke Street that year. Portland's city health officer, Dr. M. B. (Marius) Marcellus, and his wife Vinnie purchased Edwin Lockwood's house on Clarke Street and dubbed it Skookum Tepee. Lockwood then built Hillcrest three blocks south of it. The *Oregonian* said it "equals any in this district for beauty."[63]

Judging by the ten cottages built, increased facility construction, and corresponding resort activity during 1914, Bayocean Park appeared to be progressing nicely. However, trouble had been brewing all year.

CHAPTER 3

Litigation Wreaks Havoc

(1914–1918)

In addition to funding the construction of promised resort facilities by setting up a new corporation, as he had for the Natatorium, T. Irving Potter tried raising funds via the courts. It turned out to be a terrible mistake. Though seemingly innocuous to begin with, his suits led to countersuits, adverse decisions, and negative media coverage that eventually destroyed the resort financially and removed it from his family's control.

Lot Contract Holders Sued to Collect Overdue Payments

The courts heard the case against F. N. (Frank) Derby first. The Salem realtor and insurance salesman had been an *Eastman v. PCRC* plaintiff who concurred in dropping the case in July 1911. But after paying $300 on a $600 lot, he quit mailing checks. So had a couple of hundred others, taking net lots sold down to 1,658.[1] Unlike the others, TBPRC was not satisfied with foreclosing on Derby; they wanted to force him to pay the other $300. Why? Funding the Natatorium with stock sales rather than company cash a few months earlier suggests the company was running low on funds.

In April 1914, a Marion County Circuit Court judge ruled against Derby. That would have made the Potters think this tactic would work. But Derby's appeal delayed payment. And a year later, the Oregon State Supreme Court reversed the decision:

> In the case at bar, where the whole agreement seems to have been drawn advantageously to the seller, it is not unreasonable to assume that the purchaser intended to reserve to himself the one small privilege of losing what money he might at any time have paid, and thereby be automatically released from further obligation.[2]

TBPRC would get no more money from Derby or any other contract holder who chose to let go of their lot.

Another case filed in December 1913 was making its way through Multnomah County Circuit Court while Derby's was heard. TBPRC had sued Portland chiropractor Dr. George Breitling to collect $600 on four repossessed lots purchased for $2,950 in 1909 and 1910. Breitling countersued, charging the company with fraud and demanding a refund of the $1,440, including interest, which he had already paid. As a result, the case took nine months to be heard by a jury on September 9, 1914. After three days of testimony from eleven witnesses, they decided in Breitling's favor on the 12th. The Oregon Supreme Court reversed the Breitling decision a year and a half later, saying he had waited too long to charge fraud, but TBPRC got no additional funds from him for the same reason as Derby.

Guests riding the dinky train. BOP-6, TCPM.

In addition to the significance of its outcome, the 229 pages of testimony, maps, sales pamphlets, and photos submitted during the Breitling case provide a behind-the-scenes look at Bayocean Park of 1914 not found elsewhere. Breitling testified for the first day and a half, guided by his attorney, G. G. (Gustav) Schmitt. He said the brochures A. J. Jones brought to his office during six months of regular visits made him an avid booster as well as a buyer. But then Breitling heard troubling news from a friend who visited Bayocean Park, stopped payments, and visited the spit to see for himself in July 1913.[3]

Breitling bushwhacked across the northern hills guided by an off-duty dinky engineer to find his lots located on opposite shores of the spit. He was distressed to see no signs of activity anywhere near them. Water pipes were strewn about the areas where work was going on. He thought many of the cabins were shacks unbefitting a high-class resort. The exterior of the Annex looked fine, but inside, it was "junk… a cheaply constructed building." He saw no plunge or bathhouse on the bay side. David Baker corroborated Breitling with photos of water pipes suspended among the trees on Cape Meares. He agreed the Annex was poorly built but judged the Natatorium as fine as any despite its wave generator not working.[4]

P. D. Hance claimed to have built thirteen cabins. He was confident that had TBPRC accepted his bid of $17,500, the Annex would have been a much nicer hotel. He challenged the company's claim to have spent $100,000 annually since January 1, 1909, because its tally included the Natatorium, which a different corporation had built, and the pier and Bayside Inn stood on tidelands outside the subdivision. Presenting photos of cobbly streets, Hance said, "I would not call it pavement, but it is an attempt." David Baker and Francis Mitchell hauled two chunks of pavement up the courthouse steps to make the point with the jury. Swan Hawkinson explained the inferior quality: his street crew had to lower the cement-to-sand ratio because cement sacks were running low.[5]

Harkness Chapin was TBPRC's main witness. Attorney J. C. (Jesse) Veazie led him through the company's many achievements on the spit and submitted a plat map highlighting four miles paved and three miles graded of the fourteen miles of streets in the subdivision. Harkness thought being more than halfway finished with half of the roads was as good as might be expected. Chapin explained each instance of shoddy concrete work, though when shown one photo, he admitted, "we are not proud of that street at all." Harkness gave several examples of expensive houses on the ridgeline and said the only buildings he considered shacks were a couple that Hance and Baker built, including their office. William Clemens said streets on Bayocean were as good as any near his Portland home.[6]

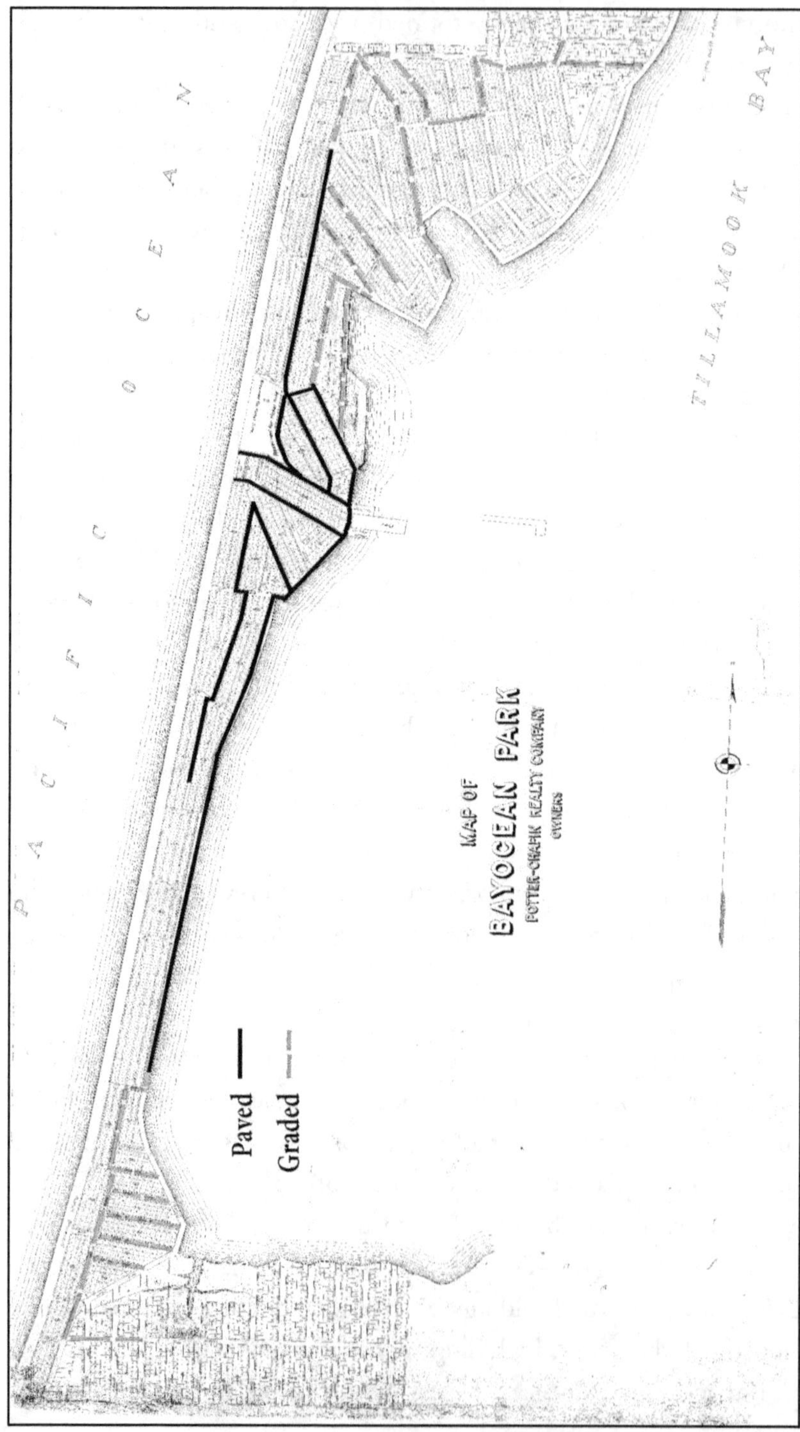

1910 Bayocean plat map cropped to the extent of roads paved and graded by the end of 1914. Adapted from Plaintiff Exhibit 6, Folder 3, *TBPRC v. Breitling*, OSA.

As for the water system, Chapin said the main pipe was four inches in diameter, feeder lines half that. Pipes were strung above ground on Cape Meares to make them easier to enlarge as demand increased. They were cast iron but looked like cheap plastic in photographs because they were dipped to prevent rust. All lines on the spit were buried initially, but storms and construction activity had uncovered a few. Crews paved streets and extended water lines to lots as soon as owners expressed an intent to build, which is why Breitling had seen neither near his lots. Harkness testified that Breitling said he was pleased by what he saw, had no intent to build, and quit paying because of financial difficulties.[7]

According to Chapin, TBPRC deserved credit for every expenditure made regardless of land titles and corporate distinctions. All guests of the Annex thought it was first class. The company had not built Hotel Bayocean "because we have had no demand for it yet…we are using our best judgment as to what would create the most demand for the money." As for the Natatorium, Harkness said a new corporation just seemed like a better way to handle things. He approximated having spent $500,000 to date, half from selling lots and half invested by T. Benton and himself.[8]

Francis Mitchell came to the stand eager to report that he and Swan Hawkinson had measured 19,200 feet (3.64 miles) of paving. He was sure the open-air bay plunge was no more than 75 by 500 feet, not the 500 by 1,000 feet claimed by TBPRC. According to Francis, the two-inch cast iron water lines on the spit were above ground and rusting because workers had moved them there from Cape Meares after running four-inch coated pipes through the trees on the slopes. "We found scales a quarter of an inch thick that were peeled off of some of the pipes."[9]

Mitchell said that, like Breitling, he had been an early Bayocean Park booster, encouraging friends in Kansas City to buy lots while selling them for PCRC in the Administration Building. But he had become increasingly disillusioned and now felt deceived, angry, and embarrassed at having misled people. He was convinced things would have been different if T. Benton had remained in charge. The two had met during a visit to Kansas City and shared complaints about Harkness Chapin.[10]

Mitchell blamed T. Irving for being "unable to carry out the plans outlined by his father [and make a] success of the place now…he has bottled up Bay Ocean." The latter referred to a barbed-wire fence strung across the pier to keep Axel Anderson, P. D. Hance, Swan Hawkinson, and David Baker from using it. Francis promised to "pay out every dollar I have if it is necessary. I have got $6,000 invested in Bay Ocean and I am going to keep on fighting for myself and my friends…I am here to fight this to the end." As Mitchell continued to rant, the judge interrupted to ask Veazie if he had any additional questions. He replied, "No, I don't think I had better ask any more."[11]

Local Lawsuits Activate Francis Mitchell

The barbed fence blocking the pier involved a case filed by TBPRC in Tillamook earlier that year against Axel Anderson. In May 1913, Anderson and Carl Shagren had retired from the Life-Saving Station at Barview and purchased the *Henrietta No. 2* to ferry passengers around Tillamook Bay. Sometime after that, they contracted with TBPRC to transport passengers from the dock it had built near the Garibaldi train station in 1913 to shorten the trip from Portland to Bayocean Park. In March 1914, Axel purchased a small fishing boat of his own called the *Bobby* to haul cargo. He tied it up to the pier each night.[12]

The trouble began when Harkness Chapin learned Anderson was bidding against him on a four-year contract to deliver mail from Garibaldi using TBPRC's dock. It seemed to Harkness like Axel was biting the hand that fed him, but the boatman disagreed. Chapin asked P. D. Hance and David Baker to intervene, but they refused. When Axel's bid of $25 a month won, Harkness assessed him a $25 moorage fee which, of course, he could not pay. T. Irving gave Anderson final notice in person on July 8th. Eight days later, he asked Tillamook County Circuit Court to issue a restraining order and filed suit against Francis Mitchell.[13]

These lawsuits lit a fire inside the Missourian that would never go out, and young Potter would soon regret having held the match. Mitchell immediately published a manifesto in the *Herald* detailing every dastardly deed of Harkness and T. Irving. He asked the public to support Bayocean

Park businessmen, saying TBPRC "seeks to injure and interfere with them and to monopolize every avenue of access and profit." P. D. Hance and David Baker joined Francis and Axel in signing the paper. They distributed copies locally and mailed them to lot owners across the nation.[14]

On July 28th, Tillamook County Circuit Court decided against TBPRC. It acknowledged company ownership of the dock and said it had the right to charge for moorage, but the fee had to be reasonable. The *Herald* wrote, "We are sorry to see such a spirit displayed." That was significant because TBPRC had run an ad for the first time in the local

The Mitchell soon after completion. July 1912, *Surf*, 1. Bayocean Booklets. TCPM.

paper on July 21st, in response to Mitchell's manifesto.[15] The *Herald* had stood up for the company in the past, but it would not tolerate the bullying of local businessmen. Instead of backing off, TBPRC filed another suit against Anderson in Tillamook County Justice Court. That judge sent it back to the circuit court judge. The case lingered until newly appointed Judge George Bagley Sr. dismissed it in October 1915.[16]

The action filed by TBPRC against Mitchell was to collect back payments of $606.44 owed on three lots and $9.10 for the sidewalk poured in front of The Mitchell in March 1911. Francis insisted he had paid for the sidewalk and acknowledged owing money on the lots. But he refused to pay more until the company honored its contractual obligations to pave all streets and sidewalks, build a first-class hotel, run utilities to all lots, and construct two additional piers. Attorneys exchanged papers for a couple of years until Judge Bagley dismissed the case in October 1916. Francis and Ida had moved to Portland by then.[17]

The Mitchell had been the key to Francis and Ida's plan to make Bayocean Park their new home when they left Kansas City in 1907, but they ran out of money by the time materials needed to build it could be shipped there. A $500 loan from the Tillamook County Bank and promotion by the *Surf* got them to the finish line, but The Mitchell must not have provided enough income for them to live on because they moved to Tillamook in October 1911. Whatever they did while there was enough to convince the bank to loan them $1,200 to pay off the first loan and raise additional cash in January 1913. They moved back to the spit in January 1914, just in time for Francis to get tangled up in the Axel Anderson affair.[18]

In August 1914, soon after TBPRC filed suit against Francis, the Mitchells sold their mercantile to Dr. G. W. Rice of Kansas City for $2,000, who also assumed their loan. Rice leased out The Mitchell during the 1915 resort season but paid nothing to the Tillamook County Bank. So, it foreclosed, purchased the mercantile at auction for $1,461.85 owed, including interest, and sold it to William George of Kansas City in June 1917 for $1,374.30. By then, Francis and Ida were living in Portland, where he sold insurance while using profits from their sale of The Mitchell to wage a battle to wrest control of Bayocean Park from the Potters and Chapins.[19]

On October 9, 1914, the *Herald* published a letter from T. Irving about the "considerable criticism of the T. B. Potter Realty Company by a few individuals over the fact that we have placed a charge for the use of our dock at Bayocean by commercial boats." Using the same argument his father had used with Reis Tract residents a decade earlier, T. Irving said contracts required TBPRC to build the pier, not maintain it. It had done so for too long "at a heavy loss." It was only fair to ask commercial users to "pay a small proportion." He offered those who objected a free lease in exchange for taking over maintenance.[20] No one took T. Irving up on his offer.

Bayocean Park Forced into Receivership

On November 25, 1914, sixty-four contract holders represented by Gustav Schmitt made another effort to force TBPRC into receivership, this time in Multnomah County Circuit Court with Judge William Gatens presiding. Unfortunately, the earliest papers in the *Marsh v. TBPRC* case file are dated December 10th, so newspaper coverage provides the only source of information before that.[21]

As had Eastman and his Salem cohorts in 1911, the plaintiffs accused T. Irving and Fannie (not T. Benton) of spending money on extravagant entertainment, excessive advertising, and high salaries that should have gone to building the resort facilities that had been contractually guaranteed. Based on press coverage, the complaint said the company was insolvent, that it would cost $2,500,000 more than TBPRC had to finish the resort, and that it was selling equipment because it had no intention to do so and needed to pay down debts. The plaintiffs accused Harkness of returning to the company in July 1912 to make sure he got the money owed him by T. Benton, who had "became mentally unable to retain management."[22]

In their response, TBPRC's attorneys Palmer Fales and Robert Platt portrayed plaintiff accusations as "spite work" from a few troublemakers, thirty-three of whom were behind on contract payments; others were disgruntled ex-salesmen. The affidavit filed by Harkness Chapin said he was the only one of the principals still drawing a salary—$450 a month—and that his contract with T. Benton was a private agreement. Jesse Veazie filed cooperatively but independently on behalf of a hundred lot owners who intervened on behalf of the company. He also convinced five plaintiffs to withdraw after showing them how Mitchell, Baker, and Hawkinson had misled them.[23]

The company claimed a net worth of $979,172.37. As of November 1st, they had sold 1,648 lots worth $890,336.15. Of that, $573,020.80 had been collected and $556,259.76 spent. The company valued 1,152 unsold lots and unplatted tracts at $869,366. Attorney Palmer Fales told the press TBPRC's largest debts were loans from the Potters—$34,899.12 from T. Benton and $183,829.41 from Fannie—and estimated the cost to complete Bayocean Park at $165,000.[24]

One reason for the disparity in net worth is that TBPRC valued unsold lots at their last offering price while plaintiffs used Tillamook County's assessments, which were ninety percent lower. Another reason was that plaintiffs included Hotel Bayocean among the work remaining while the company did not.

News coverage did not include cash on hand or a profit and loss summary. During the Breitling case a couple of months earlier, Harkness Chapin had testified to spending $500,000 on the resort, half from lot sales, half invested by himself and T. Benton. It is not too surprising that Harkness had discovered another $56,259.76 in expenditures, but now he was saying it had all come from lot sales. If so, where was the $250,000 Chapin and Potter had invested? How about the $218,728.53 lent by the Potters? In July 1911, T. Irving had told *Oregonian* reporter E. C. Sammons the company would spend $650,000 by the end of that year. The most reasonable explanation for the disparate numbers is that nearly a million dollars had passed through PCRC and TBPRC by the end of 1914; half to resort construction, the other half to operational expenses like commissions, salaries, and marketing.

Judge Gatens should have asked for an independent audit of TBPRC's books, but he did not. What he did do was refuse to set up a temporary receivership as requested by the plaintiffs or throw out the lawsuit as requested by the defendants. Instead, he told the parties to work out the terms of a permanent receivership. Fales and Platt tried twice more to quash the suit and then sued Francis Mitchell and Swan Hawkinson for slander and Gustav Schmitt for assisting them. That did not play well in the press. TBPRC had spent so little on advertising in 1914 that publishers had nothing to lose in going after the company.[25]

In January 1915, Gustav Schmitt filed a supplemental complaint listing every plaintiff's lot number and payment history. Most of them lived in Portland, where Francis Mitchell and his cohorts were active. Schmitt also listed more problems, like water pipes drooping, leaky joints causing low water pressure, and paving equipment sitting idle for over a year rusting away. The cost of dealing with these additional problems increased liabilities to $2,900,000 more than assets. To plaintiffs, it made no sense to continue making contract payments until a receiver could ensure they would be used to finish the resort.[26]

Fales and Platt denied Schmitt's new allegations and filed individual suits against the plaintiffs behind in payments—thirty-seven by then. Jesse Veazie provided his sixty-one interveners' lot numbers and payment history. Only ten lived in Portland, with thirty in Spokane and twenty-one in Salem. Their concern was that a receiver would make it harder to finish the resort.[27]

Meanwhile, fellow circuit court judge Henry McGinn presided over two cases in which Bayocean Park contract holders demanded full refunds from TBPRC. On February 11th, Frank McNurlen reported paying $603 in principal and interest on an $850 lot purchased from Christian Lauritzen at Umatilla, Oregon, in February 1910. The super salesman had told the young railroad engineer his lot was "level and laid beautifully for a nice business" in the commercial district around the north pier. But when McNurlen visited the spit in July 1914, he found nothing but sand and brush.[28]

McNurlen's star witness was S. B. (Sydney) Vincent, chief field examiner of the Oregon State Commercial Division. He had inspected Bayocean Park in November 1914 after hearing fraud charges. Vincent testified to having measured twenty-eight miles of streets on the plat map of which just three and a half miles were paved. And the concrete was so inferior it would not bear regular traffic whenever a road reached the spit. The water system was equally shoddy and incapable of handling much more demand.[29] The internal report Sydney had filed earlier was more damning:

> The paving apparently has been done for its advertising value and not for its utility... if Bayocean is ever to attain the substantiality in growth promised for it by the promoters, the paving already laid will have to be replaced...The so-called reservoir is nothing but a poorly constructed dam. Rocks thrown up form a small pool less than 3 feet deep in the deepest part... if Bayocean attains the city-like proportions promised lot owners, the water system will have to be replaced and an adequate reservoir constructed.[30]

Jesse Veazie ignored both the complaint and Vincent's testimony and pointed to a clause in the sales contract precluding grievances based on a salesman's verbal statements. That did not impress Judge McGinn. He made TBPRC cancel the contract, refund everything McNurlen had paid, and reimburse his travel expenses. He then told the press, "Gentlemen, there isn't an honest thing in this case excepting the hard dollars this engineer boy earned in working for the O. W. R. & N. Company that these people stole from him."[31]

Gustav Schmitt then filed a similar lawsuit on behalf of Minnie Schmidt. She had purchased a lot in November 1909 after a year of solicitation from a salesman who said it would be a fantastic location for the restaurant she wanted to build. But in August 1914, Minnie discovered it was in a high elevation sand gap, later dubbed Rabbit Hollow, far from commercial lots. Jesse Veazie planned to use the same defense as he had with McNurlen until Judge McGinn was assigned the case. On March 23, 1915, Veazie filed a supplemental answer saying, "Defendants are informed and believe, and therefore allege, that since the filing of the defendant's answer…the plaintiff herein sold, assigned, and transferred, for a valuable consideration, all of her right, title, and interest in and to said contract."[32] TBPRC must have given Schmidt what she wanted to avoid another public reprimand.

At this point, litigation was going so badly for the Potters that going into receivership would serve to protect them from reimbursing anyone else asking for their money back. So, on their behalf, William Clemens suggested setting up a seven-member receivership committee to manage Bayocean Park. Each side would appoint three men. Gatens would appoint a seventh to serve as chairman. Plaintiffs' representatives L. E. (Lyman) Latourette, who was Portland's City Attorney, Francis Mitchell, P. D. Hance, David Baker, and Swan Hawkinson agreed to the plan after Clemens agreed to modifications: the chairman would be a full-time, paid receiver; at least five committee members must agree before a policy was implemented; every current employee of TBPRC would be fired; and all related suits would be dismissed.[33]

Gatens implemented some of the terms agreed to, but he reduced the number of votes required to set policy from five to four, gave the receiver the final say on everything, and fired no one. The plaintiffs' representatives felt betrayed, especially Latourette, who had taken the lead. It had been his idea to initiate the lawsuit originally, on behalf of his mother, who had inherited several Bayocean lot contracts from a friend.[34]

On March 23, 1915, Judge Gatens hired Sydney Vincent as the receiver. Before ferreting out fraudulent operators in Oregon, Vincent had been a reporter with the Associated Press, president of the Portland Press Club, and secretary of the Oregon Manufacturers' Association. What Vincent had not done was run a business. That and his previously expressed opinions on the resort made Vincent a questionable choice to shepherd it to completion and financial viability.[35] To make up for Vincent's lack of business experience, all the men Gatens appointed to his advisory committee were prominent Portland businessmen. Horace Ramsdell managed Lipman, Wolfe & Co. Jay Smith ran Marshall-Wells Hardware, and B. O. Case was a wholesale milliner. These men would represent lot owners. TBPRC's representatives were William Clemens, Mortimer Fouch, and Otto Schwerdtmann.[36]

The receiver's first act was having the judge place a restraining order on the five men who had negotiated with Clemens because TBPRC employees complained that they were interfering with work and creating discontent among lot owners. In his response, Francis Mitchell blamed those employees for losing The Mitchell, which means one of the unnamed parties was Harkness Chapin. P. D. Hance was upset that none of the advisory committee members representing lot owners were plaintiffs and that Ramsdell served on T. Irving's Coin Machine Manufacturing Company Board of Directors. Conflicts with the employees had cost Hance $1,000 already, and another $1,000 invested in a house was at risk. Judge Gatens vacated the restraining orders but made no changes to the stipulations or appointments. And he replaced Hawkinson with R. J. Marsh as the lead plaintiff despite Marsh being one of the contract holders Jesse Veazie had convinced to withdraw.[37]

The advisory committee's first recommendation was to pay Vincent $300 per month. Though it was less than Chapin had received, it was still five times the average male salary in 1915. The receiver showed his appreciation by appointing William Clemens as president and Mortimer Fouch as secretary of TBPRC. He retained T. Benton's long-time secretary E. V. (Elizabeth) Reardon and bookkeeper A. C. Strahl before showing everyone else the door. Vincent hired brothers Samuel and John White to represent the receivership in legal matters. He started writing deeds for lot owners who paid off contracts—at about the same rate as preceding months—for Judge Gatens to approve. At the end of July, the judge approved Vincent's recommendation to offer delinquent contract holders the option to sign new contracts for the remaining balance with covenants accepting things as they were at Bayocean Park.[38]

After a few months, seeing no financial reports from the receiver, Lyman Latourette and his cohorts asked Vincent to look at the books. All they got was "a general, verbal statement made on June 18, 1915, that he had collected about $7,000 [$3,000 a month], that his expenses were from $800 to $1,000 per month, and that he had paid about $3,000 on old bills of the company."[39]

Activities described in Bayocean Park's society page column during the summer of 1915 sounded the same as they always had, with no mention of a change in management. However, the typically positive news was interrupted when an elderly fellow died of a heart attack while bathing in the Natatorium and two men camping on a lot owned by one of them drowned crossing the bar in a small boat. Sydney Vincent rented a place for the summer and enjoyed the resort with his family as best they could, considering its lousy paving and leaking, above-ground water pipes. He exchanged cabins with Harkness Chapin in 1916, suggesting a close relationship. T. Irving and his family stayed in their cottage for just a week in 1915. He stayed alone at the Annex just a couple of times in 1916.[40]

Two years of litigation press coverage had slowed down cottage construction. Only three went up in 1915, and they would be the last until 1927. D. T. (Daniel) Van Tine, the principal of Portland High School, had Lorelie built on the east side of Clarke Street just south of Green Gables,

Harkness Chapin's place. Thelma Swank's cottage was on the ridge above Bay Street between 6th and 7th Avenues. The Pagoda—named for its upwardly curling cupola and rafter ends—was built for Portland's first female osteopath, Dr. Gertrude Lord Gates, and her partner, Dr. E. Tracy Parker.[41]

Dr. Parker's younger sister, Helen (Parker) Alexander, later recalled what it was like spending a summer on Clarke Street:

> Our kitchen windows faced the grandeur of the bay and the forested mountains surrounding it. Our meals were eaten with a changing scene, day after day. Looking north, down the peninsula with its winding road, bordered by tortured pines and blossoming salal, Oregon grape clung to the ridge as if to mold it. From all directions it was a Japanese print, with the soft fog wafting through the draws to separate partly the ridges…At the end of the day someone would call: "The sun is setting." We would all rush to the glass windows across the end of the living room, and stand there for twenty minutes just to see what shape the sun would take that day [and at other times to see] the little fishing boats which would go completely out of sight behind the swell and then always appear again; the schools of whales spouting with glee [and] the magic phosphorus, which outlined the breaking waves and lighted up the shimmering green water.[42]

No resort facilities were added in 1915, but the *Oregonian* reported that work started on a 350-foot-long, six-foot-wide, concrete promenade. The famous Seaside Promenade was one and a half miles long and fifteen feet wide, but it was not converted from wood to concrete until 1920, so this would have given Bayocean Park bragging rights. However, no promenade was ever built along the spit. Receivership books later recorded $857.48 contributed by "adjacent property owners" in a "sea-wall account." Bayocean Park lot owners would not have paid for a promenade for guests to enjoy. The need for a seawall means erosion was already evident, just a year after north jetty construction had begun. Vincent's objective would have been to keep TBPRC men working, but it cost $1,478.88, which made things worse. He then conceived a better idea—building the west end of Bayocean Road—that fall.[43]

Bayocean Road's First Section Built

County Surveyor U. G. (Unno) Jackson had surveyed the entire route for two weeks in 1911. From the west end of the Tillamook River drawbridge, he followed existing wagon ruts for a mile across the estuary and north to Memaloose Point, where the river met the bay and the ruts ended. No wagon had ever travelled the next four and a half miles west from there to the sea because rocky bluffs, riparian areas, and forested slopes ran into the bay. Before they could, culverts and bridges would need to be built to navigate creeks, and material dredged from the bay would have to be pumped behind bulkheads or riprap set out in the bay.[44]

Fred Baker, the publisher of the *Headlight,* was the first to petition county commissioners for the construction of Bayocean Road on August 9, 1912. The commissioners appointed W. B. Alderman, J. H. Hathaway, and Unno Jackson as road reviewers. When Jackson showed the other two men his survey and discussed the challenges encountered, they decided to take his word for it. The men recommended construction "because there is at present, and in the future will be, a greater demand for a county road to the Bayocean territory." Since Bayocean machinery and men with experience were readily available, the commissioners paid TBPRC to improve the first 4,800 feet of wagon ruts for $2,000 in August 1914. It ran past one of the two tracts along the road owned by Fred Baker and ended at Hathaway's barn.[45]

In August 1915, Sydney Vincent's bid of $11,997 to build a section at the east of the road, where it met Bayocean Park at 13th Street and 1st Avenue, was the lowest, but the commissioners had only budgeted $7,750. The two parties worked out a daily rate to apply until year-end, or the money was gone. An onshore crew dynamited the rocky bluffs into boulders small enough for the dredge crane to lift and stack them in a line offshore. The dredge crew then pumped bay sediment into the space between the shoreline and riprap, where the shore crew graded into a dirt road.[46]

Keeping two crews busy until January 1, 1916, was the best Sydney Vincent managed. After eight years of activity, the spit must have seemed eerily quiet to the half dozen residents remaining when the last worker left. The following summer, Edwin Lockwood sold Hillcrest to Kate Smith, the wife of Vincent's advisor, Jay Smith. Jim O'Donnell kept Whiteaway and returned to enjoy it with his family during the summers. That and staying neutral during "Mitchell's war" endeared him to locals.[47]

Barview Destroyed as North Jetty Extends Seaward

Unlike Bayocean Park, north jetty construction was on a fast track. Geibisch and Joplin Company of Portland had finished eighty percent of the trestle by the end of August 1915. Rockfill was only thirty-six percent complete because the seventy-five men working at the company's Miami River quarry could not keep up despite rail cars delivering five to eight

Rocks carried by rail cars filled the space between wooden trestles on the north jetty, which caused the destruction of Barview during construction. Both viewed from the south. Barview Jetty Images 20 (above) and 57 (below), TCPM.

hundred tons daily. That November, storm surges scoured away five hundred feet of shoreline twelve hundred feet east of the jetty base, destroying the resort town of Barview. Waves carried some of Southern Pacific's railroad tracks away and covered others with debris, as they did the Life-Saving Station grounds. The residence of the station's commanding officer, Captain Robert Farley, was one of many lost.[48]

In 1923, Southern Pacific sued the United States in its Court of Claims to recover the $80,916.38 cost of laying tracks twenty-two feet behind the new shoreline and protecting them with bulkheads and riprap. It argued that the jetty's projection into the sea had redirected high waves from the southwest, which previously continued up the coastline, directly into Barview. That was a taking of private property prohibited by the Fifth Amendment to the Constitution. The court disagreed strictly on the legal question without mentioning the jetty, and Southern Pacific did not appeal.[49] The Tillamook newspapers kept silent—they had lobbied hard for the jetty that had just destroyed one of their communities. They could only hope this was the end of it.

Fannie Potter Sues the Receivership

On January 3, 1916, Fannie Potter sued in Portland's (Federal) District Court to recover the $183,829.41 loan TBPRC's attorney Palmer Fales told the press she gave the company back in December 1914, plus $25,000 in anticipated attorney's fees. Nothing was said of the $34,899.12 supposedly lent by T. Benton, whom the press reported living in a sanitorium. Fannie hired William Bristol to handle the case because of his experience in federal court, where the case had to be heard because she lived in a different state than where TBPRC was incorporated. Going beyond that to say Fannie was "a resident and citizen of the state of California, and not, and never has been, a resident and citizen of the State of Oregon" suggests that Fannie wanted to avoid the case being heard in Multnomah County Circuit Court at all costs.[50]

Judge Gatens authorized Sydney Vincent to hire federal litigators, John Sedgwick and Charles Fulton. They argued that Fannie's mortgage was an attempt to convert equity into debt by falsely claiming that she and T. Benton had lent the money to TBPRC after seeing the money they had invested disappear. That is supported by the timing of Jesse Veazie's notarization of the mortgage on September 12, 1914—the same day as the Breitling verdict. And during that trial, Harkness Chapin had mentioned no mortgage while testifying. If the company had received the money since then, where had it gone? Sydney Vincent certainly did not have it.[51]

Attorneys on each side exchanged papers during the spring of 1916. Judge Charles Wolverton made no decisions. But two of William Bristol's declarations are noteworthy. To explain Fannie's acting alone, he wrote, "since the 4th day of July 1910, said T. B. Potter has been absolutely mentally incapacitated, at times violently insane and at others passive, but nevertheless has continued to be and is now a lunatic." Second, before August 25, 1914, Harkness Chapin had taken ownership of one thousand shares (forty percent) of TBPRC stock instead of foreclosing on the $99,000 T. Benton still owed him, having received just $8,000 of the $107,000 agreed to on January 1, 1910.[52] Harkness had more at risk than anyone other than the Potters.

While not selling insurance, Francis Mitchell worked closely with Lyman Latourette and others to organize lot owners. They recruited members and solicited contributions with ads explaining the threat Fannie Potter's "illegal mortgage" posed. With the increased support, they got Judge Gatens to replace their representatives on Vincent's advisory committee in March. He offset that by replacing Mortimer Fouch with Harkness Chapin a month and a half later.[53]

In June 1916, William Bristol asked Judge Gatens to remove Sydney Vincent on behalf of Fannie Potter and two lot owners who had been ignored by the receiver and his committee when they asked for their money back. The judge did not remove his receiver, but he did honor Bristol's demand for a financial accounting of the receivership's first twelve months. The report he filed in September showed that by April 1916, Vincent had just $779.21 in the bank, which explains why taxes had not been paid and no progress had been made on resort facilities. New plaintiff attorneys Andrew Crawford (Oregon State Attorney General during the Eastman case) and his brother James reviewed the report in December. They accused Vincent of spending "nearly three dollars to collect and expend one dollar," alluding to wages consuming most of the income. That prompted Judge Gatens to order a more detailed accounting, but the Whites somehow convinced the Crawfords to retract their request.[54]

In the fall of 1916, Sydney Vincent offered to extend Bayocean Road two miles westward from Memaloose Point to McCoy Creek for the $18,000 remaining in the county's 1916 road budget and $8,000 of their 1917 road budget. The commissioners turned him down. They must have regretted doing so when Ambrose Arstill submitted the lowest bid in May 1917 for $28,507.78. Vincent would never submit another Bayocean Road bid. His inability to pay the property taxes due on September 30, 1915 complicated things between the two parties because property taxes funded roads. Vincent and successive receivers never paid taxes. Penalties and interest assessed increased the debt to the largest owed by the receivership. Resolving that would eventually be the key to completing Bayocean Road.[55]

Desperate for cash in December 1916, Vincent foreclosed on 155 delinquent contract holders en masse. He had written to every contract holder several times during the previous twenty months, offering to grant them a deed for a cheaper lot in exchange for payments they had made on an expensive one or trade one lot for payments made on multiple lots. Many accepted. But some had filed suit, like McNurlen and Schmidt, to cancel the contract and get a full refund. Though they had been unsuccessful, Sydney decided it was time to "quiet clouded titles" for contract holders outside Oregon because they were the most challenging and expensive to handle. Over the next fourteen months, forty brought their payments current. Twelve others voluntarily canceled theirs. On February 4, 1918, Judge Bagley foreclosed on 103 who did nothing.[56]

Sydney Vincent's mass foreclosure had raised much-needed cash and reduced the receivership's liability. But many of the people who lost their lots and accrued payments were friends of Francis Mitchell in Kansas City. When he and Ida returned to Bayocean for the 1917 summer season, no fractious encounters between the two men were reported, but after returning to Portland in the fall, Francis made so much fuss in the press that Judge Gatens eventually felt compelled to defend his handling of "the tangled affairs" that October:

> There is no doubt in the world that the T. B. Potter Realty Company has not carried out the terms of its contracts with lot purchasers in Bayocean [but the Supreme Court decisions on Derby and Breitling] hold in effect that a contract holder who permits his contract to become delinquent automatically cancels the contract, thus relieving the company of its obligations and the property involved reverts to the company and becomes one of its assets. My sympathies have always been with the property holds [*sic*] for the reason that they are the injured parties. If they can point out any legal manner in which I can grant them relief I will most certainly do so.[57]

Sydney Vincent pointed out that Fannie Potter's suit precluded selling lots because they were being held as collateral for the mortgage. His only source of income was payment on existing contracts, and they were insufficient to make improvements. Despite his legal obligation to TBPRC, Vincent said he had done what he could to accommodate contract holders by trading central lots for those distant ones and giving them lots free and clear in exchange for payments made whenever possible.[58]

Vincent did not mention resort operations as a source of income because it was losing money. Despite the Bayocean Natatorium's popularity, high admission price, and booming economy, it had run at a loss since opening in July 1914. TBPRC lent the Bayocean Natatorium Company $13,644.27 the first summer. Vincent lent it another $1,072 in 1915. Judge Gatens converted the loans to equity in October 1915 by issuing TBPRC an additional 136.5 shares of BNC and granted Vincent the proxy vote on all 686.50 shares in May 1916.[59]

On September 19, 1917, BNC filed suit against TBPRC for fraud on behalf of its other 750 shareholders. It said the $100 paid for each share totaled $75,000, which left $15,000 after spending $60,000 on the Natatorium. So, TBPRC should have contributed $55,000 for their 550 shares. The $70,000 excess was plenty to cover any initial shortfall in revenue and pay the dividends promised by salesmen. Because they shared the same office, staff, and officers, the plaintiffs accused TBPRC of setting BNC up as a sham corporation to make others pay for something it had promised.[60]

In his response, Jesse Veazie said the five lots under the Natatorium, its power plant, and future utility revenue, which TBPRC had given BNC, were worth at least $55,000. But what got the case dismissed on November 15th was Veazie's point that BNC could not file suit on behalf of individual shareholders. A month later, J. B. (John) Keefer, the company's president, and others sued as individuals.[61]

With Bayocean Park legal wrangling getting all the attention, north jetty completion got none. Sometime in October 1917, a Geibisch and Joplin Company crane placed the last of 429,000 tons of stone 5,400 feet out to sea 16 feet above the waves. It had cost $766,000.[62]

Weary of lot owner grievances fomented by Francis Mitchell, Judge Gatens held a hearing on March 16, 1918, to address them in person. The attendees attacked Sydney Vincent for his mass foreclosure, paying Fannie Potter interest on her phony mortgage, and making no progress on the resort. Gatens agreed to replace Vincent with three receivers selected by lot owners at the end of the meeting. He immediately appointed Lyman Latourette and school principal R. R. (Robert) Steele and authorized them to choose a third. Daniel Van Tine joined them at the end of May. Latourette managed daily affairs, with Steele and Van Tine providing support and signatures when necessary.[63]

Before the meeting broke up, the audience asked Latourette and Steele to prioritize the completion of Bayocean Road. Since the road was not a contractual promise and getting a start on it had been one of Vincent's few achievements, he and Gatens must have convinced them Fannie Potter's federal suit precluded dealing with their main grievances. Vincent aggressively defended himself in his resignation letter yet sounded relieved to be handing Bayocean Park over to receivers willing to work without pay. Though he had continued paying Reardon and Strahl, Vincent had not taken a salary for more than seven months. Judge Gatens issued him a "receiver's certificate" for $2,242.66, but it had remained due when Vincent died of complications from surgery in 1926. His obituary said nothing of Bayocean Park.[64]

Potter and Chapin Families Leave Bayocean Behind

As of March 16, 1918, the Potters had no say in Bayocean Park operations, and if anyone knew it would not survive much longer financially, it was them. Fannie might yet recover some of what she and T. Benton had invested from her mortgage suit, but she was not pressing the issue.

T. Benton did not live long enough to see his worst fears come true, having died at fifty-one on April 29, 1916, without ever finding a cure to his mental illness. Fannie scattered his ashes onto San Francisco Bay, perhaps as the *Bayocean* cruised nearby. In his obituary, all the *Oregonian* had to say about Bayocean Park was, "the project was a pretentious one. A fine hotel was built, and streets paved." Fannie delayed initiating probate until August 19, 1917. By then, she had married Lewis Thomas, a University of California dental student who had been a champion swimmer at Portland High School.[65]

The only assets in T. Benton's estate were 1,251 shares of TBPRC. Fannie placed them in a trust as instructed by his will. There was no income to support his family, nor the thousand dollars willed to his long-time secretary Elizabeth Reardon, who returned to California after Sydney Vincent left Ironically, the man who had made a fortune selling real estate never owned any of his own, though Fannie purchased their last house in Alameda, California. In September 1919, she and Lewis (by then Dr. Thomas) moved to Pebble Beach, California, where she continued to hold out hope until February 6, 1920, when she reported TBPRC stock's value as "nil" and closed probate.[66]

Harkness Chapin had no hope of recovering the $99,000 owed him because Fannie was unlikely to share any proceeds if her mortgage suit was successful. So, in September 1917, he and Ina sold their mansion in Northeast Portland. They quit paying Bayocean property taxes and sold Green Gables in 1920. By the time Ina died in 1921, they had moved to Wolf Creek, Oregon. Harkness passed away at seventy-one on May 23, 1935, in Reedsport, Oregon. Neither estate was probated. When their son Leland visited Bayocean in August 1950, the author of its *Headlight-Herald* community column did not know who the Chapins were.[67]

T. Irving lost no money on Bayocean Park, but he had watched his grand idea drain his parents' wealth. In 1918, he left Portland and his Coin Machine Manufacturing Company to work for the Federated Engineers Corporation in New Jersey. Before departing, he and Bess sold their Bayocean Park cottage to Carl Jackson. In 1929, they returned to Portland, and T. Irving set up a company to sell and manufacture a more efficient refrigerator that he had invented. After they divorced in 1934, T. Irving moved to Buffalo, N. Y. and remarried. He was busy developing products for his new wife's cosmetic company—some of which are still sold today—out of an office on 5th Avenue in Manhattan when he died at seventy-six on December 16, 1963. An extensive, standalone obituary in the *New York Times* said that Potter owned over sixty patents. It did not mention Bayocean Park.[68]

CHAPTER 4

Receivers Runs the Resort

(1918–1926)

The new receivers had little time to get Bayocean Park ready for its 1918 seasonal opening on July 4th. Their main challenge was getting the power turned on. Previously, BNC's titular president had automatically signed leases for the power plant and Natatorium that had been written by TBPRC, which then credited the net proceeds against BNC's debt at the end of the season. But John Keefer now claimed that debt was illegitimate and insisted on cash. Lyman Latourette resolved the dilemma by having another BNC officer sign the old deal, and Judge Gatens approved it on July 3rd. Daniel Van Tine drove to Tillamook later the same day, boated out to the spit, and lit the boilers with the help of Bert Biggs and Swan Hawkinson.[1]

A more significant long-term challenge for the receivership triad (Latourette, Steele, and Van Tine) was the lack of revenue. To supplement the resort income their first year, they leased out the dredge, donkey engines, scow, iron drill, and a mule team for seventy dollars a month to Feeney and Bremer Foundry, which was building the steamship *Bedloe* at Dick Point. By February 1918, Ambrose Arstill had extended Bayocean Road to the shipyard a mile west of Memaloose Point so employees could drive there. Tillamook locals used it to watch the hull of the *Bedloe* launched in January 1919 and towed to Astoria for completion.[2]

The *Bedloe* could not be built at Bayocean Park because the pier had not been maintained nor the channel dredged regularly. Ocean-going vessels had not docked there since TBPRC finished the Natatorium in 1914. Shallow draft launches still delivered railroad passengers there from across the bay, but by the fall of 1918, pilings at the end of the pier had rotted to the extent that a severe storm might tear away deck planks that were still in good condition. Judge Gatens authorized removal of the decking for temporary storage, but the triad did not have enough money to hire anyone to do the work.[3] That rotting pier would have discouraged visitors from returning, and the time would come when no planks were left. Everyone would have to hike across the mudflats like Ida Mitchell if Bayocean Road was not finished by then.

Motorized road-building equipment like that used to build the first stages of Bayocean Road. Album 11 (1918-1922), TCPM.

Francis Mitchell's Star Rises as Bayocean Park's Falls

After winning his four-year battle with TBPRC, Francis Mitchell worked out a deal with William George to lease The Mitchell and headed back to the spit with Ida. The Mitchells celebrated their victory with a small ad in the *Oregonian*.[4] Unfortunately, the grand resort they had been promised was still not there. Francis was forty-eight and Ida fifty. He had convinced her to invest everything they had in the Potters' dream, so perhaps he felt he had no choice but to stay and continue a war he had no chance of winning. Francis quietly supported the triad for the next few years. But he would eventually view them and others as enemies to fight.

The Mitchell was Francis's primary weapon. As in most small towns, the mercantile was the first place visitors saw, and its proprietor's local expertise was the first sought. The Mitchell sold metropolitan and local newspapers, so editors and reporters contacted Francis when they needed a scoop. The Bayocean Post Office was there, too, between 1918 and 1946. Seeing the position open when they returned, Francis got appointed as postmaster. Ida took over in 1926. For three years between them and two years during Ida's two decades of service, others held the role officially, but Francis had no qualms about handling the mail for them and telling everyone what was what while doing so.[5]

The media said nothing of the resort's change in management, dire financial situation, lawsuits, or rotting dock during the summer of 1918. Instead, Bayocean Park's society page column spoke of soldiers enjoying the Natatorium while on leave from cutting spruce for army airplanes. The Bayocean Annex, Bayside Inn, and Bungalow City sounded as busy as they had been. But the activities of the Latourette, Van Tine, and Steele families displaced those of the Potters, Chapins, and Vincents, and William Clemens was notably absent. The auto enthusiast who had been Bayocean Park's greatest booster had taken ill at the end of 1917, made no trips in 1918, and died that October.[6]

When Otto Schwerdtmann replaced William Clemens as the president of TBPRC, he attempted to retain some authority over resort management by refusing to rubberstamp deeds granted by Latourette. Judge Gatens took care of that by removing that step. Schwerdtmann then quit paying TBPRC's corporate fees, and the state dissolved the company on January 8, 1921.[7] No one seemed to notice.

Early in 1919, the triad took a deep dive into the TBPRC records Sydney Vincent turned over to them. Their tally of funds transferred from Kansas City to Portland between 1910 and 1912 matched the mortgage Fannie claimed to have granted TBPRC. That supported Sedgwick and Fulton's accusation that she was trying to convert equity into debt. Without explanation, Judge Wolverton ignored this information and continued the case. But Fannie had been put on notice that the new receivers would use company records in ways Vincent had not.[8]

The Kansas City transfers were additional evidence that Potter and Chapin had not had "unlimited funds" as claimed in 1907. The half-million they invested initially was substantial, but they were counting on contract payments and revenues to fund the rest. And they might have pulled it off if the grand Bayocean Park they promised everyone had been operational within a couple of years. But that was never a realistic expectation, and the Panic of 1907 made it impossible. T. Benton and Harkness were operating on a shoestring since the start, with no allowance for contingencies.

The resort opened early in 1919, on June 15th, despite the theft of linens and utensils from bungalows. Swan Hawkinson learned ex-TBPRC employee Charles Blazer was one of the culprits and got him to return everything. Hawkinson continued serving as Bayocean Park's unofficial sheriff after he and Othelia quit managing Bungalow City.[9]

The triad ran small ads just quoting rates that year. Society page coverage shrank in concert with reduced newspaper advertising. Articles once spanning several columns were just a few inches. Anyone reading Bayocean Park's column for the first time would have thought the resort was nothing special. But Saturday night dances at the Annex, swimming in the Natatorium, playing on the beach, and hiking to Cape Meares remained popular. Families continued booking bungalows for extended stays, and the Annex usually had a few guests. However, the indoor dance hall was not mentioned in 1919 or ever again. The tale of its demise that is most likely true is that it burned down during a party one night.[10]

On October 1, 1919, the triad filed a financial report detailing every receipt and disbursement going back to the start of the receivership in 1915. Sydney Vincent had used a fiscal year ending April 1st to match its inception. Closing books in the fall made more sense for a resort, but Lyman Latourette may have done so to hide a negative balance at the end of March 1919, which he resolved with personal funds.[11]

The decline in revenue was striking. During Vincent's three-year reign, receipts dropped from $29,047.41 to $15,962.48 and $9,177.88. The triad did even worse during their first twelve months, taking in just $3,051.69. Through September 1919, $2,362.16 received on thirty-four contracts made up for two summers' operational losses of $2,128.77. Though they paid no property taxes and worked without pay, only $233.39 was in the bank.[12]

No contract holder made every payment during the triad's first seventeen months. Francis Mitchell mailed three checks. Many sent one, over two hundred none. Like Vincent, Latourette offered those with multiple lots a warranty deed on one of them if payments already made justified that. With some, he negotiated lower prices, to the extreme of asking some contract holders to simply make up delinquent taxes and pay the $10 recording fee. In February 1920, the triad and Judge Gatens felt they had been lenient long enough and foreclosed on 234 contract holders who had not responded to any appeals.[13]

The Bayocean Natatorium was the most significant drain on cash, running at a loss in 1918 and 1919 despite Daniel Van Tine managing it for free. The triad got $408.33 from Mrs. H. J. (Alma) Martin , which was half of what she made operating the Bayocean Annex in 1919. But the advertising and maintenance costs they were responsible for must have exceeded that. The only profitable operation was Bungalow City, which had a positive cash flow of $939.50 after paying Swan and Othelia Hawkinson $1,167.00.[14]

Alma Martin refused to return in 1920, saying the money she made running the Annex in 1919 was insufficient to justify her effort. Despite enticing her replacement by including the Amusement Pavilion and bungalows, and the *Oregonian* saying, "the largest crowd in years thronged this resort" on July 10th, profits were less than one hundred dollars, which—based on the profit-sharing terms of the lease—meant the receivership got nothing.[15]

The only revenue from the Natatorium in 1920 was the sale of "excess equipment." Despite Bert Biggs's constant tinkering, the power plant failed so often that Carl and Maud Jackson installed an electrical generator at Maudy-Carlo. At the end of 1919, federal Judge Wolverton had granted permission to sell construction machinery, narrow-gauge rails, excess cast-iron pipes, and other rusting materials scattered about the spit. But the triad had to put what little they got from that in an escrow account. Decking continued to fall off rotting pier posts, forcing those arriving by boat to disembark closer and closer to shore.[16]

Contract payments and settlements covered resort losses through September 1920, but Lyman Latourette funded increasingly greater losses out of personal funds every year after that. He listed them as "additional disbursements" alongside debts like property taxes, attorney bills, and Sydney Vincent's certificate.[17]

Despite the personal cost, Latourette advised Judge Gatens to keep the resort operating because Tillamook County commissioners continued funding work on Bayocean Road. Their coffers had grown steadily since 1907 when Bayocean Park publicity prompted resort construction up and down the Tillamook coastline. Most of the new landowners, including those on Bayocean, paid taxes. Even in its diminished state, the commissioners expected Bayocean Park to draw motorists who would do business on their way through town. They budgeted $24,000 in 1920, hoping that would be enough to finish the road, but setbacks left more to do.[18]

Reed College Students Study Resort Management

In 1921, the triad came up with an idea they hoped would solve their revenue problem permanently—they handed Bayocean Park operations over to twenty-five Reed College students. Each student received room and board at the Bayside Inn and the opportunity to apply academic lessons to real life in exchange for four and a half months of work. Their enthusiasm and service drew extensive, positive media coverage. The *Oregon Journal* called it "one of the most unique business ventures by college students to defray their own college expenses." The ten percent discount they offered Portland teachers increased Bayocean Annex bookings to a dozen or more each week.[19]

The first thing Reedies did was build a dance hall across from Bayside Inn. Six student musicians accompanied patrons twirling about the room every Wednesday and Saturday night. Graduate electrical engineering student George Henny set up a radio transmitter to broadcast a Portland station and published a daily newsletter. Two male engineering students got the Bayocean Natatorium boilers and power plant working. A female scholar tended wounds when not managing the retail bakery set up in the Annex. Many others had roles and titles to match based on their academic major. But some cut driftwood hauled from the beach to feed Natatorium and power plant boilers the requisite three and a half cords of wood each day—until their saw broke. A barge rented to deliver sawn timber sank during its first trip across the bay, forcing Reedies to spend a night retrieving it.[20]

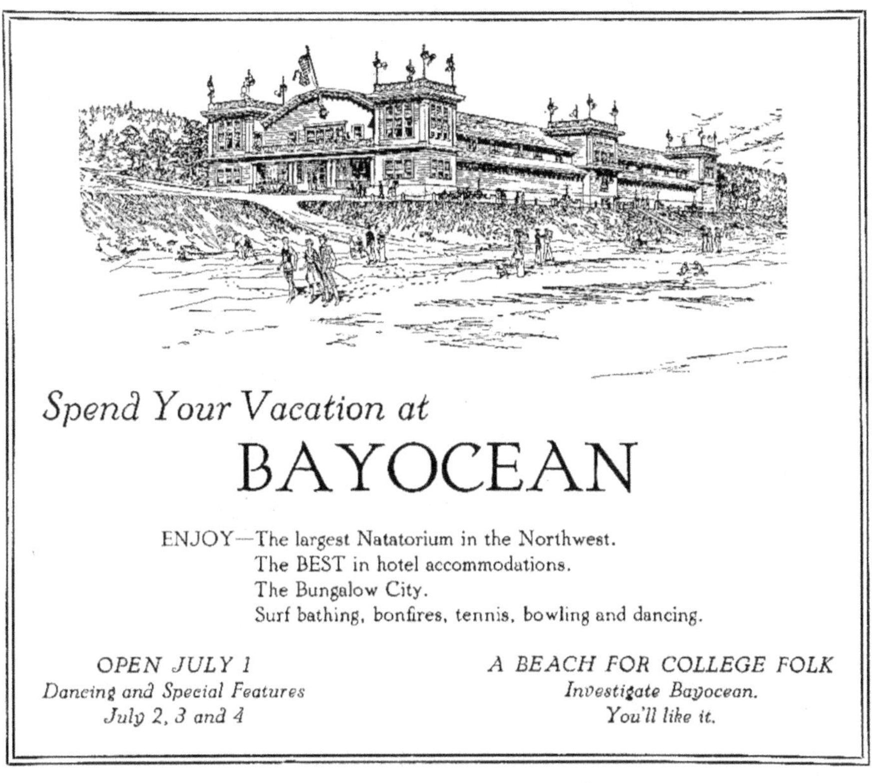

Spend Your Vacation at
BAYOCEAN
ENJOY—The largest Natatorium in the Northwest.
The BEST in hotel accommodations.
The Bungalow City.
Surf bathing, bonfires, tennis, bowling and dancing.
OPEN JULY 1
Dancing and Special Features
July 2, 3 and 4
A BEACH FOR COLLEGE FOLK
Investigate Bayocean.
You'll like it.

Advertisement in the 1921 *Griffin*, Reed College's yearbook.

In addition to broadcasting and printing, George Henny repaired telephone lines. On July 25th, a rotten pole toppled over with him hanging onto it and fractured his skull. When Dr. Robert Boals of Tillamook saw the severity of the injury, he telegraphed Dr. A. E. Rockey in Portland. The surgeon drove through the night to operate on Henny the next day with the assistance of Boals and Dr. Marcellus, who was vacationing on the spit. Afterward, Rockey said, "chances for his recovery are about even." Henny fully recovered, changed his major, and became a physician.[21]

Unfortunately, Bungalow City again produced the only income sufficient to require Reedies to share it with the triad per their profit-sharing arrangement. Though they chose not to repeat it, the students valued their experience enough to hold a reunion dinner in December 1922 and invite Bayocean residents.[22] If twenty-five young adults working without wages could not eke out a profit running Bayocean Park, how could anyone else?

While Reedies were running the resort during the summer of 1921, Ambrose Arstill's eight-man crew camped at the abandoned Feeney and Bremer shipyard. They blasted rock, cleared brush, and cut trees all summer to grade the middle section of Bayocean Road. Only a mile and a half remained when they left on the first of October.[23]

Fannie Potter-Thomas Settles Out of Court

On June 1, 1922, two weeks before her federal trial was scheduled to begin, Fannie Potter-Thomas settled out of court. She received Bungalow City and the rest of Block 56, the Amusement Pavilion and the tideland tract it sat on, fifty lots, and $1,750, half of the escrow account. The receivership received the remaining lots and resort facilities. Judge Gatens instructed them to give $1,175 of the money remaining in escrow to individuals owed $6,000 on a prorated basis and keep the rest. When Fannie received her deed on July 14th, she immediately transferred everything to her daughter Arleta's husband, John L. Dobbins, for "$10 plus other valuable consideration."[24]

The settlement did not improve the resort's financial situation. For the first time since 1910, Bayocean Park had no Fourth of July celebration, and it did not open to the public until July 12, 1922. It took that long to convince a shipowner to carry railroad passengers across by guaranteeing them $600 in revenue. The receivers got Alma Martin to return to the Annex by promising her at least $300, all profits above $600, and three rooms in the Bayside Inn to use as she liked. They also assured her at least one toilet and one sink would be operational in each of the men's and women's bathrooms by July 20th—without saying what guests would do for the first eight days.[25]

Despite the Reedies having repaired its machinery, Daniel Van Tine chose not to manage the Bayocean Natatorium in 1922. He sold Lorelie that fall. Lucien Harvey struck a hard bargain to replace him. In addition to keeping all profits, he got a maintenance allowance, five rooms at the Bayside Inn, and use of the resort's mule team and wagon five hours per day to haul wood for the Natatorium and power plant.[26]

On August 12th, while Lucien tended to the Natatorium, his wife Ida boated over to Tillamook and filed suit against Fannie Potter-Thomas. She claimed Fannie hired her in October 1921 to help negotiate a settlement on her federal lawsuit but then refused to pay her $5,000 owed. Because that court's procedures would keep the case open for a couple more years, Judge Bagley referred the suit to Judge Wolverton, who promptly dismissed it. The average annual salary for women was only $360 at the time, so Ida was not about to drop it. She filed another lawsuit for $2,995 in a manner Bagley accepted in January 1923.[27]

Families enjoying their favorite bungalows. BOB-9, TCPM

On July 1, 1923, Arleta Potter-Dobbins signed a deed in Tillamook transferring Bungalow City to Portland's Security Savings and Trust Company for an undisclosed amount. Lyman Latourette notarized it, and Lewis Thomas witnessed it, suggesting Fannie was there. Arleta took the deed home for John to sign, which he did a few weeks later. But it was not recorded until the first day of Harvey's trial, March 4, 1924. On July 28,

1923, Security Savings sold the bungalows to Lyman and Lillian Latourette for "$10, less than $100," a transfer not recorded until September 11, 1926. Latourette claimed Bungalow City was worth $9,000 twenty-three years later, suggesting he worked out a side deal with the bank.[28]

Depositions taken in Portland on March 1, 1924, provide insight. Dr. Gertrude Gates said she had discussed ways to get rid of the triad at a meeting with Ida and Fannie in Portland on November 11, 1921. One of the triad's negotiators said he tried hard to get Potter-Thomas to take the Annex rather than the bungalows because its value was higher but ran at a loss, but she would not go for it. William Gatens, who had returned to private practice after losing to Louis Hewitt in the general election of November 1922, said he would have supported any settlement:

> It was the only piece of litigation while I was on the bench that gave me real worry…I was annoyed so much by it and it seemed to be a never ending thing [and I] would not give you a dollar and a half for those lots over there.

Harvey disagreed with Gatens. She thought the property Fannie received was worth at least $75,000. Trial testimony is not extant, but after listening to it for two days, the jury awarded Ida $2,200 on March 5th.[29]

When Potter-Thomas refused to send Harvey the money, Judge Bagley ordered Sheriff John Aschim to sell her Bayocean property at public auction on August 30, 1924. Aschim soon discovered Fannie had transferred everything to her son-in-law. None of the parties, including Latourette—who had testified for Harvey—had mentioned it.[30]

Undeterred, Ida filed another suit on September 16, 1924, charging John Dobbins and Fannie Potter-Thomas with fraud and requesting invalidation of the original deed. Harvey accused the two of conspiring to transfer the property to elude debtors because Potter-Thomas was insolvent. She did not mention the subsequent transactions, so she was unaware of them. But they were sure to come out during testimony at a second trial, and that would have been—at the least—embarrassing for Lyman Latourette. And if the second jury found in favor of Harvey, Fannie's debtors could go after what little she had retrieved of the money she and T. Benton invested in Bayocean Park. So, Potter-Thomas and

Dobbins settled with Harvey out of court for an unspecified amount, and Bagley dismissed the case on January 30, 1925.[31]

John and Arleta Dobbins kept the lots north of the bungalows but never revisited the spit. Nor did Fannie. She divorced Lewis Thomas in November 1928 and never remarried. After John Dobbins died in 1935, Fannie moved in with Arleta. Given her personality, and Bayocean Park's financial demise most likely having caused T. Benton's insanity, Fannie probably enjoyed hearing of its physical demise shortly before her death, at eighty-four, on December 4, 1952. Arleta kept paying taxes on one Clarke Street lot until 1952, making her the last Potter to maintain any connection to Bayocean Park. On December 7, 1973, she died at eighty-one in Berkeley. Neither her estate nor Fannie's was probated.[32]

Bayocean Lots Hard to Sell

Once Fannie Potter-Thomas was out of the picture, the triad was free to sell foreclosed lots. And that was the only way they had left to offset Annex and Natatorium losses. Unfortunately, no one wanted to buy them.

The last order William Gatens had signed as a judge, on October 21, 1922, approved a deal with Francis Mitchell to sell lots en masse. Mitchell accepted a five percent commission rather than the twenty-five percent typically paid brokers in exchange for giving local investors the first chance to buy lots in groups of twenty or more at a twenty percent discount. Francis was sure his plan would raise the cash needed to extend Bay Street north and 1st Avenue east to meet the west end of Bayocean Road at 13th Street. Only a quarter mile remained unfinished because another mile-and-a-quarter had been completed that summer. No buyers materialized.[33]

The first court order signed by Judge Hewitt on February 10, 1923 gave the Smith-Wagoner Company of Portland a thirty percent discount on lots sold. Smith-Wagoner did no better than Mitchell. In August 1924, it canceled the contract. Francis then asked for a twenty percent discount and the exclusive right to sell specific lots. Judge Hewitt turned him down. Mitchell sold a few lots for the standard five percent commission, as did Henry King, but they made more money buying and reselling foreclosed lots purchased from the county. In 1925, Henry King led a group of locals in setting up The Bayocean Company to the same end.[34] Few lots were ever sold by any of them.

Meanwhile, the Annex and Natatorium continued to lose money. Alma Martin returned in 1923 and 1924, but no one leased it longer than one year after that. The triad found no one to operate the Natatorium in 1923, and those who ran it later refused to renew. After losing Bungalow City in 1922, total resort revenue dropped to $1,696.77. Two years later, it shrank to $742.53. With expenses exceeding two thousand dollars, Latourette had to pay most of them. By the end of 1924, his additional disbursements had grown to $3,749.90. Seeing no intent by the county to complete the last quarter mile of Bayocean Road, Lyman held on only because he thought maintaining resort facilities sufficiently to interest a buyer would cost more than its operational losses.[35]

So few families lived in the area by 1925 that the Tillamook School District made the Barnegat School District part of Bayocean's. The little Barnegat schoolhouse, which no students attended after 1917, succumbed to a landslide in the 1930s.[36]

Receivership Ends

Lyman Latourette's benefit to cost analysis changed in 1926. His hope that lots would sell once Fannie Potter-Thomas was out of the way had not panned out. Receivership debts had grown to $20,000—not counting property taxes—and his share was becoming too much to bear. Worst of all, the county had funded no work on Bayocean Road in 1925. So close to the finish line, their coffers had run dry. Robert Steele and Daniel Van Tine concurred. So, in March, they asked Judge Hewitt to approve the sale of Bayocean Park to the highest bidder, and he agreed.[37]

Hewitt and two other Multnomah County Circuit Court judges rejected the only bid submitted before the original April 19th deadline without stating any reasons. A request for outstanding claims accompanying the request for proposals may have scared off bidders. The only claim accepted was $2,480.39 from ex-TBPRC attorneys Fales and Platt. The judges dismissed an $84,000 appeal from the Bayocean Natatorium Company because it no longer existed. They tossed out

Francis Mitchell's request for $63,200 when he did not show up for a special meeting scheduled to provide more details.[38] The sums requested by ex-Natatorium shareholders and Mitchell may have seemed ludicrous to the judges, but they and the triad were the only ones who knew just how bad Bayocean Park's finances were.

On May 17, 1926, M. D. (Mig) Ackley of Tillamook submitted a proposal directly to Judge Hewitt on behalf of himself and anonymous associates. In exchange for taking ownership of all properties previously owned by TBPRC and BNC, both of which no longer existed, they would take care of county property taxes and all other verified debts. Existing lot contracts and transfer requests would be honored. They promised to put twenty percent of all lot sales in an improvement fund, part of which would purchase a new floating dock at least thirty feet wide by fifty feet long. The Annex, Bayside Inn, Natatorium, power plant, and water system "shall be repaired and put in condition for use for the present season." Bay and 1st Streets would be improved by the end of the year. A $25,000 surety bond guaranteed performance. Judge Hewitt thought the offer worthy and published a notice asking those with objections to submit them in writing.[39]

BNC and sixteen lot owners led by Francis Mitchell objected. They wanted to give Tillamook County more time to improve Bayocean Road to get higher bids. The triad liked Ackley's offer and dismissed the objections as frivolous. They argued that receiverships were not designed to last forever, and the mechanism had proven unfit for Bayocean Park. They said the resort would be worth $200,000 once Mig's group carried through on projected expenditures of $95,000. It was a deal that would benefit everyone.[40]

Judges Hewitt and Robert Tucker heard testimony from both sides on June 1, 1926. Tucker published their decision the next day. After twelve years in limbo, he wrote, "the buildings are going to ruin; the electric light plant and waterworks systems are both disintegrating." While acknowledging that the developers had made promises that were reckless and impossible to honor, he said that buyers should have realized that. No one was to blame, least of all the receivers. It was time for everyone to move on. Hewitt and Tucker accepted Ackley's offer after he agreed to pay delinquent county taxes in full immediately, increase the surety bond to $50,000, and begin bringing Bayocean Road up to market road standards within sixty days and finish doing so by April 1, 1927.[41]

Mig's cohorts balked when he showed them the judges' conditions, especially the market road stipulation. The purpose of attaining that status was to bring state assistance for maintenance, but it required two graveled lanes with prescribed dimensions, drainage, and bridges. Little of the completed part of Bayocean Road qualified. More importantly, it was a county road. The Tillamook group's responsibility should be limited to streets within the subdivision. So, they countered with an agreement to bring 1st Avenue, Mears Street, and Bay Street up to market road standards within thirty days of the county doing the same with Bayocean Road.[42]

The group also hedged on paying delinquent taxes. They promised to work something out with the county, which might be something less than payment in full immediately. They were unwilling to increase the surety bond and—understandably—refused to be held responsible for any delay caused by litigation. Finally, Ackley's cohorts wanted to be given until July 1, 1927, to find another way to provide power to the resort other than repairing the power plant. After consulting with Francis Mitchell and Lyman Latourette, Judge Hewitt approved the counterproposal on July 9th. Three days later, Mig Ackley transferred his contractual rights and obligations to the newly incorporated Tillamook-Bayocean Company (TBC). And on July 13, 1926, Hewitt instructed the triad to hand them the keys.[43]

Lyman Latourette, Daniel Van Tine, and Robert Steele were done managing Bayocean Park. They had served twice as long as Sydney Vincent, and without pay, so they were probably happy to get the news. However, the receivership continued until Bayocean Park property was transferred, TBC met their conditions, and Judge Hewitt approved their final report on May 25, 1931.[44]

CHAPTER 5

Locals Take Control
(1926–1932)

As of July 13, 1926, the fate of Bayocean Park was in the hands of six Tillamook businessmen. They had hobnobbed with the Potters and Chapins and resort guests at local events and sold them a few products and services, but none owned a lot on the spit before 1926. They had no use for a summer cabin on the bay and ocean beach they could visit any time, and they were not speculative types. Their objective was making money.

Tillamook-Bayocean Company Introduced

Mig Ackley's lead role in organizing TBC stemmed from an early interest in Bayocean Park construction. His are among the earliest photographs of its construction, facilities, workers, and visitors held by the Tillamook County Pioneer Museum. E. M. (Everett) Condit co-owned the Tillamook Garage with Ackley. C. L. (Connie) Dye was the hard hat in the group. He owned a construction company, a logging operation, and a dairy farm. H. T. (Hosea) Botts, an attorney, was the TBC shareholder most familiar with the resort's financial and legal history, having represented the Bozorths and Potters in Tillamook County Circuit Court. And in 1911, he was president of the Port of Tillamook during negotiations with the Corps of Engineers and Port of Bay City. G. P. (George) Winslow was Hosea's law partner and Tillamook's state representative.[1]

Arthur Beals was the most prominent of the TBC shareholders. He had built a small empire of dairy, oyster, and timber operations after arriving in Tillamook in 1891. In 1907, he served alongside William Clemens in Oregon's House of Representatives. He chose not to run for office in 1911 but won Tillamook's state senate seat in 1924. Senator Beals and Representative Winslow were TBC's political tag team.[2]

When Beals introduced TBC to the *Oregonian* on August 8, 1926, he said the resort would be open for the rest of the season because they had repaired the Annex, Natatorium, and power plant. Arthur reported several lot owners planning to build cabins, adding to the thirty already there, and encouraged others to join them by spending $50 to $500 on one of 1,800 lots available. Given Harkness Chapin's report of 1,152 lots available on November 1, 1914, Beals's tally meant that receivers had repossessed 648 more lots than they had sold during the past twelve years. And only 1,000 of the 2,800 lots south of 22nd Avenue were owned by everyone else, including the county.[3]

TBC had given fourteen lots to Lyman Latourette in exchange for $5,600 of the $5,835.40 they owed him: $4,335.40 to clear his "additional disbursements"; and $1,500 for "services rendered" to the group before May 1, 1926.[4] The only service Lyman could have provided TBC was assistance in making their proposal. Since Judge Hewitt said nothing about a conflict of interest when he approved the report where Latourette showed this transaction, he must have been just as anxious to be rid of the receivership as Judge Gatens had been.

Latourette's willingness to accept all but $235.40 of the amount owed him in lots valued at an average of $400 explains why he tried so hard to keep Bayocean Park afloat—he loved the place as much as Francis Mitchell. As for Bungalow City, Lyman and Lillie changed its name to Bayocean Bungalettes and started running small ads on June 27, 1926. The weekly rate was $12, the same as in 1914. With inflation averaging 5.15% annually during those years, it was the equivalent of a 55% decrease.[5]

Automobiles Drive to Bayocean for the First Time

TBC ran a few Bayocean Park lot advertisements in the *Herald* the last two weeks of July 1926. So did Henry King. But that was it. The company's marketing strategy was to get metropolitan press coverage on Bayocean Road. On July 3rd, Portland auto mechanic Fred Dundee led a caravan of three automobiles to Tillamook using the southern route and on out to The Mitchell via Bayocean Road. The *Oregon Journal* and *Oregonian* ran stories crediting Dundee with being the first to drive to the famous resort. Though intended to encourage others to do the same, the photos of planks the cars were crossing may have had the opposite effect.[6]

According to Dundee, Francis and Ida "were tickled pink to think that after waiting 19 years their dream had come true. Mr. Mitchell claimed to feel 10 years younger." Mitchell also claimed to have built the last section between Bayocean Road and Bay Street—with Ida's help—after "meeting with disappointment when he attempted to induce public officials" to do it.[7] His exuberance is understandable, but Francis took too much credit. Though locals would report them maintaining the road leading into Bayocean in the years ahead, the Mitchells had no road-building equipment.

Before leaving in 1915, Jim O'Donnell's men had graded from the paved end of Bay Street, up through Jackson Gap to Mears Street, south to 1st Avenue, and west to the edge of Bayocean Park at 4th Street. On June 20, 1925, Mitchell wrote lot owners, "at our own expense, Mr. Biggs and son, and the writer have opened up First Avenue from the ocean to the East line of Bayocean and on to the Biggs home. As soon as mud dries it will be passable for a light car during dry weather." Bert Biggs and his son John Albert Jr. (Albert) were farmers with the equipment needed. Francis had helped the Biggs men resurface work previously done inside Bayocean Park, then grade from the end of 13th Street out to Biggs Point, which included the last quarter mile of Bayocean Road. Whenever it dried out after June 20, 1925, anyone willing to pay Albert Biggs a toll to open the gate he installed could finally drive to Bayocean Park.[8] Whoever was first, it was not Fred Dundee.

Senator Beals told the *Oregonian* in August 1926 that the drive from Tillamook took forty-five minutes because the road was admittedly rough; but he had initiated state legislation to complete and improve both the Wilson River Road and Bayocean Road. The commercial benefits the former would bring to Tillamook had motivated his return to the Oregon Senate in 1924. The latter would do the same and help recoup his investment.[9]

Henry Ford's assembly lines had made automobiles affordable to the middle class. Railroad lines no longer determined where families spent their vacations. They could pack a tent, drive to the coast, and set up camp in many locations. The road from Portland to Forest Grove, up Gales Creek, and down Wilson River to Tillamook was the shortest, but it was also the worst. When it first opened as a toll road for wagons in 1893, the ride between Forest Grove and Tillamook took twelve hours. Replacing horses with an engine made the trip even longer. The first attempt in 1906 took six days.[10]

Everyone drove to Tillamook County resorts using the longer southern loop because it was faster and—usually—navigable. But by the 1920s, new campgrounds and resorts had sprung up in Lincoln County, and they were closer to the junction at Grand Ronde than Tillamook. Given Bayocean Park's rundown condition, most families had little reason to turn north. Improving the Wilson River Road would change that—if Bayocean Road was ready. Beals informed the *Herald* on August 12, 1926, that twenty men were working to that end.[11]

A day earlier, Arthur Beals had let the *Headlight* know Portland realtors Keasey and Humason had signed a contract to purchase 339 lots and a ninety-acre tract at the southern end of the spit where they would build an eighteen-hole golf course. The first nine holes, including "an ocean hole, which will give a splendid view of the Pacific from a commanding elevation," would be ready within a year. On October 10th, Dorr Keasey told the *Oregon Journal* he had already put men to work because the state highway commission had approved the Wilson River Highway. The other nine holes would be installed after it was finished. "With the resort located as it is just off the main route of the Roosevelt [Oregon Coast, US 101] Highway, it will become one of the popular playgrounds of the Oregon Coast."[12]

When the Oregon legislature met in January 1927, Senator Beals and Representative Winslow introduced a bill to allow funding of state highways via tolls, beginning with the Wilson River Highway. The legislature quickly approved the bill, but Governor Isaac Patterson vetoed it. The fiscal conservative feared the state would end up holding the bag if tolls collected were less than projected costs. Legislators from the state's interior had supported the bill because they could later take advantage of it themselves. But they were unwilling to allocate existing highway funds to help their Tillamook colleagues because they felt coastal communities had already received more than their fair share to construct the Oregon Coast Highway. The Wilson River Highway would have to wait. Keasey and Humason dropped their plans for a golf course.[13]

Cottages Rise Again

In February 1927, the *Headlight* announced the first cabin going up on the spit since receivers took over, which was more significant than its 750 square feet. The owner was Portland railroad conductor O. P. (Orin) Brigham. He had purchased a lot from TBC for $275 just north of the meadow where Tillamook lodges had once stood.[14] Though Keasey and Humason's golf course location had not been specified, this meadow was likely at its center.

Swan Hawkinson also put up two houses that year when he was not busy shuttling people across the bay in a launch he had acquired. One was a two-story home built for himself and Othelia. They paid TBC $200 for the lot north of their first house, which they turned into a rental. Swan also put up a little 650-square-foot cottage for Corinth Crook on a lot she bought for $350 from a private party two lots north of the Hawkinson's new home. Corinth had rented a bungalow each summer while running the language arts department at Lewis and Clark High School in Spokane, but she chose to spend retirement as a neighbor of the Hawkinsons.[15]

Brigham, Crook, and the Hawkinsons had purchased their lots after Beals had said several lot owners planned to build in August 1926. So, whoever he was referring to had changed their minds. Probable reasons were the failure of Wilson River Highway legislation and TBC keeping the Annex and Natatorium doors closed in 1927. Later, they told Judge Hewitt that the Bayside Inn had sufficient capacity to meet the demand and that they had been unable to lease the Natatorium. They did not mention the Rockaway Natatorium having opened in 1926. Though much smaller than Bayocean's, it was easier to get to and brand new. Potential lessees would have known that it would be hard to compete with that.[16]

TBC also admitted to having left the lights off because too few residents were willing to pay for the electricity generated by the power plant. However, Mountain States Power Company promised to run lines to the spit in 1929 if Bayocean Road could handle their trucks and heavy equipment by then. When challenged about their contract obligating them to repair and reopen the resort facilities, they said that that requirement only applied to 1926. That satisfied Judge Hewitt.[17]

TBC shareholders were tight-fisted businessmen. They had purchased Bayocean Park to make money. So far, it had not. And, unlike Lyman Latourette, they would not continue funding a losing cause. As a result, 1926 was the last year that guests would rent a room in the Bayocean Annex or splash about in the Bayocean Natatorium. It was also the last year that Bayocean would have a column in the summer society pages of metropolitan newspapers. However, the story about Brigham's cottage appeared in the first regular column dedicated to Bayocean in the *Headlight*'s Community News section. TBC ownership had changed Tillamook's perspective. It now considered Bayocean a local community rather than a resort that was owned by and catered to Willamette Valley's elite.

Tax Compromise Funds Bayocean Road Improvement

In May 1927, Francis Mitchell made local headlines again when he learned that Tillamook County commissioners were considering a proposal from TBC to cut Bayocean's delinquent property taxes—which had grown to $50,000—in half. He quickly gathered 507 signatures from lot owners on a petition demanding that the commissioners make TBC pay in full or return half the taxes paid previously by responsible lot owners.[18]

On July 15th, county commissioners announced that in exchange for TBC contributing $5,000, $10,000, and $10,000 over the next three years, they would add $15,000 to raise the $40,000 necessary to bring Bayocean Road up to market road standards. The commissioners promised to revalue all Bayocean Park lots at current values to lower taxes. They immediately zeroed out the value of all lots in the hilly central section in exchange for TBC giving the county the dune tract north of 27th Avenue. Albert Biggs received $258 for a right-of-way. By Friday, the 29th, work on the road had begun and the tollgate removed. Francis Mitchell was so pleased that he helped organize a parade through downtown Tillamook and gave a speech alongside Mayor Sam Moulton that evening. The next day, seventy-five cars drove out to Bayocean on the toll-free road.[19]

Two weeks later, F. D. Mitchell Realty placed an ad titled "Bayocean Is Coming Back" in the *Headlight* offering prime building lots. It said, "Visitors from Portland and other cities are coming in large numbers each week." TBC hosted a dance in the Annex dining room on Saturday night, August 20th, and a picnic the next day. A month later, the Mitchells took a trip to Kansas City. After returning in November, they had a 550-gallon Texaco gas tank and pump installed outside The Mitchell to serve the influx of automobiles anticipated in 1928.[20]

Ida and Francis Mitchell in front of their car with their Texaco gas pump in the background, as viewed from the south. BOP-21, TCPM.

Volunteers Improve Wilson River Road

With little hope of state funding, Tillamook locals took it upon themselves to improve the Wilson River Road in March 1928. It had been impassable since McNamer Bridge collapsed seven years earlier. There was no other way around the seventy-six-foot gap in basalt walls on either side of rapids thirty feet below because it was just west of where Elk Creek merged with the South and Devils Lake Forks of the Wilson River. At the end of May, Francis Mitchell, Connie Dye, Everett Condit, George Riechers, and a dozen others put up a 142-foot-long bridge in eight days using timber cut and sawed at the site. The Tillamook Chamber of Commerce provided tools, and a farmer nearby lent them a team of horses. The county commissioner funded the removal of seventy-one fallen trees and overgrown foliage elsewhere along the route.[21]

On June 14, 1928, three men drove a Ford stripped to its "engine, four wheels, steering gear, a seat and enough room for fishing tackle and other bare necessities" the fifty miles from Gales Creek to Tillamook in nine hours. Ten days later, two men and their wives slid a hundred feet to the Wilson River after hitting nasty ruts eight miles east of Tillamook. Surprisingly, they suffered only minor injuries, but they returned to Portland using the southern loop after being treated in Tillamook.[22]

Additional improvements enabled Tillamook County Engineer Stanley Coates to reach Forest Grove in six hours in August, slowing down in just one spot to get through encroaching bushes. Farmers along the route told him forty-four cars had passed that week, and thirty-five the week before. If Coates had continued to Portland, it would have taken him another hour.[23] So, at best, the Wilson River Road took three hours longer than the southern loop, and drivers risked scratching the sides of their cars. Most families would continue driving to Lincoln County via Grand Ronde for their vacations.

Bayocean Military Academy Plans Big

George Riechers, who helped rebuild McNamer Bridge in March 1928, was a Tillamook realtor. He and truck driver Fred Klinehan had bought into TBC the same month. Whatever they invested was not enough because the company had to take out a bank loan the following month to make that year's $10,000 road payment. They also hired Arthur Beals for "a salary to be agreed upon later" to manage their affairs. He kept track of his Bayocean activities in a lumber company journal.

During the summer of 1928, most of his notes concerned the Bayocean Military Academy, which leased the Bayocean Annex, Bayocean Natatorium, and Bayside Inn from TBC, and the Bayocean Bungalettes from the Latourettes.[24]

Dr. William Harroun of Portland was the man behind the academy. On May 8th, he told the *Headlight* that from June 20th to August 2nd, forty military reserve officers would train 250 boys with "physical defects" aged five to twenty-one in infantry and cavalry skills with the help of fifty horses. When not drilling or attending classes, the boys would fish, boat, swim, and surf to build stamina. Some of the boys would continue their military training while attending school at the Annex during the off-season.

Harroun planned to repair the Natatorium and build a golf course, parade grounds, armory, and landing field the following year.[25]

Beals and Harroun got off to a bad start. On June 14th, the senator was disturbed to find that the doctor had set up an office inside the Amusement Pavilion, which was not part of the lease. Later, when Harroun asked Beals what it would cost to buy the resort, his answer was $150,000. A realtor Harroun consulted thought that was too much, but Beals refused to negotiate.[26]

The Bayocean Military Academy ran classified ads in the *Oregonian* and *Oregon Journal* every day for a month ahead of the event, and both dailies ran feature stories immediately beforehand. On June 21st, as Harroun prepared to drive some of the boys to the spit, he told the *Journal* nearly 150 recruits had signed up. Yet neither newspaper said anything during or afterward. And when Beals checked things out on July 3rd, he found "no one in charge." His journal records him driving to Portland to find out what was going on but finding no answer to the question. He makes no mention of any activities on the spit that summer, only that he turned down Harroun's request to extend the lease. On July 17th, after a check bounced, Beals drove out to the spit and threatened Harroun's wife with criminal charges to convince her to ride back to Tillamook and withdraw cash from a bank.[27]

Beals may have had good reasons to end TBC's relationship with the Bayocean Military Academy, but Dr. Harroun was no charlatan. He was well-known for his philanthropic efforts before and after the academy. Harroun later served as the Oregon State Director of the National Association of Physicians and Surgeons. Given that Beals was a Republican, doing business with a strident Democrat may have been the issue. Harroun was a friend of Harry Truman, and he later spearheaded Franklin Roosevelt's campaign in Oregon.[28] In any case, if Beals had given Harroun more leeway, Bayocean Park might have had a sponsor with the means to maintain and improve its facilities.

Oscar Swanson was remodeling Bayside Inn in June 1928 when he heard that they had considered selling the resort to Dr. Harroun. He and his divorced stepdaughter, Inez Walter, offered to buy the inn. On July 11th, the parties agreed to a $6,500 price, paid by installments at eight percent with a $4,400 balloon payment in December 1931. Swanson and Walter also agreed to help renovate the Natatorium and lease it for $300 a month starting on June 1, 1929. Oscar and his wife had a teenage daughter, two adult daughters, and two adult sons. Inez had a teenage son and a daughter. In August, Inez began offering a Sunday brunch and invited the Potawatomi Campfire Girls of Tillamook to "make the Inn their headquarters and provided a club room with [a] fireplace for their use" each month.[29] That and Prohibition made the new name Walter's Tavern a curious choice.

Bayocean Road improvements had made it possible to schedule events like Campfire Girl meetings, but it had also enabled looting and vandalism. Eight-year-old R. H. (Bob) Watkins recalled waking to the noise of some boys tossing toilets from the third floor of the Annex down the concrete stairs at the south end not long after his parents and two sisters moved into the Bayocean Bungalettes in 1928. Others reported, "The grand piano was shoved down a flight of stairs and wrecked. In the pantry where thousands of plates, cups, saucers, glasses, and other pieces for table settings were stored, vandals smashed them until the pile on the floor was nearly three feet deep."[30]

Bob's father, R. W. (Pop) Watkins, worked odd jobs in Tillamook while his mother Betty gave Ida Mitchell a break running the Bayocean Post Office. In 1930, Pop and Betty bought property in the Oceanview subdivision on the mainland, which they would go on to promote as much as the Mitchells did Bayocean Park. The ability of workers to commute was another positive aspect of Bayocean Road, but gap washovers made driving to and from the spit unpredictable during the winter.[31]

Bayocean Road Improvements Celebrated

Arthur Beals drove out to the spit after the Bayocean Road upgrades scheduled for 1928 were completed on Friday, July 13th. He noted the trip taking forty minutes in his journal. The five-minute improvement since 1926 was good enough for TBC to host a "Bayocean Road Completion" celebration. They hoped to attract three to four hundred people during the weekend of August 11th and sell some lots.[32]

Festivities began with a dance in the Annex dining room on Saturday night that over four hundred people attended. Sunday's schedule included car races on the beach, a bathing beauty contest, several sports competitions, a clambake, and a marshmallow roast in the evening. The *Headlight* estimated that a thousand cars carried three to five thousand people to the spit that day, many with Washington and California license plates. The *Herald* tallied 1,500 vehicles and 6,000 people, claiming half the county showed up.[33]

Francis Mitchell gave the first speech at a ceremony on the beach on Sunday night. He reported finding nothing equal to the splendor of Bayocean Park during two trips taken that year. County Judge Fritz Beltz assured everyone that the county would finish improving Bayocean Road in 1929. That must have made the audience wonder what they were celebrating. His comment about collecting higher taxes from increasing valuations likely deterred others from buying lots. Mayor Moulton promised to continue working on Wilson River Road and, perhaps to offset Judge Beltz's faux pas, said he planned to buy a lot. Judge Louis Hewitt, who had driven from Portland to see how things were coming along, said he was pleased with TBC's progress.[34]

Great Northern Investment Company representatives were not as impressed as the speakers. They were the only realtors who had shown any interest in buying lots in bulk at wholesale prices and reselling them. After attending the event, their best offer was to sell lots at a ten percent commission plus costs, not to exceed $200 per week, which TBC accepted. Great Northern ran a couple of advertisements in the *Headlight* and *Herald* the following week promising to have salesmen on the spit to show prospects the fifty best lots. Henry King did the same.[35] Great Northern was not heard from again.

Like Potter and Chapin, TBC shareholders knew that residents of Willamette Valley, not Tillamook County, were their target market. They could only hope that lowering lot prices and the ability to drive to Bayocean would change that, but it just made it easier to spend a wonderful day at the beach and return home at night. In 1930, TBC contracted with Mig Ackley's brother Ralph, a Portland realtor. But the only ads he ran there were classifieds for a "campground site facing the beach" and "a painter to paint 200 or 300 squares [and] take part of his pay in lots."[36]

On August 13, 1929, the Tillamook County Road Inspector approved improvements to Bayocean Park's streets. Fulfilling that part of their agreement prompted TBC to host another celebration on Labor Day. The *Headlight* reported 3,000 partaking in the festivities that day. One was Ernest Peterson, another Portland auto mechanic whose article and photographs filled the first page of the *Oregon Journal*'s September 2nd automotive section. On the second page of his article, Peterson provided a mileage log of his trip via the southern loop. Those who have driven from Portland to Bayocean recently will appreciate the differences:

00.0—Portland.
100.0—Tillamook (improved road entire distance).
111.0—Tillamook River (end of pavement; gravel road begins).
111.4—End of gravel. Plank road starts.
111.7—End of plank. Gravel road resumes.
112.3—Plank road resumes.
113.5—End of planks; beginning of new grade (dirt road).
116.8—End of dirt road; loose gravel.
118.2—End of gravel; Bayocean pavement starts.
119.4—Bayocean post office.
120.5—Northern end of pavement skirting beach.[37]

Calling Bayocean Road "a very restful drive" elsewhere suggests Peterson had a sense of humor, given that a mile and a half of it was wood planking.

Peterson introduced Francis Mitchell as "prominent among the early settlers who never lost faith in this enterprise," which was true. "Purchaser of the first lots in Bayocean" was not. Francis had purchased one lot in Kansas City on July 30, 1907, the day after sales began.[38] An auto mechanic may not be expected to fact-check, but his editor should have done so. Not doing so encouraged Francis to repeat this false claim with future reporters who should have questioned it but did not—so it became an erroneous part of Bayocean history.

Francis was enthusiastic about Bayocean Park's future and said all facilities were operational. Peterson subtly questioned both. His caption under a photo of the Natatorium said it might reopen in 1929. Another photo showed rotting pier posts reaching out past TBC's new little floating dock. The note under a picture of Peterson's car parked on a paved street said, "In 18 years, nature has almost covered the pavement with a carpet of grass." He did let Mitchell off the hook regarding the Annex, taking no photo of it or saying anything about its being shuttered.[39]

Peterson's story drew interest "as to [the] sale of Bayocean as a whole [for] $200,000 net to us [with] $50,000 cash payment" according to Beals. The deal would have included everything except Walter's Tavern. His $25,000 share would have brought him a tidy profit, given that his involvement had cost $4,271.25 to date. Nothing became of it.[40]

Tillamook-Bayocean Company Criticized

Having heard Judge Hewitt publicly compliment their progress in his speech on the spit a month and a half earlier, TBC asked him to cancel their $25,000 surety bond at the end of September 1928. Granting the request would effectively release them from court supervision, so the judge offered interested parties a chance to comment. He got an earful from attorney Paul King, the second husband of Thora Trommald, who represented her, her sister Agnete Bates, the Jacksons, the Hawkinsons, Gertrude Gates, and Kate Smith.[41]

King's letter suggests why two prospective buyers thought Beals wanted too much for the resort. The first complaint was unpredictable water service caused by slipshod repair of water pipes and debris regularly plugging the reservoir outlet on Cape Meares. Next,

> That the hotel has not been repaired except for a single coat of paint. That the same has not been placed in a condition fit to be used, and is and has been in a dilapidated condition, the same has been dismantled, windows on the ocean side thereof are out allowing the wind and rain blowing through the building; all or most of the furniture, fixtures, linen, silverware, dishes, bedding, and other equipment necessary to use the hotel as such, have been removed therefrom.[42]

The Natatorium was in even worse condition, with pools full of dirty, stagnant water and its roof sagging. A bulkhead meant to keep sand off the west wall had "rotted away, leaving the building in unsafe condition." Also rotting were its front doors and siding along the east wall where sand had piled up. Interior fixtures had rusted from exposure to rain blown in through broken windows. The boilers and power plant were inoperable. Power lines and poles lay strewn about the spit.[43]

As for Bayocean's streets, "no substantial road, nor any reasonably useable road has been built by the Tillamook-Bayocean Company." King disagreed with the county road inspector, saying the four-hundred-foot section at Jackson Gap that a contractor "attempted to construct has been entirely washed away, is now underwater at all tides and impassable." Because of improper grading, gravel laid thinly elsewhere had already disappeared into the muck.[44]

George Winslow and Hosea Botts responded, saying water service had only been interrupted while making repairs. The Annex was habitable, but there was not enough demand to reopen it, so TBC had stored most of its furnishings elsewhere. They acknowledged the rotting bulkhead and sand accumulating on the Natatorium's exterior walls but insisted its interior was in good condition and cited a state inspector's recent certification of a boiler. Mountain States Power Company would soon be delivering power to residents, mooting the power plant and power grid issues. A crew was in the process of removing logs and repairing the section through Jackson Gap. After hearing from both sides in person on December 17th, Judge Hewitt declined TBC's request and told everyone to work things out.[45]

One problem that may have come up in the hearing but not in written testimony was that BNC was still the owner of record of the Natatorium despite having not existed since 1921. TBC's solution for the dilemma was Byzantine. On December 29, 1928, Botts notarized a statement from Fred Dundee claiming to be "President of the Board of Directors or Stockholders Committee of Bayocean Natatorium Company, a dissolved Oregon Corporation." Dundee then asked H. S. Brimhall, Tillamook County Clerk, to issue a duplicate certificate of title for Block 53 because he could not find the original. Brimhall did so on January 2, 1929. On April 6th, Dundee, Riechers, Ackley, Botts, and Beals set up a new corporation with the same name as the dissolved one. Brimhall then issued a new certificate of title with a different number and mailed it to Botts on July 20th.[46]

Crowds Witness Facility Closures and Homes Missing

In May 1929, Tillamook County commissioners awarded a contract to remove the remaining planks and gravel the remaining dirt sections of Bayocean Road. A decade later, their counterparts would claim that the road had cost the county between $150,000 and $200,000 to build. Though thousands of cars had driven on it the previous fall, winter rains had made it impassable again. By Sunday, July 28th, the road had been improved enough for the Tillamook County Fish and Game Protective Association to hold its annual picnic on the spit. Sheriff John Aschim, who oversaw parking at the event, estimated three to four thousand cars took 7,500 people to Bayocean that day.[47]

Doors to the Annex and Natatorium remained closed the day more people visited Bayocean than any other. And those strolling north on the beach who had done so in years past would have noticed at least two cabins missing. May and Enrique Mallory and Georgia DeWitt lost theirs during the winters of 1926 and 1927. Elmer and Alberta Burns's place fell in 1931. Reports of closed facilities and cabins being taken by the sea would not help sell lots.[48]

On June 29, 1929, Paul King's group agreed to let Judge Hewitt reduce TBC's surety bond to $2,500 after the company guaranteed to repair the Natatorium roof, install a new reservoir on Coleman Creek, and make additional street repairs. On November 14th, with repairs completed, Hewitt released the bond. TBC was then free to do as it liked with Bayocean Park.[49]

Despite the Natatorium repairs, it stayed closed in 1929. Only The Mitchell, Walter's Tavern, and Bayocean Bungalettes were open. David and Jennie Baker returned after an absence of several years to help the Latourettes recover bungalow business lost while the facility was in limbo. Lillie and their children stayed there all that summer, with Lyman joining them on weekends. Walter's Tavern held dances so often that Oscar installed a new floor. They typically had a couple of paying guests, as did The Mitchell. On Sunday, October 6th, Oscar and Inez hosted a luncheon for Tillamook dignitaries to celebrate the completion of Bayocean Road.

Despite the recent stock market crash, Francis Mitchell predicted a revitalization of Bayocean Park.[50]

New Bayocean School Built for Commuters

In August 1929, the Tillamook School District allocated $1,800 to build a new schoolhouse for Bayocean. There were just six students at the time, but the class would double in 1930 and grow steadily in the years ahead as families moved into District No. 58 because Bayocean Road now enabled commuting. Bob Watkins later explained the need for a new building.

Second Bayocean School, as viewed from the west. Sherwood 57, Lorraine Eckhardt's collection.

During the 1928–1929 and 1929–1930 school years, he attended classes in three different buildings: a summer cabin, the cafeteria in Walter's Tavern, and a garage in the clearing at the south end of the spit. Near the garage was "one of the old buildings, or what was left of it, just timber or so, of the original settlers."[51] The garage was the first schoolhouse built by TBPRC in 1912. The timber was cedar planking from the Tillamook Indian lodges that had once stood there.

Construction had to wait until school officials purchased four lots from TBC at the end of December for $1,500, but the schoolhouse was ready for the 1930–1931 school year. It was twenty-four feet wide by thirty feet long. Upstairs was a classroom, a library, and a small office for the teacher. The basement had bathrooms for each sex, a furnace, a storage room, and enough open space for students to play during recess in inclement weather—except when the toilets overflowed. Parents supplied wood, which the older boys chopped and fed into the furnace. Older girls helped younger classmates with lessons.[52]

Barbara (Schlegel) Bennett, who attended Bayocean School in the 1940s, recalled searching for arrowheads among seashells in the midden on the bay east of the school. A playground with a Maypole, swings, and monkey bars was on the west side. Perry C. Reeder Jr. recalled Cockle Street and 3rd Avenue forming a one-way loop from Mears Street to the edge of the playground and back out, passing pine trees and a baseball diamond along the way. Jim O'Donnell's men had graded but never surfaced the streets, so they were bare sand. Children typically walked to school, but their parents drove in for community events, church services, and summer bible school. The new school's first teacher was Otta Biggs, the wife of Albert. The salary was not much—between $75 and $110 annually—but anything helped during the Great Depression.[53]

Bayocean Bungalettes Becomes Cottage Park

In December 1929, the Bakers, the Mitchells, and Marian Stevenson bought the Bayocean Bungalettes from Lyman and Lillie Latourette for $8,550 on contract at six percent interest. They changed its name to Cottage Park. Three months later, Stevenson sold her share to the Bakers to focus her attention on getting a house built on the ocean side of the corner where Mears Street headed out to the spit at 1st Avenue. As 1930 progressed, Mitchell got increasingly frustrated with TBC for refusing to repair streets, so he asked

David and Jennie to join a campaign to fight them. When they refused, he went after them.[54]

Francis's favorite tactic during the 1931 resort season was to stop cars before they reached the town center and tell occupants the Bakers "were crooks, robbers, thieves, and grafters; that the entire place had gone to the dogs." With others, he used a friendlier approach of informing them that Cottage Park was full, but there were rooms available at The Mitchell. David had seen him use similar tactics against TBPRC when they were cohorts. He did not like it any better than T. Irving Potter had and, like him, sued Francis. Judge Bagley held hearings on June 24th and 25th. The parties could not work things out, so he hired a manager to run Cottage Park in July, audit the books, and sell the Latourette contract at auction on August 3rd. The Bakers submitted the winning bid of $5.00.[55]

Francis then went after his other competitor, Walter's Tavern. David Baker joined Oscar Swanson in suing both Mitchells. Judge Bagley exonerated Ida but enjoined Francis from continuing his behavior and charged him $91.80 in court costs. Francis told Oscar afterward that he had no money to pay judgments, so lawsuits did not frighten him.[56]

The press said nothing of Francis's shenanigans or the resort during the summer of 1931. However, the *Oregonian* noted Ida starting a 4-H Club in February and a sewing club just before Christmas, both at Bayocean School. The day after Christmas, it said that a 30,000-cubic-yard landslide buried a steam shovel at Pitcher Point and closed Bayocean Road.[57]

Natatorium Collapse Initiates Disaster Tourism

The next time the media mentioned Bayocean was during the third week of April 1932, when waves undercut the Natatorium's foundation during a storm, causing its west wall to collapse. Thirty years later, locals recalled this event as a milestone, the point at which erosion escalated. Viewing the Natatorium's collapse soon became as popular as swimming in its pool had once been. Tourists continued snapping photos of people standing on its septic tank until it sank below the beach in the 1980s.[58]

Carl Jackson was not there to watch as the first disaster tourists drove by Maudy-Carlo because he had died in January. Swan and Othelia Hawkinson bought the house from Maud to use as a rental later that year

West wall of the Natatorium after collapsing in 1932. BOB-68, TCPM.

but then sold it to Mig and Maud Ackley in 1936. The gap continued to bear the Jacksons' name.[59]

In August 1932, election officials moved the Bayocean Precinct polling station from Walter's Tavern to Bayocean School because more voters lived on the mainland. Judge Bagley stayed at a cabin he had purchased for $200 at a county foreclosure auction the same month. This had been Otto Schwerdtmann's place. The judge later bought adjacent lots and paid $300 for a garage. He spent nearly every weekend there for several years.[60]

Another landslide blocked Bayocean Road in December 1932, this time at Dick's Point. Though this forced Bayocean Park and Oceanview residents to boat to Tillamook for a while, it gave them a break from filling potholes along 1st Avenue. In September, Pop Watkins had written a letter to the editor of the *Oregonian* supporting a state bill reducing load limits on state highways. He was upset with "trucks coming head on at a speed of better than 40 miles, taking up two-thirds of the curves, throwing gravel off your face. It makes you want to head right out into the bay." The trucks were hauling rocks crushed on the beach below Cape Meares "nine miles to the Wilson-Kilchis rivers pavement project." Pop complained that TBC and the county refused to provide so much as a wheelbarrow to repair the damage, leaving it up to "the guy that is broke but don't know it."[61]

Bayocean Park Divvied Up

Pop Watkins wrote his letter unaware that TBC shareholders had distributed Bayocean Park amongst themselves on August 16th and 17th. Bayocean Park would continue as the name of the subdivision, but not the resort because it was no longer a consolidated unit. Different individuals would own each facility in the resort town known simply as Bayocean.[62]

In his memoir, all Arthur Beals had to say was that TBC "sold a few lots." It was not false humility. The company granted just twenty-six deeds in seven years: one in 1926; three in 1927; three in 1928; five in 1929; three in 1930; one in 1931; and seven in 1932. The final year's spike came from settling remaining contracts, which they had to do before dissolving the company. Hosea Botts said only, "the inroads of the ocean had dashed our vision of a lot of wealth from this matter."[63] The Natatorium's collapse may have prompted TBC to call it quits, but erosion was not apparent until their last year, so it is not the reason they failed. Some have suggested the Great Depression was to blame, but more deeds were issued after it started, and TBC closed the Annex and Natatorium before it began.

Though he did not say so, Beals knew TBC failed for the same reason as its predecessors—the lack of transportation. Bayocean Road improvements had resulted in more theft and vandalism than lot buying. Beals had counted on the Wilson River Highway to get Portland families to drive to Bayocean Park instead of other resorts. After Governor Patterson vetoed the bill that would have enabled that in 1927, Arthur did not introduce another, and he did not run for re-election in 1928.[64]

Wilson River Road improvement would have to wait until 1936, when Works Progress Administration (WPA) workers funded with state and federal taxes started blazing a new route north of the old one east of Camp McNamer, established just east of the bridge. They built massive steel bridges across deep gorges and dynamited tunnels through hillsides to straighten the course and lower the summit. Others working out of Camp Wilson No. 1 (now the Charles Sprague Memorial Wayside) did the same along the previous route. It took five years and thirty-five hundred men to complete what would then be known as the Wilson River Highway (OR 6) in November 1941. Tillamook was finally the closest coastal city to Portland in minutes and distance—far too late to help Bayocean Park.[65]

What TBC principals distributed amongst themselves were several tracts and 1,270 lots. Having sold just 26 of the 1,800 lots Arthur Beals referred to in 1926, the county must have foreclosed on 504 of them for non-payment of taxes. He received the largest share of those remaining, probably as compensation for a more significant financial contribution and managing company affairs. Beals selected 621 lots in Blocks 1 to 39 on the mainland and at the southern end of the spit and a Biggs Cove tideland tract. Hosea Botts got 94 lots in Blocks 38 to 49 and the tideland tract north of Bayside Inn. Connie Dye received 51 lots in Blocks 43 to 54 and the tideland tract under Bayside Inn. Fred Klinehan got 43 lots in Blocks 37, 41, and 59. Everett Condit, Mig Ackley, George Winslow, and George Riechers shared the Bayocean Annex, tideland tracts between Bayside Inn and Biggs Cove, and 461 lots from Block 58 out to 27th Avenue.[66]

Direct deed indexes indicate that five TBC shareholders never sold a lot, letting the county have them all. Salvage rights brought some of them a few dollars. Dye eventually sold the Bayside Inn but nothing else. Botts peddled a few lots and bayside tracts but let the county foreclose on most. Beals clearly came out the best by choosing the right location. He continued paying property taxes and buying and selling lots until giving them away before his death.

CHAPTER 6

Erosion Escalates
(1933–1939)

The big news of 1933 came on February 8th, when the Houser Construction Company finished repairing and extending the north jetty. Tillamook's lumber industry welcomed the news. But Bayocean and Oceanview residents would later report that shoreline recession had become increasingly more evident after Houser began in May 1931.[1]

North Jetty Extension Blamed for Dune Shrinkage

By 1927, the sea had worn the last 1,900 feet of the north jetty down to below sea level at low tide, which created an obvious navigation hazard. Closer to shore, gaps in the trestle allowed sand collected north of the jetty to enter the channel, reducing its depth from eighteen to fourteen feet. Shifting shoals created more obstacles for ships to work around. The Army Corps of Engineers agreed to repair and extend the jetty by three hundred feet to its full authorized length of 5,700. The Port of Bay City agreed to maintain the channel beyond the turning basin at Garibaldi instead of sharing the cost. Tillamook's congressional delegation secured funding in 1930.[2]

While lobbying for north jetty repairs and extension, Garibaldi lumbermen asked the Corps to revisit the construction of a south jetty. It agreed to do so, and at about the same time as Houser finished their work, the Portland District Engineer recommended a 5,400-foot south jetty, saying it would deepen the channel to twenty-two feet and benefit commerce more than the cost. The Pacific Division Engineer concurred, but the Board of Engineers did not. This would have been the right time for Bayocean Park and Oceanview residents to tell the Corps that they believed the north jetty was causing erosion, but for whatever reason, they did not. As a result, the issue was not discussed.[3]

The owner of the northernmost cabin on the spit had been closely tracking erosion. In 1915, David and Vesta Williams purchased the Woodhouse cabin. Vesta and their five children spent each summer there while David ran his plumbing business in Portland. On weekends, he joined them. After arriving at the pier, it was a mile-long hike to his place, but it was worth it to sit on the porch each evening and watch the sun drop below the waves. David and his family had the viewshed to themselves, for no one ever built north of them, and the Hughsons were a thousand feet south and higher up the dune.[4]

Summers were grand for the Williamses until their front yard began to disappear. When the dune edge approached the porch in 1926, they hired Swan Hawkinson to move it back and uphill as far as possible on the same lot. They would be the first of many to do so. David then set up a stake and began measuring the rate of erosion. It held steady at one foot per year until 1932 when they arrived to find the edge six feet closer and right up against the porch again. They returned home.[5]

David returned alone in 1933 to find another six feet lost and the porch hanging over the edge. He sold the cabin for salvage and never returned. The Hughsons did the same. So did Fred Dundee, for the Bayocean Natatorium had not been distributed amongst TBC principals because they did not own it. They had paid for its roof repair only because the second Bayocean Natatorium Company had no money, and they wanted out from under Judge Hewitt's oversight. Fred Dundee's gratitude for TBC paying that bill would have collapsed along with the Natatorium's west wall in April 1932. All he got for his participation was a share of salvage proceeds.[6]

George Jones, Bayocean Park's first construction superintendent, bought the salvage rights to all three buildings. After leaving the spit, he had sold real estate in Portland for a few years before moving to Rockaway Beach in 1915 and setting up a tent city. In 1930, George and his second wife Orrilla (Rilly) moved to Oceanview. Most of the first row of Bayocean Park lots, 125 feet long, had disappeared during the twenty-one years since he had helped survey it, so he was not about to build there, but he had no qualms about taking advantage of those who had.[7]

Though seventy-two years old, Jones spent most of 1933 and 1934 taking the structures down and using the materials to build a large two-story home. Columns from the Natatorium extended above the roofline, giving it a distinctive look. So did the old buggy he placed above the front porch next to a signboard that read Buggy Knot Inn. George and Rilly rented out a couple of rooms upstairs. Downstairs, they sold picnic goods to vacationers.[8]

Locals Fight Over Water

George Jones must have felt even better about choosing Oceanview over Bayocean Park when residents began feuding over water in the fall of 1933. TBC principals had set up the Bayocean Water Company to charge residents to pay for maintenance after repairing the resort's water system in 1929. In the spring of 1933, new water commissioners David Baker, Oscar Swanson, and Hosea Botts raised rates. Bayocean residents felt the same way about that as Reis Tract residents had in 1907. And when they refused to pay, Baker, Swanson, and Botts shut off their water just as T. Benton had. Bayocean's thirsty objectors complained to the Oregon Public Utilities Commission.[9]

In early August, the Salem YMCA held a week-long campout at Oceanside, a resort on the south side of Cape Meares. Two chaperones led a group of younger boys over the cape to spend a day on Bayocean, where they were greeted by "women 'totin' guns' in approved wild west fashion" on each side of the streets leading into town. The weaponized women were courteous to the boys while badmouthing their opponents. The "headman of the 'honest' group," likely Francis Mitchell, ranted about grievances going back "nigh onto 25 years," of which water was the most recent. The boys had fun regardless, playing in the Bayocean School playground and rummaging through the Annex and Natatorium ruins.[10]

On August 20, 1933, the Public Utilities Commission held a hearing in Tillamook. Whatever was said quieted things down because an article about the Veterans of Foreign Wars Labor Day picnic on the spit mentioned no pistol-packing mamas. However, the Swanson clan left soon afterward—perhaps because Francis Mitchell had just convinced County

Judge Beltz of his sanity when Oscar Swanson and David Baker tried to commit him to the Oregon State Hospital. A few years later, on May 15, 1936, the Public Utility Commission declared the Bayocean Water Company a public utility because it served every user in the area. Jay Smith, Swan Hawkinson, and Bill Coats set up the Bayocean Cooperative Water System to replace it on December 21, 1936.[11]

In December of 1933, the dune ridge was getting uncomfortably close to the Pagoda, so Dr. Gertrude Gates bought two lots—one from the county, the other from Hosea Botts, each for just $50—seven hundred feet north, on the east side of Clark Street, just south of the Hawkinsons' first house. A couple of months later, Swan Hawkinson moved Gertrude's cabin (Dr. Parker did not participate), reversing its orientation to keep the front door facing Clarke Street. The large windows in the back continued providing a grand view, but of the bay instead of the ocean. Swan added a porch to protect the front door from the winter storms that would now pound away at it. He then added a smaller version of the Pagoda south and east of the original. A short hallway connected them at the corners where they met, but they were separate units, so locals referred to them as the Pagodas. In 1937, Gates sold equal interests in them to schoolteacher Lutie Cake and librarian Lena Brownell, both of Portland.[12]

Artisans' Cooperative Community Livens Things Up

As the Pagoda was being readied to move, on February 16, 1934, eighteen men, women, and children in an old car and a rickety pickup pulled up to The Mitchell and introduced themselves as the Artisans' Cooperative Community. They had been camping and fishing their way along Bayocean Road when they heard the Bayside Inn was vacant and sat next to excellent crabbing, clamming, and fishing. Connie Dye agreed to let the Artisans stay rent-free while tradesmen in the group improved it. During the next two and a half years, Bayocean would bustle with activity, renewed hope, and more controversy.[13]

Louise Smith was the Artisans' driving force. With $10 of the collective $20 they had arrived with, she bought a clamming license, loaded their car with clams, and headed to the Willamette Valley to set up a trade route.

Smith exchanged some clams for food, clothing, and supplies but sold enough to buy a crabbing license. By May, she was trading and selling an average of "300 dozen clams a week, besides 30 dozen crabs and six gallons of crab meat." The Artisans purchased four vehicles, a fishing boat and nets, and a salmon license with the money raised to expand their operations.[14]

While making her rounds, Louise Smith visited newspapers to promote the Artisans. She said they were industrious, skilled craftspeople who had run into tough times like many others during the Great Depression. Rather than taking government handouts, they had pooled their meager resources. Louise insisted the Artisans were registered Democrats and Republicans with capitalistic ideals, not Communists. She encouraged others like them to join. They planned to buy the Bayside Inn (which they had renamed Bay Ocean Tavern), lease a farm at Mayger, Oregon, and set up a branch office at Salem. Positive press resulting from Smith's pitch increased membership to forty by the first of June, and she made sure the media knew that.[15]

Artisan activity during the summer of 1934 must have been a relief after the previous year's water war. But Jennie Baker died on June 12th, leaving David to operate Cottage Park and fend off Francis Mitchell alone. And as Artisan membership grew, so did internal discord. Louise Smith said nothing about that to the press, but Blanche (Parrish) Sweger wrote of it in her diary.[16]

On October 20th, the twenty-one-year-old woman rode into Bayocean with her older brother Derewood, his new wife Angy, and their parents from the northern dust bowl of South Dakota, seeking a better life in the west. The day after arriving, she wrote that the "biggest storm in history [had hit], the water came up to the kitchen door and even flowed down main street." Natatorium Gap had breached again, and again the media had missed it. So, Henry and Susie Snyder were clueless when they bought a tideland tract from Hosea Botts just north of the Bay Ocean Tavern a couple of months later and built a cabin.[17]

Blanche enjoyed having a room to herself after camping alongside the road for a month. She hiked up to view the ocean from Clarke Street, collected glass floats on the beach, and played kitten ball on the tennis court next to the Annex ruins. She loved playing games in the inn's lobby, listening to President Franklin Roosevelt on the radio, and dancing on nights the tides did not allow them to work. Artisan children attended Bayocean School. The Mitchells and Coatses brought them treats on Christmas Day, and everyone enjoyed a Christmas Party at the schoolhouse.[18]

Angy Parrish, left, and Blanche (Parrish) Sweger, right, posing in hip waders in Tillamook Bay while Artisans' Cooperative Community members, in 1935. Joyce (Sweger) Loftis's collection.

Catching, cleaning, and preparing fish and seafood was not fun. Blanche did not mind the work, but she hated waking at a different time each night to match the changing tide. Problems began when some Artisans refused to work after being voted into the community. The same people let their children run wild, waking Blanche and others who were trying to sleep. Sleep-deprived Artisans forced to do more than their fair share of the work grew increasingly agitated at membership meetings. In her last entry, on New Year's Eve, Blanche wrote that her parents had left because of the discord.[19]

Despite strife among the Artisans, Louise Smith applied for a $3,900 equipment grant from the Division of Self-Help Cooperatives at the Federal Emergency Relief Administration (FERA), which was replaced by the WPA at the end of 1935. She solicited Tillamook's congressional delegation and First Lady Eleanor Roosevelt. A few months later, on April 10, 1935, the Artisans received their grant. It would be the only FERA self-help grant issued in Oregon. The money bought boats and fishing equipment, got the Mayger farm going, and rented a house and offset printer in Salem, where stationery and brochures were produced and services were sold to the public. The problematic Artisans had been shown the door by then, so things quieted down.[20]

In August, FERA inspector Albert Wheelon made his first inspection of the Artisan Co-operative Community. He told the *Headlight-Herald*, "everything was very satisfactory" and stated that "it is now the only cooperative of the kind in the United States which is not on relief." However, Wheelon's internal report said that bookkeeping was inadequate, rooms had no heat, and customer orders were falling behind because membership was dropping. He also noted Oregon State Relief Administrator Elmer Goudy being "skeptical of the success of this cooperative in particular and desirability of all cooperatives in general. While he is not antagonistic, it will be necessary to sell Mr. Goudy on the idea of cooperation before his active support can be secured." But Goudy's attitude worsened after new members, who were disdainful of government assistance, were appointed to the Oregon State Relief Committee (OSRC), for which he worked.[21]

On October 1, 1935, the *Oregon Journal* covered a meeting at which the OSRC ordered a full investigation by their Tillamook affiliate after the ousted Artisans accused them of misconduct. Louise Smith immediately sent FERA a letter accusing Goudy and the OSRC of prejudice and wrote a letter to the editor of *Oregon Journal* saying she had done so. A flurry of communications followed, but Albert Wheelon could do little because he had already sent the money to Oregon. [22]

The *Oregonian* got into the act a week later by sending Ralph Stuller to interview the Artisans. He described the Bay Ocean Tavern as having a "modern foyer, lounging room, electric lights, toilets, baths and showers, music room, modern kitchen and office for business records." The lobby was full of books, magazines, and newspapers available to visitors. During interviews, a terrier scampered about the foyer, a typewriter clacked away in the adjacent office, a child cooed in the bedroom above him, and dishes rattled in the kitchen. Stuller described the Artisans as a diverse group of "painters, carpenters, cobblers, clerks, white-collared men, seamstresses, cooks, farmers, railroad men, and mechanics." In exchange for their labor, members received shelter, medical, work clothes, and $1 per day in a private script accepted by a few Tillamook stores. A couple who met there planned to get married that winter. Though Stuller did not name the couple, they were Blanche Parrish and Alvin Sweger.[23]

Artisans' Cooperative Community script. Joyce (Sweger) Loftis's collection.

An inspection conducted soon after Stuller left was less complimentary. Customers liked Artisan products, and members were content. The problem was a lack of proper accounting for the equipment purchased with grant money. Tillamook's relief committee resolved that by providing the community's treasurer with lessons. Meanwhile, Louise Smith drove to California to seek greener pastures and found some by January 1936, but that state's officials wanted nothing to do with the Artisans. That empowered Goudy and Tillamook detractors who, in May 1936, said that the five remaining Artisans were stealing oysters and violating fishing regulations to fill orders. Smith vehemently denied that but admitted to Albert Wheelon, "Our housing conditions have been so wretched that we have lost most of our members on that account… …This hotel life does not suit many people, as there is practically no privacy for anyone.[24]

Wheelon approached Washington State officials, found them receptive, and convinced Goudy that transferring remaining Artisans' grant funds was in everyone's best interest. A Washington field inspector was inspecting the Artisans' operation on July 21, 1936, when the remaining Artisans packed up and left. They showed up in Port Angeles, Washington the following day, rented a couple of houses, and went to work. Federal and state officials were upset by the Artisans' abrupt departure but had no choice but to make it work. After an Oregon auditor drove to Port Angeles and found everything in order, Elmer Goudy sent the Artisans' remaining grant balance to his Washington counterpart.[25] He and Louise Smith were finally rid of each other.

Later, Albert Wheelon learned that the Artisans had left so abruptly because Connie Dye had sold the Bay Ocean Tavern to the Mitchells for $400. While the Artisans were there, Francis had stayed out of the limelight. Later, he summed up their impact on Bayocean by telling Charles Carson that the town had been "rejuvenated for a short time by the WPA fiasco during the depression."[26]

Looking east down 12th Avenue at the Bay Ocean Tavern (Bayside Inn) in 1938. The Mitchell is on the right. Culp 11, Lorraine Eckhardt's collection.

WPA Projects Benefit Cape Meares and Arthur Beals

When the Artisans left in October 1936, they drove down a Bayocean Road resurfaced with fresh gravel and reinforced with new bulkheads by a WPA crew. The same crew finished the Cape Meares Loop Road, which connected Bayocean Road with Netarts Road at Oceanside. In addition to providing a pleasant Sunday drive for tourists, it gave communities on both sides of the cape alternative access when landslides blocked the primary route.[27]

Arthur Beals got some work done for himself included in the loop road contract. Seven men, plus a foreman he provided, spent much of 1936 digging a 1,500-foot ditch to straighten out the lower part of Coleman Creek and build a 350-foot-long dike across its mouth. A tide gate in the four-foot-wide by seven-foot-high structure automatically opened to let creek waters flow into the bay during low tide and closed during high tide, converting both sides of 1st Avenue from estuary to meadow. The ecological value of wetlands not being recognized back then, the community would have welcomed the additional, developable land. It just so happened that all of the land on the north side of the street belonged to the ex-senator.[28]

Beals brought in twenty dairy cows to graze the new meadowland. Over the years ahead, he bought ten additional acres, filled gaps between the lots and tracts he already owned, and consolidated his Bayocean dairy farm by vacating streets between 1st Avenue and Biggs Cove. In 1933, he and his wife Grace had purchased a house David Baker had built in 1931 and 1932 just south of Bayocean School. Howard Sherwood Jr.'s family lived in it from 1938, prior to buying George and Rilly Jones's home in 1940.[29]

This WPA project was one of the first things covered in the Bayocean News column initiated by the *Headlight-Herald* on November 5, 1936. The *Headlight* and *Herald* had run them intermittently, but the *Headlight-Herald* had not since their merger in April 1934.[30] The *Headlight-Herald* never attributed the column, but everyone knew Betty Watkins was its author.

In early December 1936, Betty introduced Byron and Jesse Randall as the new managers of Cottage Park. David Baker was still living on the spit, but he had given up on the enterprise after Jennie died, so the Latourettes took it back. Social events hosted by the Mitchells frequently appeared in Bayocean News the rest of that winter. In February 1937, Swan Hawkinson finished a cabin on Bay Street just north of 9th Avenue for Judge C. F. Richardson of Milwaukie.[31]

On August 19, 1937, Watkins added Bayocean—Oceanview as a subtitle to her column, then changed it to Bay Ocean—Oceanview a month later. She and Pop had lived in Oceanview for seven years by then and were promoting it as fiercely as Francis Mitchell did Bayocean Park. She reported everything from earaches to erosion. In October, she wrote about two cabins on the spit being moved to avoid falling into the sea. One belonged to Dr. Peter Reid, a Spokane physician, who had paid $2,500 to have a forty-by-thirty-foot house built on a $750 lot overlooking the ocean on the west side of Mears Street in 1928. Nine years later, as the dune edge approached, he hired Swan Hawkinson to move it back on the same lot. Conrad and Elvira Mueller had put up the other one across from Judge Bagley's house in 1930. Early in 1937, they bought a lot on the west side of Bay Terrace and paid David Baker move it down the hill that fall.[32]

Locals Demand Action from the Corps of Engineers

On January 27, 1938, Bayocean News blamed erosion on the north jetty publicly for the first time:

> It is the opinion of a good many of the residents here that the last extension of the Barview Jetty is the main cause of the change in currents that has washed out so many residences and valuable building sites in the last few years where, formerly, the sand had continued to build up. A solution to the problem is earnestly sought by all those interested.

Johan Poulsen's son-in-law Paul Bates, a Portland insurance agent, took up the challenge and asked Dr. Marcellus, Bill Coats, Judge Bagley, and Hosea Botts to join him on a Bay Ocean Erosion Committee. Their lobbying of Tillamook's congressional delegation secured $120,000 for "a preliminary survey of Tillamook Bay, Oregon, with a view to protection of

1918 state highway map showing southern loop to Tillamook from Portland via Grande Ronde. Oregon State Archive, June 6, 2022, https://www.facebook.com/OregonStateArchives/posts/392736162895071.

Natatorium ruins on the shore. Annex ruins on the ridge above. Dorian Studio images, Jon Chaix's collection.

Bayocean, and property thereon, from erosion and storms." After taking a quick survey and some photos on the spit a month earlier, the Portland District held a hearing in Tillamook on September 27, 1938. Many people submitted written testimony to District Engineer Major Cecil Moore ahead of the meeting, including thirty-one Bayocean cabin owners solicited by the Bay Ocean Erosion Committee.[33]

Paul Bates submitted six photographs to the Corps showing how much had been lost since the north jetty extension and said that only chunks of concrete remained where the Natatorium had once dominated the viewshed. George Riechers took the opportunity to complain about vandalism destroying the Annex, which he and his cohorts had sold for salvage earlier that year. Only the concrete walls and floor of its first level remained. The shoreline was creeping closer to the ruins, but for now, parents considered it safe enough for their children to use as a skating rink.[34]

Oregon State Highway Engineer R. H. Baldock wrote that Bayocean had "declined in use largely through the rapid advancement of transportation facilities to other beaches…if the beach can be preserved, it would appear safe to predict a secondary highway would be extended north along the sandspit." In the same vein, Dr. Marcellus wrote that if America went to war again, a highway along the spit's ridgeline would shorten the drive up the coast and speed military transport.[35]

Arthur Beals submitted no testimony in 1938 but later wrote, "The Coast Highway Association has gone on record supporting a connecting bridge link between Cape Meares and Bayocean Peninsula. This action would be in line with the original plan of the Roosevelt Highway." That may be the case, but since 1918, state maps had shown the coast route, as approved by the Oregon State Highway Commission, running through Tillamook, not Bayocean. But his perspective gave Francis Mitchell a new "if only" to bring prosperity since Bayocean Road had failed to do so. It also provided him a new enemy to focus on—Tillamook leaders—even if they were a completely different group than those who had convinced the highway commission to run the coast route their way twenty years earlier.[36]

David Baker said five cabins had been lost north of the Natatorium and two on the ridge above them. They had been owned by the Mallorys, DeWitts, Burns, Hughsons, Williams, Hylands, and Turners, respectively. By September of 1938, the dune's edge abutted the west side of High Street for most of its extent. Swan Hawkinson wrote of moving the summer cabin Harkness and Ina Chapin once owned on Clarke Street for Ava Garrigus to a lot closer to Bay Street before ex-Tillamook Mayor Alton Swett bought it in 1935. In 1938, David Baker and his new wife Mary were living there.[37]

George Jones wrote that at least sixty more feet of Bayocean shoreline had disappeared since he returned in 1932 and that the loss in some spots was 150 feet. Bill Coats's testimony corroborated Jones's. Since finishing the Fo'c'sle in 1932, 60 of the 120 feet between it and the dune's edge had disappeared. His and Betty's house was too big to move; he expected it to be gone in four years.[38]

The hearing held in the Tillamook County Courthouse on September 27, 1938 was packed. Oregon State Treasurer Rufus Holman represented the state. Southern Pacific sent officials. Forty locals were there, including several Bayocean and Oceanview residents who relayed their observations and concerns. Francis Mitchell bragged of being the first lot buyer and complained about Bayocean's "present desolate conditions," never mentioning erosion. County Judge Harland Woods complained about not being able to fish near the bay inlet because the north jetty had quickened the current. County Engineer Stanley Coates presented a map with shoreline recession ranging from 50 to 200 feet since the extension of the north jetty.[39]

On October 2nd, Ralph Stuller authored another story for the *Oregonian* titled "An Oregon 'Ghost City' Stirs in Its Grave." This time he gave a detailed history of the rise and fall of Bayocean Park, including photos of the ruined pier, streets with cracks hosting weeds, chunks of the Natatorium strewn on the beach, and the concrete shell of what had been the resort's "palatial hotel." Stuller reported a few homes ready to fall to the shore but did not include photos of them. Despite its state of ruin, he hoped completion of the Wilson River Highway and construction of a south jetty would bring "Oregon's most fashionable resort" back from the dead.[40]

Gap Breaches Threaten Garibaldi

Three weeks after Stuller's article, on October 26, 1938, a storm "washed away about three-quarters of a mile of sand at the end of Bay Ocean…with the result that for the first time in history huge swells are being carried across Tillamook Bay, resulting in severe damage at Garibaldi." Major Moore and other Corps officers assessed the damages and held another hearing. In late November, Tillamook County commissioners asked WPA engineers to dump boulders in the path of the waves to create a sea wall, but federal administrators nixed the idea.[41]

Things calmed down in December, but on the first day of January 1939, "mountain high waves" hit the Tillamook Coast at the same time as the "worst high tide in close to thirty years." On January 3rd, breakers tossed Southern Pacific tracks sixty feet onto the Coast Highway where Barview had stood before the same forces had destroyed it in 1915. Ten men sent to repair the damage were swept out to sea by another storm surge. Fortunately, they all managed to dodge floating debris and reach shore safely.[42]

As for Bayocean, waves crashed through several gaps for the first time in recorded history. Bertha (Weaver) Morgan and Blanche (Parrish) Sweger had noted Natatorium Gap breaches in 1909 and 1934. Others later recalled waves pouring through Jackson Gap in 1909 and 1915. In 2001, Oregon State University oceanographers learned that the sea had washed over Tillamook Spit regularly before white settlement since 1700.[43] But most people knew none of this, which made the January 1939 breaches seem even worse than they were.

No Bayocean buildings were directly in the path of washovers. Harkness Chapin had platted the sand gaps as streets simply because they did not require grading. But waves carried sand scoured from them and detritus from the ocean onto Bay Street and into Tillamook Bay. The Natatorium Gap was the only paved gap. That protected the sand below the concrete but made it easier for torrents to reach The Mitchell and cover its first floor with sand gathered from the sides of the gap.[44]

Maudy-Carlo had sat right on the edge of Jackson Gap, but in March 1938, its last owners, Mig and Maud Ackley, had deconstructed it. Their son Walter, a future mayor of Tillamook, was a teenager then. Despite knowing that his parents had acted wisely, he was so distraught when the cabin came down that he never returned to Bayocean.[45]

Newspapers had warned readers that a storm was coming, but some headed towards Bayocean instead of away from it in search of an exciting way to bring in the new year. They were not disappointed. Winds tossed burning logs from campfires on the beach and blew out cottage windows. Sneaker waves carried a few temporarily out to sea. Those who could not wait for road crews to clear debris and repair washouts timed breakers and quickly splashed through cluttered gaps to reach Bayocean Road and hitch a ride.[46]

Several hundred automobiles drove out to witness the carnage the following week. On January 8th, they lined 1st Avenue for a mile from its junction with Mears Street. Folks living on the mainland cheered as road crews cleared streets on the spit on January 12th so future spectators could drive into the Bayocean town center and stop clogging theirs.[47]

Engineers Survey Storm Damage

Soon after the storm, Major Moore led a team of engineers to Tillamook. On January 10th, he sent a preliminary report directly to Chief of Engineers Major General J. L. Schley. It included a map and description of each "wash," the term he used to differentiate sand gaps that had breached from those that had not. Moore said that some residents had moved elsewhere temporarily because the main water pipe had broken where it crossed Jackson Gap. The dune's edge had receded ten to twenty feet during the storm, bringing it close to several houses. Tillamook County commissioners told Senator Charles McNary that those homes ranged in value from $5,000 to $15,000. They argued for a south jetty as the best way to save them, pointing to the sand accumulating three to four miles south of the jetties on the south side of the Nehalem and Columbia Rivers after they were built as proof.[48]

Moore let Schley know that locals blamed the north jetty for the erosion that had lowered four gaps enough to allow storm surges to wash through them, and that they wanted the Corps to construct bulkheads in

Corps engineers surveying Natatorium Gap on January 4, 1939, as viewed from the south. The Mitchell, Judge Bagley's second cabin, and Bayside Inn are in the background. Folder 1 (Bay Ocean), File 7402, Box 96, Civil Works Project Files, 1902-1968. POR-81, RG 77, NARA, Seattle, WA.

each gap to correct the problem immediately. Moore thought doing so "a worthy project for local interests in conjunction with emergency appropriations" and the $120,000 cost, "emergency work which is considered advisable in the near future." Seeing the impact of erosion on people appears to have affected Major Moore. Perhaps he regretted having deleted "the interception by the jetty of the southward moving sand supply has doubtless contributed to the recession along the south land point" from the Oregon section of a national report on jetties recently reissued in his own name. He had repeated an observation that the north jetty had been "fairly successful" in maintaining the inlet channel without a south jetty to match."[49]

Another storm hit the Tillamook Coast on the first of February, removing another swath of dune and undercutting the houses on its edge. Alton Swett's Green Gables fell later that year. So did George Bagley's place. In May 1938, the judge had hired David Baker to build a new house on a tract just north of the Bayside Inn and abandoned his place on the ridge. A year later, Baker returned to do more work while Mary cared for the ailing judge. The couple then left Bayocean for Portland, where David died on March 19, 1975.[50]

George Baker (one of the taxidermy brothers) had purchased one of Henry King's cabins in 1921 and retired to Bayocean in 1930. He nearly lost his life while watching the storm on High Street near Judge Bagley's house when a 600-foot section of pavement slid to the shore. Somehow, he managed to arrest his fall and scrambled back to the top. Another 500-foot section of the street collapsed the following week.[51]

The *Oregonian* sent staff reporter Herman Edwards to Bayocean in mid-February. Residents gave him their theory on what was causing the erosion. The north jetty now forced all the bay's outflow, previously dispersed north and south, towards Cape Meares. Currents there pushed the doubled volume towards the shore where it swung north, "creating four distinct eddies that gnaw ceaselessly at the narrowing beaches, all gravel now, and at the yielding sand dunes. Fishermen relate there is a fearsome pull in these whirlpools as they churn away at their work of destruction." According to locals, gap bulkheads could provide temporary protection, but the Corps needed to build a south jetty and a seawall running the length of the spit to correct the problem it had caused.[52]

Edwards's full-page article featured several images, including the first map of Bayocean showing breach locations available to the public. Like Major Moore, he numbered each "wash," but in parentheses after naming each "gap." South Gap (Wash #1) started at 2nd Street on the beach, ran northeast along Shell Street, and entered Biggs Cove at the west end of Beals's dike. Jackson Gap (Wash #2) spanned 3rd and 4th Avenues where Mears Street on the ridge dropped down to meet Bay Street on the bay. Rock Crusher Gap (Wash #3) spanned 7th Avenue; its namesake having once stood where it met the bay. Natatorium Gap (Wash #4) spanned 11th Avenue.[53] "Gaps" caught on with the public, whereas "washes" did not.

Edwards's article was also the first to show a house hanging on the edge of the dune, owned by E. H. (Harry) Roberts, proprietor of the Roberts Brothers department store in Portland. He had purchased Westview from William Clemens's estate in 1919. Another photo showed the crater in High Street where George Baker had slid down the dune a few weeks earlier.[54]

The Bay Ocean Erosion Committee lobbied Tillamook's congressional delegation relentlessly in pursuit of the bulkheads, south jetty, and seawall. As a result, General Schley shared Moore's initial report with them but said the Corps had no funding or authority beyond the study already in the works, which would take a couple of years. He offered to assist other federal agencies that had any money available. John Aschim, then secretary of the Tillamook Chamber of Commerce, got the same response when he lobbied Schley on behalf of Tillamook businesses at risk of losing everything without the protection afforded by the spit. All that came of their combined efforts was nine WPA workers placing sandbags in the gaps.[55]

Bayocean's erosion having become a Tillamook Bay-wide concern, Bates and Aschim set up a Bayocean Committee. They served as chair and secretary, respectively, and County judge Harland Woods served as vice-chair, with each interested group, including the Bay Ocean Erosion Committee, having a representative. With the help of Governor Charles Sprague, they lobbied President Franklin Roosevelt, Representative James Mott, Senator Rufus Holman, and Senator Charles McNary. Mott guided a bill for $120,000 through the House, but the Senate Commerce Committee stripped it from their version of the bill.[56]

Harry Roberts's cabin (first owned by William Clemens) nearing the dune's edge in 1938. Ben Maxwell Photo ID 5507, Salem Public Library Historic Photograph Collections.

CHAPTER 7

Wartime Community
(1939–1947)

As spring arrived in 1939, conditions on Bayocean improved. While Corps engineers surveyed the spit, near-record crowds dug for clams in beds exposed by an extremely low tide. The Randalls set up a store in one of the bungalows. George Sanders, the retired manager of Tillamook's Pacific Telephone and Telegraph Company, and his wife Myrtle must have thought that the washovers were a fluke because they built a house on the north side of Jackson Gap.[1]

Greta Forbish Meets the Mitchells

Greta Forbish and her family visited Bayocean for the first time in the summer of 1939 when a booked-up Netarts resort owner assured them that the Mitchells would have rooms available. They wondered why he said it with a chuckle until they drove up to the dilapidated buildings in the town center after bouncing over ruts for the last mile. Before they could turn around and leave, a "sprightly gnome" scampered out to direct them to a parking spot between several other cars. Francis Mitchell was "delighted at the resurgence of activity."[2]

Francis and Ida had moved into the Bayside Inn and closed The Mitchell. Surely, they must have shoveled out the sand, but there had been too little business to keep it open for a long time, and Texaco had removed its gas pump. Francis searched for old cans of food in the shuttered store for his guests to cook in the inn's kitchen without success. So, he wrote down what everyone wanted and drove into town to fetch their groceries while Ida dried out their mattresses and bedding with a warming pan.[3]

The families shared a communal dinner that evening. Later, they retired to the foyer, where Francis fired up the stove as one lady sang while another played an old reed organ. Their level of talent drove Greta outside.

She was pleased to see that the tide had covered the mudflats seen and smelled from her room earlier.[4]

Francis's attempts to sell lots to his guests irritated Greta enough that she was a bit unkind in describing Ida as a "dark, heavy, and placid wife [who] seemed like an immovable rock about which a sprightly lizard scuttled." But the Mitchells grew on her. Greta liked Ida's chiding of Francis when he got carried away: "You don't know that for sure. You might be exaggerating." And she found their manner of addressing each other as Mr. Mitchell and Mrs. Mitchell endearing. So, the Forbishes returned, which endeared them to the Mitchells because the other families did not.[5]

In July 1939, thirty-five Boy Scouts from Baker City, Oregon camped on the spit and spent a day fixing Bay Street. In September, the Bayocean Cooperative Water System buried several hundred feet of new pipe at Jackson Gap several feet below the new, lower road level. On November 1st, Kate, and Jay Smith abandoned Hillcrest. It fell into the sea a few months later. Whenever a storm hit the coast that winter, people drove to the spit in hopes of witnessing more destruction. Fortunately, the WPA sandbags were enough to prevent washovers through the end of that year. Lillie Latourette died on December 23rd and Judge Bagley on December 26th.[6]

Homes Continue Falling

On January 5, 1940, storm surges tossed the WPA sandbags into the bay and scoured the dune cliff within forty feet of the Marcellus home. Marius and Vinnie decided to abandon Skookum Tepee a few months later and moved to a 258-acre estate at Kilchis Point, from which they could at least keep an eye on the site of the cabin they had enjoyed for twenty-six years.[7]

Another storm at the end of January took the cabin H. M. and Clara Madden had bought from Thelma Swank in 1923. Harry Roberts's Westview survived, but it was hanging over the edge, so he hired Swan Hawkinson to move it closer to Bay Street. George Higgins also hired Swan to move his house back from Mears Street in Oceanview.[8]

On May 24th, county commissioners agreed to maintain 1st Avenue, Mears Street, and Bay Street to 12th Avenue. Though this did not commit them to improve the streets, locals were pleased, especially Swan

Hawkinson, who was busy moving and deconstructing homes in Oceanview and Bayocean Park as their shorelines moved east.[9]

Severe storms wreaked havoc again the following winter, washing through Jackson Gap so often that in January 1941, the *Headlight-Herald* noted, "a delta formation is being built along the roadway on the bay side by the action of the breakers." Arthur Dolan put some of that sand to use in his concrete business after purchasing a tideland tract in the bay east of Jackson Gap from Arthur Beals in September 1942. He had purchased several lots at the ocean end of South Gap for the same purpose in October 1940. Despite Dolan excavations, the bay side of the spit would be known for its "white sugar sand" thereafter, as first promised in sales brochures, rather than the mudflats recalled by Bertha (Weaver) Morgan and Greta Forbish.[10]

On February 15, 1941, George and Myrtle Sanders's place slid into the sea. They had removed their belongings beforehand, after enjoying their place for only two years. Beachcombers grabbed the rest over the next few days. Early in the new congressional session, Representative Mott reintroduced another $120,000 gap defense bill, and Rufus Holman, who had been elected to the Senate, introduced legislation to purchase all spit property for $250,000. Neither were passed.[11]

Engineers Judge Bayocean Not Worth Saving

At the end of March 1941, as Mott and Holman were trying to convince colleagues to spend more money on Bayocean, the Chief of Engineers proclaimed it not worth saving. The Board of Engineers provided Senator Charles McNary, Representative Mott, and Arthur Beals an opportunity to plead their case in Washington, DC on June 30th but did not change its stance.[12]

Major Moore had finished his report at the end of August 1940. District geologist Lloyd Ruff Jr. was the first to provide him feedback in March 1939. Ruff dismissed the offshore eddies described by locals as too irregular to explain the spit's erosion. Anecdotal reports of winter storms approaching from the southwest and milder northwest winds and currents in the summer led Ruff to theorize that sand pulled offshore in the winter returned in the summer. He saw evidence of both north and south littoral drift, the latter being sand accumulated north of the jetty. But he was sure that the Bayocean dune had stabilized and had been shrinking for more than a century. So, if the north jetty was causing erosion, it was only accelerating a natural process. Ruff concluded, "the most efficient solution of the problem would be the relocation of the entire Bayocean community." As for Tillamook Bay, he thought runoff from the Tillamook Burn—four fires that destroyed 554 square miles of forest between 1933 and 1951—posed a more significant threat than Bayocean washovers.[13]

Six engineers spent April through July 1939 in the field. They studied sand composition, measured elevations to create Bayocean's first topographic map, interviewed locals, took photos, and gathered information

Harry Roberts's house on February 6, 1940. Army Corps of Engineers photo. Bayocean 1924–1956, Box 1B, Historic Photos 1903-1953, POR-57, RG 77, NARA, Seattle, WA.

from the Tillamook County Assessor. They put up experimental groins—wooden bulkheads set perpendicular to the shoreline. Mild summer waves destroyed them within a month. The sturdier ones that took their place had deteriorated appreciably by the time the engineers left. The "remains of a concrete bulkhead 1,000 feet north of Jackson Gap," below Westview, suggests William Clemens was the only landowner Sydney Vincent had built the seawall for in 1915.[14]

On May 22, 1939, engineers placed twenty-four chrome-yellow fire bricks on the shore at the spit's midpoint and recorded their movement. After two days, the nine bricks remaining had shrunk to half their original size and moved 2,400 to 3,800 feet north, which supported the prevailing belief that sand migrated north along the Pacific Coast. This took place while the sea was calm enough for Bob Watkins to paddle a kayak two miles out to Lion's Head (a rock west of Cape Meares) and back.[15]

Of all the factors leading to the Corps' no-action decision, the most important was that Tillamook Bay navigation and commerce had continued unimpeded despite gap washovers because those were the objectives Congress demanded and authorized them to carry out. Moore thought the Natatorium, Jackson, and South Gaps were the only ones low enough to have regular breaches and that damage to the spit would never interrupt navigation and commerce. He said that thirty-six houses, two stores, a schoolhouse, and "an auto camp with 35 cottages" were at risk. Thirty-five residents lived in twelve of the houses year-round. During the summer season, the population grew to as much as 150. Eleven houses worth $20,000 had been "wrecked or moved" since 1927. Eight were likely to fall in the next three years.[16]

Moore could be forthright in tallying what was already lost and would be soon because protecting private property was not part of the Corps' congressional mandate. Despite that and his geologist and engineers concluding a south jetty and groins would not help, he sent a confidential report to superiors estimating that it would cost $3,000,000 to build them. Why? To show how much that exceeded the $54,610 assessed value of all property on the spit.[17] Whatever ambivalence Major Moore had felt previously had disappeared; he now felt the same about the town of Bayocean as Ruff did about the spit. They were in decline; their demise was inevitable; and the sooner everyone accepted these facts, the better.

As to whether the north jetty was to blame for Bayocean's erosion, Moore punted to the Shore Protection Board, the national panel of Corps specialists. They judged the north jetty not at fault because any sand migrating south in the summer before it existed would have been carried out to sea or into the bay by tidal flows. None of it would have reached the spit.[18] The data Portland District engineers started collecting in 1939 would later help academics prove the Shore Protection Board wrong. But in 1940, as far as the Corps was concerned, the north jetty had not been a mistake.

Naval Air Station Tillamook Spurs Growth

Lumberjacks living in the back of Cottage Park probably did not care when the Chief of Engineers rejected the south jetty in March 1941. These year-round residents certainly did not care for summer guests. Greta Forbish recalled their unfriendly glances when her family stayed in one of the bungalows that year. Walter (Shorty) Locke managed them then, the Randalls having moved to Oceanview. Like the Randalls, Shorty, Mary Elizabeth (Betty), and their three children lived in one of the bungalows.[19]

That April, Henry King asked the Tillamook County Public Welfare Commission for an Old-Age Assistance grant. He was sixty-five, destitute, and ill. King had believed in Bayocean as fervently as the Mitchells and for nearly as many years. Profits from buying and selling foreclosed lots had been so meager that he had dissolved The Bayocean Company in 1936. Henry moved to Tillamook in 1940 but did no better there, and his finances deteriorated along with his health. He was granted public assistance in July 1941 and then placed in a nursing home because he was not taking care of himself. On April 14, 1942, King was diagnosed with senile dementia and sent to the Oregon State Hospital. He told staff he had developed "a nervous condition over the last ten years over property losses" before dying of pneumonia on June 10th. No relative has claimed his cremains.[20]

In November 1941, with completion of the Wilson River Highway, Portlanders were more easily able to witness Bayocean's destruction. The next opportunity came when Bill and Betty Coats's Fo'c'sle slid to the shore ten days after the Japanese attacked Pearl Harbor, December 17th. Beachcombers rummaged through the debris the following weekend and watched men deconstruct the Marcellus home.[21]

On January 8, 1942, Bayocean News promoted "a rally and re-organization" of the Bayocean Women's Club, "since so many of the club members have left the community, having been literally eroded out." Betty Watkins then set down her pen for the rest of World War II. She picked it up on January 4, 1945, but only a few more times that year and the next two, running for the last time on October 2, 1947.[22] In August 1946, Watkins added Cape Meares as a subtitle to some of the Bayocean News columns. She wrote a standalone Cape Meares News column for the first time on September 19, 1946. It ran irregularly—like Bayocean News and, oddly, sometimes the same week—until April 15, 1948, after which it appeared most every week.

Given Betty's typically cheery tone and comment about the Bayocean Women's Club, the gaps in coverage and transition from Bayocean News to Cape Meares News might have been caused by news from the spit being too depressing. Oceanview homes were threatened by erosion too, but they were more easily moved inland than those on Bayocean, so none of them were lost. She also may have thought Oceanview more deserving of attention since its population was growing and Bayocean Park's was declining. Whatever Betty's reasoning, Cape Meares News gave residents of the mainland a community identity, rather than being referred to as residents of Bayocean Park or Oceanview. Unfortunately, another result of this transition was that the *Headlight-Herald* carried little news during the next six years about homes lost on the spit or Bayocean's transformation into a middle-class community.

During the early months of World War II, the Navy decided Tillamook was an ideal spot from which a squadron of blimps could patrol the Pacific Coast. By June 1942, hundreds of construction workers were building two hangars large enough to house four blimps and barracks for a thousand officers and enlisted men who would fly and maintain them. Support services drew even more workers. The construction of Naval Air Station Tillamook (NAST) brought an economic boom to Tillamook, much as the construction of Bayocean Park had thirty-five years earlier. But when NAST closed at the end of the war, many of its workers stayed.[23]

Those workers and their families quickly filled every vacant house and apartment despite landlords raising rent. Eventually, people discovered that

Blimps cruised the Oregon Coast daily during World War II. This photo was taken at Seaside, Oregon. NPER-179, TCPM.

Bayocean offered affordable housing. Lewis Bennett was typical of them. He had been earning $.67 an hour as a shift foreman in Sioux City, Iowa when he noticed a NAST circular in a post office offering carpenters $1.41 an hour. Bennett decided to change trades and headed west with Hilda and their three children.[24]

Others moving to Bayocean were employed elsewhere. Vern Meyers was a timberman who moved to Bayocean because of the Tillamook Burn. He and Martha bought Henry King's second cabin and moved into it with their four children. The Bennetts, who had been renting the house, moved to George Burckhard's place, which Portlanders Viola Dickson and Ethel Tatarini then owned. Before and after the wartime influx, they would spend their summers there rather than renting it out. Perry Reeder Sr. worked at several places—a dairy, a laundromat, and a bottling company—after moving to the spit in the summer of 1944. He and Evelyn and their four children initially rented a bungalow from Shorty Locke for $10.00 a month. That was the equivalent of $5.50 in 1914 when the bungalows rented for $35.00, showing how cheap Bayocean lodging had become.[25]

Bayocean Road had to provide a dependable daily commute for these newcomers. Ironically, the increased traffic made it harder for county road crews to maintain the dirt streets inside the subdivision. Fear of losing momentum pushed Francis Mitchell into action again. On March 12, 1943, he hosted a lot owner meeting in Portland. The *Oregonian* reported his pleading for money and for letters asking the Tillamook County commissioner to gravel the streets.

Francis countered doubts stemming from the news of gap breaches with, "The sea, which in recent years has been tearing chunks out of Bayocean peninsula, has been kind during the last year and is returning considerable of what it took away."[26]

There had been no letup in gap breaches, but his fib got Francis what he wanted. On July 30th, county commissioners officially designated 1st Avenue, Meares Street, and Bay Street to 12th Avenue part of Bayocean Road. But a year later, the streets had not been graveled or otherwise improved. So, on Friday, August 25, 1944, Mitchell held another meeting, but in Tillamook. He ran a Watch Bayocean Grow ad in the *Headlight-Herald* ahead of it that included, "Tillamook County now owns 1,877 lots, taken for taxes, or more than 2/3 of Bayocean. The taxpayer is in a position to dictate the future policies of this promising resort."[27]

Francis's marketing strategy is puzzling. It sounds like he was encouraging Tillamook residents to buy lots and pay property taxes so the county could afford to gravel Bayocean streets. But he knew the thousands who had visited the spit since 1927 did more looting than lot buying. Did he think the Annex and Natatorium ruins and houses falling to the shore since then would induce them? How could letting everyone know that so many people—including leaders in their community—considered their Bayocean Park lots worth less than the taxes owed help sell them?

Whatever Mitchell's strategy was, it did not work because the county sold only a handful of lots in the months following his meeting. However, in November 1944, Richard and Nellie Walton bought one of the lots Connie Dye had let the county take back for $35 just uphill from the Muellers and put up a place to live in during their retirement.[28] Bargain pricing motivated the Waltons, as it would others in the 1940s, not a convoluted argument that buying property would enable street improvements.

A Watch Bayocean Grow circular Mitchell distributed about the same time as his meeting is just as puzzling as his lot selling strategy. Judge Bagley's granddaughter Sue (Bagley) Barr posted a copy of it to the Old Tillamook Times Facebook group on October 26, 2015. Barr commented, "I think it shows the stress, disappointment, and perhaps unraveling of a man who tried to hang on to his dream of a greater Bayocean most of his adult life." She did not know which neighbor gave the circular to her mother, Elizabeth, but doing so suggested that they shared the viewpoint expressed by notes (bracketed in italics below) scribbled on it.

> TRUTH IS A MIGHTY SWORD! Distort truth and you will fail. [*I did*] No better example can be found than at Bayocean. [*than us*] Today, she is fast freeing herself of all strife and contention. [*I won't live much longer*] She can soon go forward and take her place among the best beach resorts on the Oregon Coast, without question. [*grain by grain*] Our forces are well organized and will positively oppose any sharp practices or financial injury done to any lot owner in Bayocean. [*me & Mrs. Mitchell & our black eye*] Thanks to our many friends [*which one*] for their loyal support in our fight for justice what these long, lean 22 years. We shall never forget you. [*we wish we could*]
>
> Mr. and Mrs. F. D. Mitchell

Coast Guard war dog being trained by its handler. Image 816, Box 27, Beach Patrol, Photos of Activities, Facilities, and Personalities, 1939-1967, RG 27, NARA, College Park, MD.

War Dogs Patrol Bayocean's Shoreline

A Coast Guard War Dog Beach Patrol was moving into the Poulsen complex as Francis Mitchell held his meeting in Portland in March 1943. Beach patrols were initiated in July 1942 when two teams of German saboteurs were apprehended in New York City and Jacksonville, Florida. Their plan was to destroy industrial and transportation facilities and create panic across the eastern seaboard. A submarine sighting near Santa Barbara, California and a shell fired at Fort Stevens at the mouth of the Columbia River called for action on the Pacific Coast.[29]

Beach patrols were different than most Coast Guard units. These guardsmen were farm boys recruited for their experience handling animals. They operated exclusively on land and collaborated with the Army and FBI. They manned lookouts with binoculars, radios, and machine guns from high points along the Oregon Coast as cohorts patrolled the beaches below with dogs or on horseback, like the Rockaway Beach patrol. Cape Meares hosted a Coast Guard lookout and an Army radar station.[30]

The Poulsen family homes were ideally situated at the midpoint of the spit and on a high point with clear views and streets leading down to the beach. One team patrolled north while another patrolled south, in shifts lasting six hours. Each group included a war dog, its handler, and another guardsman carrying a radio and other gear. Both men had rifles. The dogs were a variety of breeds and had been trained to be aggressive to everyone but their handler. Other guardsmen served as aggravators to maintain their ferocity. Bayocean station logs refer to each dog by number, except on February 29, 1944, when Prince the Airedale, Skippy the Collie, Tuffy the Irish Setter, and Doberman Pinschers Schotti and Ardo were listed.[31]

Bayocean's full complement of twenty-four was on board by May 1, 1943. Maintaining round-the-clock surveillance required eight dogs and sixteen men. Six additional guardsmen manned the lookout or were on liberty. First Class Petty Officer Ed Russ was in command. He and his family lived in Johan and Dora Poulsen's summer home, which Marie Kerns, Kate Thatcher, and Louise Zan inherited after their mother died in 1939. The other petty officer, who was second in command, lived in Agnete Bates's Villa Tettrazzina with his wife. Paul had no say in the matter because he had passed away in February. Paul and Thora King's house served as station headquarters. Unmarried guardsmen slept on cots in the basement until they built a twenty-five-by-fifty-foot bunkhouse in the fall of 1943.[32]

The dogs were kenneled just south of the Annex ruins. The guardsmen built a lookout shelter at the southwest edge of the hotel grounds, from which they could communicate with guardsmen on Cape Meares by semaphore. One of the handlers let little Donny Meyers tag along while feeding his war dog. Donny knew better than to approach it or any other dog when its handler was not present because a dog occasionally got loose and terrorized the neighborhood. Jesse Vance Mason Jr., the oldest boy, recalled one loping through the brush and zeroing in on him. Terrified, he climbed the closest tree to escape its teeth. The much younger Joann (Dolan) Steffey came even closer to being mauled. The guardsmen made up for it by inviting the children of Bayocean to watch movies and eat popcorn on Sunday evenings.[33]

Cameras, automobiles, and nighttime bonfires were prohibited along America's coastlines during the war. In August 1943, Oregon authorized beach patrols to enforce those rules. With guns slung over their shoulders and war dogs with their teeth bared tugging at their leashes, violators readily complied. Daylight beachcombers kept their distance regardless. That, along with the fact that no Japanese were ever encountered, made patrolling a lonely, tedious business. Lights on a nearby hillside or at sea occasionally caused a stir but always turned out to be benign. The wind and rain, which the midwestern farm boys were not used to, made them particularly miserable.[34]

When not on patrol, guardsmen performed fire drills, studied, and took tests to gain rank. They maintained the Poulsen houses, repaired streets, and helped the Army build their radar facility on the south side of Cape Meares. Whatever they did in Tillamook on liberty caused a few guardsmen to return late on occasion and face disciplinary action. Their only authorized excitement was targeting practice in Natatorium Gap. Most of the men carried .30 caliber Model 1903 Springfield rifles. Four had Smith and Wesson .38 caliber revolvers, but four others firing their .45 caliber Model

50 Reising submachine guns and a .30 caliber air-cooled Browning machine gun caused more commotion. Neighbors did not like the racket, but they appreciated the sailors shooting into the hillside. Boys loved digging bullets out of the sand after the shooting stopped.[35]

Axis powers were on the defense by the spring of 1944, making sabotage less of a threat. And Allied commanders needed every man available to invade Normandy. So, the Coast Guard phased out the beach patrols. As guardsmen transitioned out of Bayocean, those remaining moved into Thora King's house, so her sisters sold theirs. Arthur and Hazel Dolan bought the Bates house in March 1944. Kerns, Thatcher, and Zan sold their place to James and Helen McCann a month later. The *Headlight-Herald* noted, "Both homes are some distance from the ocean and appear to be safe." On September 13, 1944, the last guardsmen left Thora King's house. She sold it to Charles and Sibyl Hicks in June 1945.[36]

The McCanns, who owned the Alderwood Mill in Tillamook, never lived in the Poulsen place. They used it as a rental, as did a succession of owners. Men who lived there as boys recall the McFaddens because their daughter Mickey was a tomboy who could hold her own during their explorations and BB gun wars. All they remember about Mr. McFadden is that he was retired military and seemed to be a man of means. The same was true of the Hickses, whose butler answered the door. Charles and Sibyl owned the House of Hicks restaurant in Portland. They set up a catering business with the same name in their house on the spit after adding a garage and having a well drilled because water from Coleman Creek was not dependable, clean, or ample.[37]

Discount Prices Bring Bargain Hunters

By the winter of 1944–1945, every storm breached at least one gap. Waves washed through Jackson Gap the most often, but when they were coursing through South Gap as well, children attending Bayocean School were stuck on an island.[38]

Representative James Mott managed to get $120,000 authorized for the bulkheads locals wanted in the Rivers and Harbors Bill of March 1945. But Congress could not appropriate the money until six months after World War II ended without War Production Board approval. After hearing this, Corinth

Crook wrote to Senator Wayne Morse, "if we must wait to get that money which was promised by Congress until the war is over we shall no longer exist." She chose to write Morse instead of Mott so she could scold him for not having visited Bayocean since defeating Senator Holman in the 1944 election.[39]

On April 10, 1945, Congressman Mott toured the spit at the invitation of the Tillamook Chamber of Commerce. Laurence Hough, a civil engineer at NAST, was his guide. Hough and his wife Edith had recently purchased Marion Stevenson's house on the mainland side of South Gap from Albert and Otta Biggs.[40] They probably got less than they paid because the market value of Bayocean lots and homes decreased as gap breaching increased. Erosion publicity had made Bayocean a buyer's market.

Notable among the bargain hunters were H. W. (Harvy) and Laura E. Currin, owners of a real estate company in Hillsboro. In February 1945, they bought the two small cabins P. D. Hance had built for himself and Ella May Hutchinson in 1914. The Currins' oldest daughter later explained their reasoning: "They and all their family could have at least $600 worth of fun there before those houses, too, were washed away." The cabins were on the uphill side of Larch Street, between Alder Street and 10th Avenue. Since Larch was never graded, Harvy and Laura created a little family retreat by purchasing the seven lots between it and Bay Street over the next couple of years.[41]

While the Currins bought their cabins, Dr. Reid and Harry Roberts sold their houses for salvage because they were again hanging over the dune's edge and too large to move elsewhere. Roberts's place was so big that two men planned to build a house from its materials. They had begun dismantling the home on March 13, 1945, when it started sliding down the sixty-foot slope—so slowly it landed on the beach that evening "without even breaking a window." Beachcombers took what they could for the next few days until waves broke the house apart and carried its remains out to sea. Nine days later, the Sanderses' garage collapsed, though pieces of it would linger. Since the Ritner family, the last owners of Daniel Van Tine's Lorelie, had lost it sometime before that, no houses remained on Bayocean's southern ridge.[42]

As scavengers hauled away the last pieces of the Roberts house on Sunday afternoon, March 18, 1945, a blimp damaged by a storm barely made it over the Annex ruins and crashed into the bay a quarter of a mile southeast of The

Mitchell. Despite nasty weather and debris scattered through Jackson Gap, more than five hundred people drove out to the spit to watch the deflated airbag and gondola tossed by the waves that evening.[43]

Donny Meyers witnessed the crash. His father, Vern, and Conrad Mueller rowed out and pulled the airmen, who had scrambled into a single life raft, back to shore. Martha Meyers, Betty Locke, and others gave them blankets and coffee before a Navy truck packed them off. Boys rowed out to grab what they could from the wreckage, but they had to return the bounty when found out. Vance Mason was most aggrieved to lose a radio and maps labeled Top Secret. A Chief Petty Officer's cap and a flare gun he found later were consolation prizes.[44]

Wreckage of Blimp K103 in Tillamook Bay, east of Bayside Inn. ND-35, TCPM.

Vance recalled his engagement with the Navy airmen, who regularly cruised over the Annex ruins in their blimp, more fondly. One day, he brought a megaphone and asked them for candy, which was hard to come by during the war. As Lieutenant George Drale hovered, one of his crew sent down a box of Hershey bars at the end of a parachute fashioned out of his handkerchief. To the dismay of his comrades, Vance kept them all. Mason returned the airmen's favor by delivering notes inviting older Bayocean girls for dates. Perry Reeder Jr. enjoyed the blimp flyovers but got more excited watching fighter jets practice dive-bombing targets and firing their machine guns close to shore.[45]

In August 1945, Shorty and Betty Locke bought a lot across the street from Cottage Park from the county for $75. They then purchased the bunkhouse built by guardsmen. Shorty and Vance hauled it down the hill to the lot and remodeled and added to it before moving in.[46] The same month as the Lockes bought their lot, the Hawkinsons sold their home on Clarke Street to A. W. and Nova Bogard and moved to Bay City. The Hawkinsons sold their first (rental) house eleven months later to Birger and Asta Bugge. Swan and Othelia—seventy-four and sixty-five years old then—had spent all thirty-two years of their marriage on Bayocean. Only the Mitchells had lived on Bayocean longer. From their new home on the hill behind Bay City, they would watch what happened to their old home until Othelia died in August 1956 and Swan in December 1960.[47]

Also, in August 1945, Warren and Virginia Hinsdale began work on a market and gas station at the southeast corner of 4th Street and Bayocean Road, which was the main intersection of Cape Meares. Neighbors looked forward to having groceries nearby, but there were not enough of them to justify the investment—summer tourists were the Hinsdales' target market.[48]

Erosion Studied Again

With bulkhead appropriations going nowhere, Tillamook leaders and Bayocean residents pressured the Army Corps of Engineers until they agreed to hold another hearing on September 12, 1945. What the Portland District heard convinced them to take enough money from their north jetty maintenance budget to do another study in January 1946. For two weeks, engineers surveyed the spit, took photographs, sounded the bay, and collected information about the area's commerce, economy, and population to update data collected seven years earlier. Folks in Cape Meares and Bayocean reported the average annual rate of erosion at fifteen feet.[49]

During the second week of February, waves took out the rest of the ridge where the Roberts house had stood and widened Jackson Gap. At that point, just a few humps of sand remained above water at high tide. Later that month, county road crews improved Bayocean Road with gravel, making it easier for weekenders to enjoy the show. And the Hinsdales finished their Cape Meares Grocery just in time to serve them.[50]

In July 1946, Portland District Engineer Colonel O. E. Walsh sent the second Bayocean study upline. After the Chief of Engineers received it, he asked Walsh to take a second look because he knew folks in Tillamook would be disappointed with what it said. John Aschim, who had become Secretary of the Tillamook Chamber of Commerce, got word of this and secured a copy. In September, the *Headlight-Herald* published his detailed commentary, which confirmed Walsh's prediction. Among his many details, Aschim emphasized that the narrowing of the spit had removed five hundred lots and placed the entire Tillamook Bay area at risk.[51]

That October, Pop Watkins gave freshman Congressman Walter Norblad—elected after James Mott had died in November 1945—a tour of Bayocean. Francis Mitchell had dropped out of the picture because he had no phone. Pop did.[52]

Cottage Park Renamed Bayocean Cottages

In April 1946, Lyman Latourette sold Cottage Park to Russell E. Hoover Sr. and his wife Gladys, who had spent a week vacationing there in August 1939.[53] Russell, who had been a Portland School District custodian, told the *Headlight-Herald* he would "renovate and remodel the cottages into compact modern apartments." He turned the bungalows into duplexes by attaching them end-to-end. One became a store with an office in the back where he kept books for the Bayocean Cooperative Water System. When Ida Mitchell handed over postmaster duties to Gladys in August, Russell converted the bungalow attached to the store to a post office. They opened for business on May 1st as the Bayocean Cottages. But when the Forbishes arrived, the wooden letters on a two-foot-high sign at the entrance still read COT AGE PA K.[54]

Despite Russell being a good host, Bayocean Cottages was never busy, according to Greta Forbish. His remodeling may explain why:

> Each cabin was about the size of a railroad caboose which had been set end-to-end duplicating one another in reverse. A

> minuscule dining room-living room-kitchen with a sink and wood range, a table, four straight chairs and a rocking chair made up the furnishings. The rocker banged into one's ankles no matter where one tried to move it. There was a flimsy partition and a burlap curtain for the bedroom which was just large enough for two double beds. Through the narrow aisle one could slide to the rear where a small closet contained a bureau with immovable drawers and a toilet. This was an extremely companionable arrangement for you were separated from the people in back only by a large tin Bull Durham sign which had been tacked up to reinforce the weakening partition between the two units. Refrigeration was provided in the form of a screened orange crate which was nailed on the outside of the cottage near the door. This "cooler" was quite adequate for milk, fruits, and butter.

When the roof leaked, Russell offered the Forbishes dishpans to catch the drips. They bought parts in Tillamook to fix the toilet themselves.[55]

Blanche (Parrish) Sweger's son Theodore at the kitchen table during a stay at Cottage Park in 1945. Joyce (Sweger) Loftis's collection.

In June 1946, Jay Rinehart of Hillsboro bought a lot just uphill of the Meyers on High Terrace from the county for $50 and quickly put up a house. That fall, Dr. Jack Goldman of Portland and his wife Mamie bought the cabin

Fannie Potter had lived in near the top of High Terrace. The following spring, they purchased the twelve-and-two-thirds forested lots across the street that Arleta and John Dobbins had let the county take back for $600. In November 1947, the Goldmans purchased a tract along the bay just north of the town center from Hosea Botts for $200.[56] They had outdone the Currins in securing a private beach and park for what a single lot had cost—after adjusting for inflation—in 1910.

Bayocean Becomes a Working-Class Community

Though the blimps had left and NAST had been reduced to maintenance status by the fall of 1946, Tillamook continued to suffer a housing shortage to the degree that families were living in tents scattered around Cape Meares and Bayocean. Six preschool, nineteen grade school, and eight high school students filled Bayocean School. Thirty to forty cars commuted daily on Bayocean Road, increasing to a hundred or more on the weekends when storms wreaked havoc. One of them caused a fire that burned down Bob and Barbara Watkins's home. They and their oldest son Mike were injured, but Bob got his two youngest children out safely.[57]

New families moved into Bayocean as well, furthering its transformation from a seasonal resort town to a year-round community. After his wartime service ended, George Bagley Jr. bought a crab boat and moved into his father's cottage with his wife Elizabeth and two young daughters. In March 1946, Jack and Bertha Gillham purchased the place where Johan and Dora Poulsen had spent their summers. They lived there for the next three years while Jack worked as an electrical engineer for the Tillamook Utility District. In November 1946, Lewis and Hilda Bennett purchased the Rainbow Girls House, which that nonprofit and the Campfire Girls had used as a clubhouse since 1931. With the community's help, in January 1948, Ray and Lillian Thomas built a house just off Bay Street on Stark Street, near the new oyster beds they had been hired to work.[58]

Bayocean's wartime revitalization prompted Francis Mitchell to repair The Mitchell, restock store shelves, and rent out the rooms upstairs. Schoolchildren waiting at the bus stop across the street gave him a new audience for his rants. They had been taught to respect the elderly and could not leave for fear of missing the bus. Little Harold Bennett admired Mr. Mitchell's intelligence and audacity in berating important men like Hosea Botts and Arthur Beals. Perry Reeder had no idea what Mr. Mitchell was talking about, but he enjoyed being spoken to as though he would. The women who were girls then were less impressed. They recall Mr. Mitchell as being odd.[59]

The one thing everyone who spent their childhood on Bayocean agrees on is that it was a wonderful time in their lives. They did not know Bayocean Park had been built for the upper class or that it was intended to be much grander than it was. And when they found out later, it did not matter. The boys did not care that they had to wait outside while the Hickses' butler fetched Paul. He was just one of the gang that played among the Annex ruins—despite parental prohibitions—imagining it having been an ancient fortress. Streets graded but not paved thirty years earlier made excellent trails into the woods. Sliding down fresh sand uncovered by a slide on cardboard was as good as a trip to Mt. Hood. At high tide, sand in the bay provided a warm dip on chilly days, just as the resort brochures promised. Girls engaged in their own risky adventures, like climbing riding logs in the surf. They also had to deal with the boys throwing snakes in their midst and other pranks. The children loved living on the spit. They would have enjoyed spending the rest of their childhood there and to have been able to live there today or visit friends who did.[60]

CHAPTER 8

End Times
(1947–1952)

On April 2, 1947, the Corps of Engineers announced their decision to continue taking no action regarding Bayocean erosion. They could not explain the forces at work, being "too complex for immediate scientific analysis." But they were sure the rate of erosion was moderate and natural, having nothing to do with the north jetty. Stations set up in 1939 recorded the average annual rate of erosion varying from four feet at the north end of the spit to eight feet near Cape Meares. The angst of locals who had measured twice that forced Colonel Walsh to take a third look.[1]

New Buildings Rise as Others Slide Into the Sea

In March 1947, Del and Grace Gilkison purchased thirteen lots for $900 on contract with the county at the east end of Natatorium Gap. They must have been aware of past washovers because Del used concrete blocks to build a duplex on the west side of Bay Street in September. When finished, the Gilkisons moved into the unit closest to town and placed a sign in front advertising their facility as Kaaren Ann Kottages. The plural noun suggests they planned to add more units if things went well, but they did not. Fortunately, Del earned a living as an electrician, working out of a shop behind the duplex.[2]

Francis Mitchell did not like the Gilkisons upstaging his establishments, but he could do little about it. He and Ida went on another extended road trip to Kansas City, Philadelphia, Washington, DC, Atlantic City, and Los Angeles. On the way back, they stopped at the *Oregonian* in Portland and let the society page editor know December 29th was their fiftieth wedding anniversary. A story, including a photo honoring their achievement, ran on November 23rd.[3]

While Del Gilkison laid blocks, P. D. Hance was putting up a cabin for himself just to the south. The man who had put up so many houses thirty-five years earlier proclaimed, "Bayocean will be one of the most desirable places on the coast in the very near future." Mary and A. W. (Allen) Strowger, a federal tax accountant in Portland, must have agreed. They had purchased the house first owned by the Clacks, just north of Hance's new place in 1924, and added three adjacent lots since then. In 1947, they bought four more. In 1948, they purchased the remaining lots in Block 46 from the county for $50 each and built a rental house two lots north of their cabin.[4] The Strowgers stand alone in owning every lot within a single Bayocean Park block.

On September 4, 1947, a special edition of Bayocean News authored by Russell Hoover reported, "Bayocean is definitely on the move toward a new life." Hoover was encouraged by a busy Labor Day weekend and confident that recent repairs to Bay Street would draw even more vacationers. He used the new house Jay Rinehart was building just south of Judge Richardson's and the Gilkison and Strowger lot purchases to project that every Bayocean Park lot owned by the county would soon be gone. And the slow rate of erosion calculated by the Corps meant the "enormous pile of sand" would last a long time.[5]

Hoover's neighbors were not so sanguine. As soon as Rinehart finished his new cabin, he sold it to Joseph and Inez Wenzel and Joseph's sister Augusta and her husband Kurt Braune. Having sold his first place as soon as he had finished it to someone who immediately sold it to Carl and Naomi Haldum, Jay was done with Bayocean. More significant was Arthur Beals's decision to abandon his dairy farm. Seawater covered his meadow every time South Gap breached, killing the grass his cows grazed. And the tide gate and dike could not withstand the pressure much longer. Pop and Betty Watkins bought Beals's tract intending to build a subdivision called Hauxhurst, but that fell through due to problems with the county related to all the streets having been vacated. Not long before he died on March 27, 1952, Beals gave the few hundred Bayocean Park lots outside the Watkins tract to the Tillamook YMCA.[6]

Waves washing through gaps the weekend after Thanksgiving called Hoover's predictions into question, but damages were minimal. In

February 1948, washovers pushed the rest of the Sanderses' garage into the bay, removed gravel just laid on Bayocean Road, and left the spit's main water pipe hanging in midair across Jackson Gap again. That led the county commissioners to consider rerouting the road along the east side of Bayocean School, turning south at 4th Street instead of Mears to avoid Jackson Gap, but they had no money to do the work.[7]

As Jackson and South Gaps deepened and expanded on each side of Bayocean School, sanitation became a problem because seawater saturated the drain field around the school's septic tank. Increasing class density exacerbated the problem. As a result, the school board decided to close the school and bus children into Tillamook at the beginning of the 1948 term. Parents protested, saying the sanitary problem was infrequent. Speeding sightseers worried them more. The "Just-a-Mere club of young mothers" convinced the county to provide posts and plywood, painted them with speed limits, and held a "post-hold digging party…with the grandmother's group furnishing the coffee and other strengthening vitamins." But Bayocean School was quiet that fall.[8]

On March 24, 1948, nineteen of thirty-four voters in a district covering just seventeen square miles created the second Port of Bayocean. Its proponents wanted nothing more than to raise enough money to dredge a channel for larger boats to reach the floating dock built by TBC. George Bagley was appointed captain of the port and Del Gilkison its secretary. Byron Randall, Lewis Bennett, and Russell Hoover were the other commissioners.[9]

Meanwhile, Colonel Walsh finally got his Bayocean study approved by the Chief of Engineers on May 11, 1948. It was not much different than previous iterations. Though some of the numbers had changed, his conclusions were the same as Major Cecil Moore's in 1940: Bayocean was not worth saving, its erosion was natural and proceeding so slowly that Tillamook Bay commerce was not at risk, and a south jetty would make no difference. At least the Port of Bay City got the small boat basin at Garibaldi deepened to twelve feet and expanded to handle a hundred boats out of the deal.[10]

Tillamook Spit Temporarily Becomes an Island

Cape Meares News columns rarely mentioned Bayocean in 1948, so the reason P. D. Hance sold his place to Alex Pavlov in August—so soon after building it—is not known.[11] Fortunately, a diary kept by Jack Medcalf helps fill the news blackout between September 6, 1948, and January 20, 1949.

Medcalf was a thirty-eight-year-old artist who grew up in Tillamook and taught in Silverton, Oregon's public schools. After his father and mother died in 1946 and 1947, Jack bought two lots between 9th and 10th Avenues along Bay Street from the county for $175 total and built what he called a shack using lumber salvaged from the beach. While enjoying it during the summer of 1948, Medcalf decided to take a sabbatical.[12]

The Bayocean community welcomed Medcalf. Lutie Cake cared for his cat when Jack went into Tillamook to sell his work, visit the Tillamook County Pioneer Museum, or see friends. The Bagleys, Hoovers, and others regularly invited him to meals and card games. The neighborhood boys came by at Halloween. Sue (Bagley) Barr recalled Medcalf having "the wildest outhouse ever, with bright painted designs on every wall. It was never boring in his outdoor toilet, but I was glad we had indoor plumbing."[13]

The bus hauling Bayocean children to Tillamook woke Jack each morning as it rattled by during the fall of 1948. On pleasant days, after feeding the chickens and ducks he kept penned outside, Jack would dig clams or explore the midden near the shuttered Bayocean School. He noted the ruins of two Tillamook lodges nearby. On rainy days, Medcalf read books, carved wooden spoons and masks, sculpted rocks, painted watercolors, and created prints and collages to sell in town. Sometimes Warren Hinsdale offered him a ride to Tillamook, but he often walked.[14]

Francis Mitchell always stopped by on his way to fix potholes and check on a bulkhead he had installed in Jackson Gap, which Medcalf called "Mitchell's masterpiece." When Francis cajoled Jack into joining him, the athletic young man was impressed with the old man's pace—and glad of it because "it decreased the conversation, mostly one-sided. He talked mostly about defrauded landowners, cursed the county for not doing something to keep the erosion back, and informed me that he was not insane."[15]

On September 21, 1948, an early storm interrupted Medcalf's idyllic sojourn, bringing waves crashing through all four gaps. He wrote, prophetically, "I'm afraid this is going to be a most severe winter for Bayocean [because] this is only a seven some foot tide. What will the eight and nine bring." Jack considered the lack of a hyphen in Bayocean as a bad omen. He imagined the spit becoming a reef, visible only at low tide, that local tour guides would point to and say, "For years we told them people who used to live there that they was crazy, the sea 'ud take the place." His imagined reply would be, "We lived here Mr. and loved every minute, and even if we go out tomorrow when the tide is high, we've had today at Bayocean."[16]

Medcalf's premonition materialized on November 2nd when waves overturned a boat on the bay, drowning three duck hunters and carrying their bodies out to sea. The next day tides rose to nine feet. Waves continually washed through each gap. Jack was so anxious that he could not read the mail that Gladys Hoover handed him that morning. George and Elizabeth Bagley drove by that afternoon to view South Gap. Locals had renamed it Dolan Gap because they were sure Arthur Dolan's

People standing in and around one of the Bayocean gaps after a storm. Bayocean Image 205, TCPM.

excavation of sand from its bay side was providing "the sea a nice pathway into the bay."[17]

Medcalf hopped out of the Bagleys' car to check out Rock Crusher Gap along the way. His curiosity cost him a drenching when he was surprised by a washover. Fortunately, none of the logs it carried hit him. After returning to his cabin to change his clothes and warm up, Jack set out again, timing the crossing of each gap more carefully. At Jackson Gap, he found Mitchell's bulkhead gone and broken ends of water pipes hanging from each side of it. Medcalf was terrified and excited at the same time. He wrote, "the whole ridge from the Dolan gap on to this new one [Rock Crusher], which is at least nine city blocks from the shack, is a battered mess of driftwood, washed out banks, and the road gone. Definitely an island in the Pacific tonight." Flashlights and the yells of searchers looking for the bodies of the drowned men kept him awake that night.[18]

On November 4th, Jack watched breakers widen Rock Crusher Gap to a couple of hundred feet in width and scour it below sea level. He noted the irony of having a lifelong dream of being stranded on a Pacific Island. George Bagley brought food from the mainland on the boat named after his daughters, the *Sally-Sue*. He brought water until Medcalf and Allen Strowger got a coupler from the Tillamook Fire Department and strung a rubber water hose from the Red Cross across Jackson Gap on the fifth.[19]

The storm receded sufficiently for sightseers to view the damages on Sunday, November 7th. Jack stayed close to his cabin and made it obvious that he was home so that they would not peer into his windows or take his weathervane as a souvenir, which he overheard a group considering. His mood improved when Jim Strowger (son of Allen and Mary) arrived, though Jack had heard his greeting of "Where's Bayocean?" too often to think it funny. By November 8th, people could drive into the town center at low tide by timing breakers at each gap.[20]

The sandspit's transformation into an island was spectacular enough to put it back on the front pages of metropolitan newspapers. Russell Hoover debunked early reports of a mass exodus and the exaggerated number of residents said to be stranded. The *Oregonian* called him, instead of calling Francis Mitchell, because Bayocean Cottages had a Tillamook phone book listing, and Hoover's role as "water system superintendent" had an official ring. Hoover said there were fifty year-round residents, and the only people who had departed were Adelaide and William Haney and their sons Walter and Everett. They were the last owners of Swan and Othelia Hawkinson's second house, which had burned down during the storm.[21]

Despite Russell's proclamations of Bayocean residents being determined to stick it out, a slow, steady exodus began. The Lockes and Meyers were the first to go. On November 17, 1948, Jack Medcalf wrote of being depressed enough at seeing "no smoke from the chimneys, no lights yelling from the windows" of their homes that he considered doing the same. George Bagley enticed him to stay with an offer to install electricity in his cabin. He would not honor that promise until December 21st because storms kept turning the spit into an island, and he was busy ferrying food, water, and other supplies.[22]

Meanwhile, disaster tourists prompted Betty Watkins to write:

> Apparently, everyone knows about Bay Ocean now, and very few people within one hundred miles who had not seen the havoc the ocean caused during the last storm. On Sunday, Nov. 7, there were hundreds of cars on the road to and from Bay Ocean. The traffic jam at Cape Meares Grocery corner was serious enough to have a traffic officer called out the control the situation. One resident through curiosity, counted cars for a period of twenty minutes and reported seventy-two passed in that time. Cars were still coming at dusk.[23]

The disharmony between the people remaining and Francis Mitchell distressed Jack Medcalf even more than seeing his neighbors leaving or dealing with disaster tourists. Jack thought Francis's behavior was erratic and his ideas "very distorted and narrow…his reasoning is faulty," but he attributed it to aging. So, he listened politely for a few minutes at each encounter and then excused himself to avoid agitating Mitchell with an opposing view.[24]

When Medcalf picked up his mail on December 9, 1948, Gladys Hoover let him know that when Grace Gilkison walked past The Mitchell that morning, Ida ran out screaming, "Help, Help," followed by Francis, who "pulled her inside and slammed the door so hard the windows in the place rattled." That afternoon, Mitchell asked Jack to help him move a log off the road and chatted as though nothing had happened, but he and Ida did not attend a New Year's Eve party hosted by the Hoovers.[25]

Media Coverage Leads to Theft and Vandalism

On January 2, 1949, two articles about Bayocean filled the same page of the *Oregonian.* Staff reporter Mel Baldwin's "Breaks in Peninsula Threaten Whole Bay" presented a history of Bayocean and recent details, like the five hundred acres of oyster beds buried by sand from the washovers. He gave Colonel Walsh's reasons for rejecting a south jetty while noting the Corps of Engineers' original recommendation to build matching jetties.[26]

Freelance journalist Elizabeth Ryan's "A Queen Dies: Victim of Time and Tide" had a more personal tone because she had been visiting Bayocean since childhood. She introduced Francis Mitchell as "one old-timer…who purchased the first Bayocean lot" and passed on his conviction that the Corps was correct in believing that spit erosion was natural and not enough to threaten its existence. As evidence of Bayocean's bright future, Mitchell said that county commissioners planned to give Kincheloe Point to the state for a park. In stark contrast, Mitchell's neighbors expressed great concern, saying, "over 20 homes already have paid the penalty" for the Corps having built just one jetty.[27]

Mitchell's neighbors were infuriated when they read his championing of the Corps' position because it undermined their efforts. After George Bagley and Del Gilkison gave Francis an earful, he "came by and blew up" at Jack Medcalf who, though he agreed with his neighbors, listened without comment. Nor did Jack say anything when he saw Ida "down at the gap working on the road, shoveling sand, sawing logs, and moving others out of the way" with Francis, though it troubled him. Perhaps he would have said something eventually, but Medcalf ran out of money and returned to Silverton soon after that.[28]

Ryan and Baldwin both referred to Bayocean as a ghost town and raised the possibility of its disappearance. This and earlier reports of homeowners abandoning the spit drew souvenir hunters, thieves, and vandals. The problem got so bad that Sheriff Allan Birch assigned a deputy to patrol the spit and issued a public statement reminding county residents that Bayocean was a community with cabins, boats, and other property used only during the summer, like any other coastal resort.[29]

After surveying damages, the Corps of Engineers held a meeting in Tillamook on January 18, 1949. They heard the same concerns as in the past and repeated previous findings in rejecting a south jetty again. The Corps considered but dismissed the rerouting of Bayocean Road east of Bayocean School because it would cost $584,000, and they could not be sure that, even with riprapping, it could survive the next storm. The "4-inch main…a wooden stove pipe" described in their analysis means the Bayocean Cooperative Water System crews had switched materials when they laid new lines a decade earlier.[30]

On May 8th, the *Oregon Journal*—not to be outdone by their Portland rival—ran a two-page feature story about Bayocean with a photo captioned "Oregon's Stillborn Paradise" on the cover of its Sunday Magazine section. Reporter Charles Oluf Olsen chose "Coney Island for Clams" as his headline to mock grand plans for the resort and suggest a fun palace ghost haunting the rotten pilings depicted in a half-page photo with Francis Mitchell pointing forlornly to where ships used to dock. Other images showed the bottom of Jackson Gap above water, a cornerstone of the Natatorium sitting on the beach, and the north wall of the Annex sliding to the sea. Olsen's only interview was with Mitchell, whom he introduced as "Bayocean's most ardent booster" who "stayed with the weathered resort 41 years, during which he witnessed its stubborn losing battle with nature's elements."[31]

The Gilkisons, signing as Kaaren Anne Kottages and claiming to represent "we of Bayocean and a number of other people," wrote a letter to the editor complaining that Olsen's "Swan Song" was a "funeral dirge" when those who cherished Bayocean most needed "a Boost." They cited tourism statistics to argue that the resort was still viable and said that The Mitchell had cleared $6,500 annually in its prime.[32] The editor might have published the letter if the Gilkisons had stopped there, but they went on to say things that no editor would publish. The tone and details suggest that they had given the annotated Watch Bayocean Grow circular to the Bagleys.

Del and Grace blamed Olsen's inaccurate portrayal of Bayocean on his use of Francis Mitchell as the only source:

> None of the permanent residents here have anything to do with him as he is such a troublemaker and so erratic in his thinking. What is true today is absolutely false tomorrow. According to the story, which accounts for his behavior, some forty years ago he had a complete nervous breakdown and has never recovered from it…He has been brought before a sanity board but [he] is very cagey when on the stand.[33]

When the peninsula became an island in November 1948, the Gilkisons reported seeing "old Mitch throwing his hat in the air and dancing around shouting to the heavens that God was punishing the wicked people that live down here." When Adelaide Haney's house burned down, "he told her she was being punished for living on the hill where wicked people lived that played cards, drank, and swore." They said that Francis explained his behavior by, "saying God talks to him, tells him when to beat his wife, and brother does he beat her [and that] he has her permission to do this."[34]

According to Del and Grace, instead of Mitchell being a heroic advocate for Bayocean, he was the reason for its financial decline. They said he loved showing people a 1918 letter from the TBPRC receivership offering to give him whatever he wanted to leave and then proclaim that no price could stop him from "fighting the cause for the people." The Gilkisons accused Francis of making it impossible for anyone affiliated with Bayocean Park to succeed. He continued waylaying visitors and lie about bungalow vacancies despite Judge Bagley's injunction. He told WPA workers to stop repairing streets because he and Ida were doing it. Worst of all, they said, Mitchell had conspired with Colonel Walsh to thwart Senator Morse's effort to secure $120,000 to fix the gaps.[35]

Houses Moved off the Spit

In early March 1949, while Bayocean townsfolk were squabbling, the north end of Clarke Street slid to the shore, leaving the remaining homes inaccessible by car. Three were sold at salvage prices and hauled to Cape Meares by Woodrow (Woody) Chase, Milton Schlegel, and Milton's son

Jerry. Chase, a Willamina logger, provided the equipment, while Milton, who had moved to Cape Meares in 1943 to work on NAST, coordinated things locally. Jerry had worked for Woody since graduating from Tillamook High School a year earlier.[36]

The two Pagodas were the first to go. Gertrude Gates, Lutie Cake, and Lena Brownell received just $400 for the pair. Milton acquired permission from downhill neighbors so Woody could bulldoze a new route straight down the dune to Bay Street. Similar authorizations at the south end of the spit allowed Woody to push trees out of the way so that the Pagodas could be taken to a lot in Cape Meares where they would become the home of Bob Watkins's family. To get Woody's flatbed truck under them, the Schlegels first raised each Pagoda with jacks and supported them with eight-foot-high stacks of driftwood.[37]

The Chase and Schlegel team hauling the smaller Pagoda down Bay Street. Photo WA 33, taken by Buck Sherwood, Mike Watkins's collection.

The larger of the two Pagodas was twenty-eight feet wide by thirty feet long. The typical flatbed truck being eight feet wide and twenty-four feet long meant ten feet stuck out on each side and six feet off the end. The smaller Pagoda was twenty-two feet square, so less of it hung over the sides. Once each building was on the flatbed, Woody's bulldozer nudged, pushed, and pulled the truck—like a tugboat guiding an ocean liner—down the hill and across the gaps over to Cape Meares. Most of the community came out to observe the Schlegel-Chase team move the smaller Pagoda on April 6th and 7th, the larger one on the 9th and 10th. Bob

Watkins contributed by standing on the roof and holding utility lines out of the way with an insulated pole. While there, he sawed off the upward-curling cupolas because he considered them frilly nonsense. Later, he sawed off the curled rafter ends.[38]

The Schlegel-Chase team next moved the cabin Swan Hawkinson had built for Corinth Crook, which they purchased for $200 from its last owners, George and Merle Selfridge. After placing it in Cape Meares, Jerry received it as payment for his summer's work. On April 13th, he was jacking up the twenty-six-foot square cottage when he felt the earth shake and watched with amazement as a wave formed in Tillamook Bay and breached gaps in the spit on its way out to sea. The *Headlight-Herald* said nothing of the little tsunami in their coverage of local damage.[39]

After moving the three buildings, Woody excavated a basement for the Pagodas and then returned to his logging operation in Willamina. The Schlegels worked most of the summer pouring a concrete floor and walls and connecting the two buildings, this time with no hall separating them, resulting in a consolidated, 1,408-square-foot Pagoda. Milton and Jerry built a fireplace with bricks retrieved from fireplaces still sitting where the Pagodas had been and from other houses that had fallen to the beach. They reinstalled the dumbwaiter last. On Bayocean, the Bennett boys had used it to haul wood upstairs from the basement. But Bob Watkins afforded his sons no such luxury; they would carry wood using the stairs. He and Barbara hosted an open house for their neighbors the second week of August 1949.[40]

Bayocean Cottages Sold

Watching vandalism increase, neighbors and houses leave, and the "enormous pile of sand" shrink faster than he had expected took the wind out of Russell Hoover's sails. In July 1949, after he secured a job with the new Tillamook County General Hospital and Gladys as assistant county clerk, they "sold their interest" in Bayocean Cottages to Hugh Glenn and rented Gillham's house. Gladys continued as postmaster until they moved to Tillamook in January 1950.[41]

Hugh Glenn was a fifty-two-year-old bachelor who previously laid carpet in Vallejo, California, where he and his widowed mother Helen had lived in an apartment house she owned. Though elderly and slow to reach the counter when children wanted to buy candy, Helen managed Bayocean Cottages while Hugh delivered mail to all the communities west of Tillamook. Only half of the forty-two bungalows were habitable by then. The Glenns rented the others out to fishermen, clammers, and crabbers for daytime use.[42]

Bayocean Road was the worst part of Hugh Glenn's mail route. Logging trucks and tourists drove faster than the condition of the road allowed, especially at corners. People packed a meeting held by the Port of Bayocean on November 7, 1949, to discuss the problem. "It was the unanimous opinion of those attending that 'the road is undoubtably the worst piece of public roadway in the county, if not the state, judging from the many cars that go into the ditch.'"[43]

Navigating Bayocean Road on the spit was challenging for a different reason. In late November 1949, Mary Strowger "was bowled over by a debris-laden breaker" while walking through a gap. Fortunately, she was not injured. High tides and storms continued through the end of that month but inflicted no damage other than the occasional loss of telephone service. But timing waves to drive through the gaps was a tricky business. At two o'clock one morning, Hugh Glenn's car got stuck in one of them. While waiting for someone to pull him out, a wave engulfed the vehicle. Terrified, he jumped out after it passed and sought help from the Thomases. Hugh carried Bayocean's mail sack partway by foot occasionally after that.[44]

1950 began with the Dolan place being destroyed by fire on January 11th. Arthur Beals's son Roland and his family had not been able to find a place in Tillamook after moving from Portland, so Hazel had let them use the house as a favor to her recently deceased husband's close friend. Roland's clothing caught fire while lighting the kitchen stove one morning. He ran through the house in a panic while removing his burning attire. When it hit an oil stove in the living room, the explosion severely injured Roland and a neighbor who had come over with a water hose to help. The

Dolan house was gone before fire trucks arrived, but the firemen saved the other two Poulsen houses and took the two men to the Tillamook County General Hospital.[45]

At the end of January—the Hoovers having moved into Tillamook—Evelyn Reeder became Bayocean's postmaster. Her family had returned to the spit in 1949 and rented George Baker's garage from Paul and Nadene Zimmerman. George had died in a fire that consumed his cabin in October 1944. His siblings had then sold the lot and garage. During the summer of 1950, Perry Jr. watched George Bauman put up a tiny place at the end of the trail that was supposed to have been the extension of Bay Street that went past their garage. Bauman's house would be the last built on the spit. An addition to Baker's garage would be the final residential construction.[46]

Storm surges broke through a new, unidentified gap the last week of September, trapping a driver but doing him and his automobile no harm, and "once again huge logs were carried through Crusher Gap" in October. After viewing the damage, Senator Morse arranged for the Corps of Engineers to meet with the Tillamook Chamber of Commerce in March 1951, after which engineers surveyed Jackson Gap again. Their measurements served no purpose other than to explain why every storm surge washed over the spit. As they reminded the senator, Congress had given them no authority or funding to do anything about it. The Corps did assure Morse "appropriate remedial measures" would be taken when "a major breakthrough of the ocean was imminent."[47]

Cape Meares Community Moves Bayocean School

On March 25, 1951, several Cape Meares residents rolled Bayocean School a half-mile north to 5690 4th Street, where it would become the Cape Meares Community Association's clubhouse. Ahead of the move, they had collected logs, removed plumbing and electrical connections, disconnected it from the basement, and set the building on a set of skids. The two lots had been cleared by community members using a bulldozer in July 1950, after Tillamook County offered them free use of the building and lots.[48]

Woody Chase provided the equipment for the schoolhouse move. He and the Schlegels had just used a similar process to move Arthur Beals's rental house to higher ground on the east edge of the Coleman Creek meadow. It was the most profitable of their moves, fetching $2,000; but after seeing its front door facing south towards Bayocean Road, Arthur insisted that he had told Woody to have it face west towards the ocean. They compromised by turning the house forty-five degrees. The position was maintained in 1976 when a similar building replaced it.[49]

In October 1951, the road into Bayocean was deemed too hazardous to continue regular postal service, so the Bayocean Post Office moved into a new building at the southwest corner of 4th Street and Bayocean Road, across from the Cape Meares Grocery. As might be expected, Francis Mitchell was irate. On the first of November, he tried to convince the Postal Service to reverse the decision by arguing, "of late months, the erosion has been checked."[50]

A month later, storms proved Francis wrong by washing through every gap. Ruins of the tennis court slid down to reunite with those of the Annex on the beach. Waves coursing through Natatorium Gap flooded Kaaren Ann Kottages with two feet of water. Del and Grace Gilkison had no choice but to leave. Despite waves breaching Jackson Gap at every high tide by this point, they were determined to return and rented a house in Cape Meares while they cleaned things during low tides. Few shared the optimism of the Mitchells and Gilkisons. By the end of 1951, Tillamook County had foreclosed on all but 479 Bayocean Park lots.[51]

On January 9, 1952, as many as twenty cars got stuck crossing Jackson Gap. Each made it across with a pull from the vehicle ahead of them. On the 15th, logs in Dolan Gap wiped out a nearby power pole and blocked Bayocean Road just west of the new post office. The temporary rubber water lines—which had become permanent—that Jack Medcalf and Allen Strowger had strung across Jackson Gap three years earlier were reported floating in the bay.[52] Two weeks later, Lewis and Hilda Bennett decided they had had enough. They rented a house from Milton Schlegel in Cape Meares until November, when they bought four adjacent lots and a roughed-in cabin in Oceanview and began improving it. Their Rainbow Girls House was safe for the time being, so its deconstruction could wait.[53]

In February 1952, after the *Headlight-Herald* said, "the area looks like an atom bomb had struck or a hurricane, so terrible is the desolation," Tillamook County Judge Otto Effenberger established a new Bay Ocean Committee. As had been true of previous iterations, each interest group was represented, but Effinger and his fellow county commissioners took the lead. They hired a Portland engineer to convince the Corps of Engineers a breakthrough was imminent. They were not successful.[54]

The Bagleys could also see that it was time to leave, so they hired Lebeck and Sons of Portland to move their house to a Bayocean Park lot in Cape Meares. But when the Lebecks arrived on the first of February 1952, Charles Ross and his wife Mary (owners of the Sunset Garage in Tillamook) offered them $7,000 for the House of Hicks on the condition they move it to the mainland. The Hicks had recently sold all their Bayocean property—including the house last owned by the Gillhams—to the Lebecks and moved to Alaska. To take advantage of the Rosses' offer, the Lebecks had to act quickly because the dune edge was just forty feet away from the House of Hicks, and it was approaching fast. So, they assured the Bagleys they would return later and headed up to the ridge. By mid-month, with the help of Leonard Bales Construction and Morgan Burckard Plumbing, both of Tillamook, the Lebecks had moved the House of Hicks to Beals's meadow; but when they went back for the Gillham place, its foundation had already collapsed, so they let the ocean have it and the two garages.[55]

The Lebecks had transported the House of Hicks off the ridge in one piece, but it was too large to haul down Bayocean Road. So, they cut it in half and barged each section along the south shore of the bay and up the mouth of the Tillamook River to a point near the intersection of Fraser Road and Netarts Road. The risk of taking out high lines while being hauled down the latter led to a faceoff between state police and five-foot-tall Mary Ross, which Mary won. After reaching the property, the Lebecks built a basement and brought the two halves together on top of it. When they finished at the end of March, water flowing through the gaps prevented them from reaching the Bagleys, so they returned to Portland.[56]

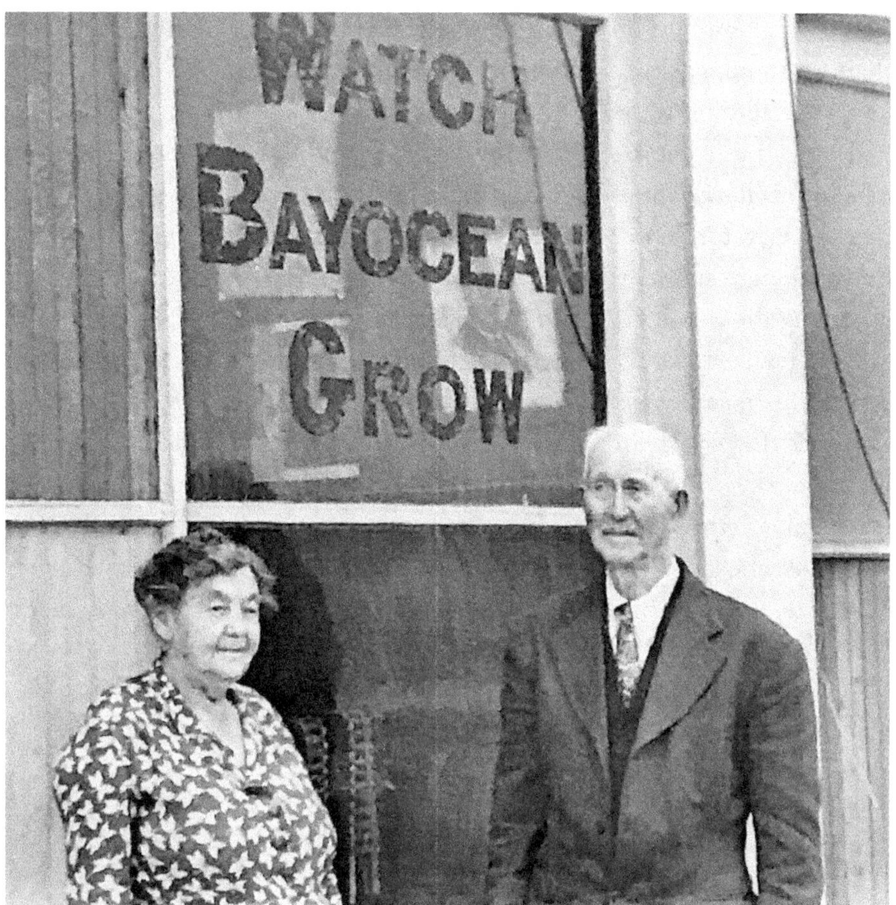

Ida and Francis Mitchell in front of the Watch Bayocean Grow sign in the window of The Mitchell. Photo taken by Greta Forbish in October 1952, Webber Research Archives, courtesy of Greta's daughter, Blithe Jensen.

The Forbishes Pay a Final Visit

When Greta Forbish and her family made their last trip to Bayocean in October 1952, the only letters on the sign in front of the bungalows read OT AG AK. Harvey Sandy greeted them because Hugh Glenn had died in an accident in July. While passing a logging truck headed east on Bayocean Road, the two vehicles got tangled up and both ended up in the ditch. Logs falling off the truck crushed the mailman. Helen left soon after her son's death and hired Sandy to manage the Bayocean Cottages. Lyman

Latourette kept him on after Helen returned the bungalows to him rather than continue making contract payments.[57]

After settling into their bungalow, Greta visited the Mitchells. They had moved into the kitchen of the Bayside Inn because the rest of it, like The Mitchell, was uninhabitable. Francis and Ida proudly show Greta their new refrigerator. The Ninety and Nine Men's Brotherhood, a boy's club in Bend that stayed there many summers, had given it to them after accepting the Mitchells' gift of a life estate in the Bayside Inn.[58]

Francis seemed worn out to Greta, and his enthusiasm was forced. "In repose, his face was sad. He looked like a bewildered child who had been punished for some infraction he did not understand." His energy level picked up as "he shyly, but not without pride, showed us sheaves of threatening letters and scurrilous anonymous notes, some couched in the most obscene language; 'I'm getting under their skin,' he chortled." Francis also read Greta a poem that she considered a sign of spirit then but "prophetic doggerel" a few weeks later:

In nineteen-fifty-one
  We've got them on the run
In nineteen-fifty-two
  They'll be through
In nineteen-fifty-three
  We'll be free![59]

Also during the fall of 1952, the Lockes moved permanently to Cape Meares, and the Meyers to Netarts. Jack Medcalf must have been pleased to see both families having returned to Bayocean when he visited his cabin in June 1950. In Cape Meares, the Lockes rented a house while Shorty put one up on 1st Avenue using material removed from their place on the spit. They moved into it in August 1953.[60] Locals recall Betty Locke taking over Cape Meares News authorship sometime after this.

Storm Surges Wipe Out the South End of Bayocean

On Friday, October 31, 1952, storm surges breached all the gaps and closed Bayocean Road for a few hours. That was an occurrence so common by then it was not newsworthy. But on November 3rd, "the ocean cut a channel through just north of Rock Crusher Gap. Now the ocean is on its way toward Tillamook." A similar channel through Dolan Gap left the Scott family stranded in the Brigham house.[61]

Orin Brigham had transferred the cabin to his daughter, Janice Apperson, in 1940. She used it as a rental until selling it to Pop and Betty Watkins in 1944, who also used it as a rental. Their last tenants were Dan and Claire Scott. Shortly before being stranded, Pop had given the Scotts notice that he would soon be moving it to safer ground.[62]

The *Headlight-Herald* later published Claire Scott's dramatic story about their escape from the island, including a sketch of the Brigham house drawn by Barbara Watkins. Claire knew the same thing had happened in 1948 and that houses once stood beyond the trees on the west side of Mears Street. But "listening only to the optimists who spoke of the usually lengthy periods of time in which erosion does [no] perceptible damage," the Scotts settled into an idyllic life. Like Jack Medcalf and others, they were determined to enjoy it as long as possible. Dan and Claire began having doubts as trees toppled into the ocean, but it was nice to have a clear view of the ocean after Woody Chase removed those remaining.[63]

At dawn on November 4, 1952, the Scotts woke to waves coursing down their driveway. The only way out was across Beals's dike. After packing a few essentials, they hiked through the woods to find waves washing across the dirt top of the dike after passing through Dolan Gap. After a moment's hesitation, they headed across, with Dan carrying their younger daughter on his shoulders. Claire held their older daughter's hand in one of hers and personal belongings in the other. It was slow going because they stopped whenever water lapped across their feet. But they made it without incident other than Dan losing his tin hat in the wind while going back to retrieve his Navy seabag.[64]

The Tillamook County Road Department bulldozed a road into the Brigham house a week later so the Scotts could retrieve the rest of their belongings and Pop and Bob Watkins could move it to a lot Pop had purchased from Arthur Beals. The Scotts found a new place to live on the hill above Bay City, from which they could watch things get worse along with the Hawkinsons and others who had done the same.[65]

In early 1949, after the storm and extreme high tide abated, the spit had reconnected. In 1952, it did not. On November 13th, another storm surge blew out everything between Jackson and Rock Crusher Gap, carrying two million cubic yards of sand into the bay and creating a new inlet at the south end of the spit. A Coast Guard crew sped over from Garibaldi to evacuate ten adults and two children stranded on Bayocean Island, but they refused to leave.[66]

With each tide change, bay and ocean waters rushed in and out, steadily widening the new inlet and changing its configuration. On December 15th, the Richardson cabin, which Harvy and Laura Currin had purchased in 1949, mistakenly thinking it would last longer than their original cabins, was lost. Fortunately, they had also bought the Mueller place—dubbed the Dew Drop Inn by subsequent owners—and moved their belongings there the previous summer.[67]

On December 16th, Francis Mitchell was helping Birger Bugge (Asta having died) move appliances from his house when a slice of sand dropped out from under its front third. A group came over from Cape Meares on Saturday the 20th to help Birger salvage what he could before the house fell to the shore that afternoon. Meanwhile, on the bay side, the Bennetts and Bagleys were removing things from their cabins before looters could steal them.[68]

Birger Bugge's house (first built and called Cypress Crest by Swan Hawkinson) not long before it fell. BOB-28, TCPM.

On December 20th, *Oregonian* reporter William Lambert and photographer W. Kirk Braun arrived on the scene. By then, the Bagleys had moved to Cape Meares so their girls could attend school. George, who was shuttling food and water to the island holdouts on the *Sally-Sue*, offered to serve as the newsmen's taxi and tour guide.[69] Francis Mitchell would not control the narrative this time around.

While Braun took photos, Lambert interviewed eight "hardy souls [who] were determined to stick it out in the hope that someone, somewhere, would do something about their plight. A few said that they would be glad to leave the peninsula but had no place to go. Others, still not convinced that Bayocean was doomed, were staying by choice." Francis and Ida Mitchell were likely the only members of the second group. The other holdouts were Richard and Nellie Walton, Frank and Alice Andrews, and Birger Bugge. Harvey Sandy fit into neither group, given that Lyman Latourette paid him to look after the bungalows. He would be the last to leave, in January 1955. The *Oregonian* article published on November 23, 1952, featured Braun's photo of Lambert placing sheets of paper over the R and the W on the Watch Bayocean Grow sign in the window of The Mitchell, which changed it to Watch Bayocean Go. Surprisingly, Francis made no fuss and let the desecration remain for others to see and photograph after the newsmen left.[70]

Frank Andrews suffered a stroke the following week and died at the Tillamook County General Hospital. Alice got a ride back out to the island with George Bagley, packed up her things, and left. The six remaining islanders acclimated to rough living conditions as best they could. Warren Hinsdale helped Bagley deliver food and supplies from their friends in Cape Meares and charitable organizations like the Elks Club. They stopped hauling water after an old well was discovered. A battery-powered radio delivered news from the outside world. The Coast Guard set up stacks of wood to light in an emergency—and they would be used.[71]

CHAPTER 9

Recovery and Resolution

(1953–Today)

Judge Effenberger's Bay Ocean Committee had attained funding from the Senate for another study of the Bayocean problem on June 20, 1952. But the Corps had taken no action until the southern part of Bayocean blew out in November. When that happened, navigation and commerce were obviously compromised. And what Corps engineers repeatedly said would not occur just had, so they acted quickly.[1]

New Southern Bay Inlet Swallows Homes as It Expands

On December 15th, no less than Assistant Chief of Engineers General C. H. Chorpening flew from Washington, DC to Portland and traveled to Tillamook with District Engineer Colonel Thomas. After four hours with Judge Effenberger and other community leaders, they toured Bayocean Island, Cape Meares, and both inlets into the bay. During the first three weeks of January, six Corps engineers conducted interviews and took new measurements. They returned in March to sound the south inlet and survey the land on both sides of it for two months.[2]

Locals reported the distance between mainland and island increasing from three thousand feet initially to a mile by the end of the year. Erosion was now attacking Bayocean from the south and the west. The new, south inlet to Tillamook Bay was not a functional one. Two lobes of sand swung towards the bay from the shoreline on each side. During high tide, waves flowed past a small island in the center of the channel. Elsewhere, depths ranged from a few inches to eleven feet. During extreme low tides, it was a swath of mudflats pockmarked with puddles of seawater. Even at extreme high tide, the channel was tricky to navigate in small boats. The uneven bed of the south inlet did serve to dissipate the energy of storm surges enough to afford the bay some protection.[3]

Oyster beds withstood the worst damage from the initial blowout, which buried a thousand acres—one-third of the bay's total—with sand. After passing over the beds, the waves fanned out. At the north end of the bay, they broke up log rafts. East and south, they expanded cracks in poorly maintained earthen dikes and flooded pastures with seawater, killing the grass grazed by dairy herds. Because the north inlet was relatively narrow, tidewaters began moving through its new wider counterpart. Lack of flushing action caused the northern channel to start filling, shrink to less than 150 feet in width, and shift dangerously close to the north jetty. Ships the timber industry depended on could no longer enter Tillamook Bay.[4]

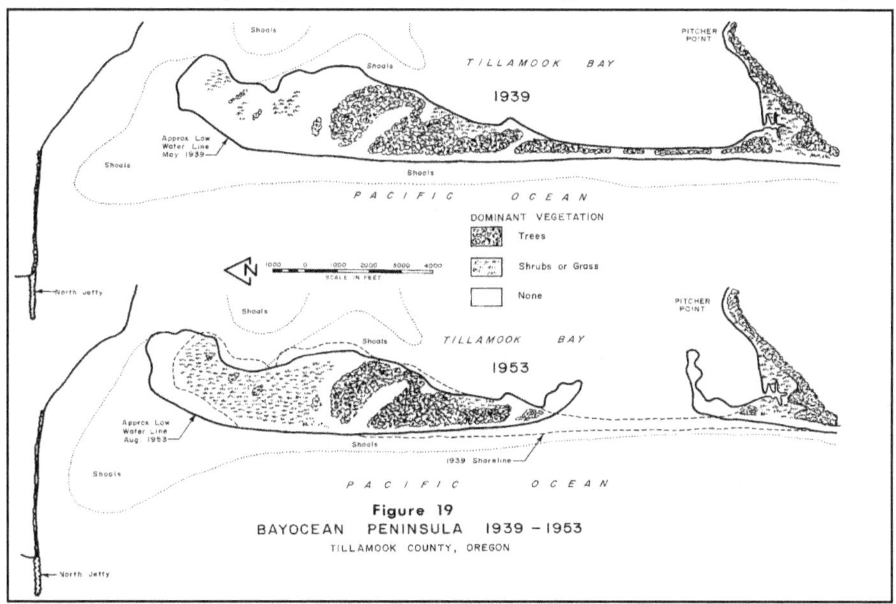

Lobes of the south inlet shown in 1953 relative to 1939. Figure 19, Appendix E, "Extension of Tillamook South Jetty, Tillamook Bay, Oregon: Final Environmental Impact Statement" (Portland District, Army Corps of Engineers, 1978).

Bayocean Refugees Start New Lives

On January 1, 1953, Gladys Hoover took over as Tillamook County Clerk, having won the position on November 4th, the same day the Scotts scrambled across Beals's dike. She would regularly be reminded of Bayocean's demise as she recorded deeds foreclosing on old neighbors in the years ahead. Gladys and Russell were among the few who continued paying taxes on their Bayocean lots until selling them in 1977.[5]

At the same time, Elizabeth Bagley went to work for the county commissioners. Instead of building a new place on their Cape Meares lot as planned, the Bagleys moved into Arthur Beals's rental house. From it, with binoculars, they could have seen the south inlet devour cabins as it expanded north, including their friend Jack Medcalf's shack on January 9th. The Wenzel-Braune cabin, being the most southerly of those along the bay, likely went before Jack's, but no one noted its demise. Evelyn Reeder set up a coffee shop in her post office the following weekend to earn extra income from disaster tourists.[6]

On January 19th, Viola Dickson and Ethel Tatarini lost their cabin, as the inlet widened to 5,600 feet. The Strowgers' two-story home and the Currins' set of tiny cabins were gone by the end of the month. The Strowger rental survived until March 19th. There to watch it fall were ten Boy Scouts from the Tillamook Christian Church, who had camped out in the Bayside Inn the night before.[7]

One of the Currin cabins on its way into the expanding south inlet. Dorion Studio negatives, Jon Chaix's collection.

Evelyn Reeder stamped the last Bayocean postmark on March 31, 1953. She opened the same doors the next day as postmaster of the Cape Meares Post Office. Betty Watkins honored the occasion by writing a history of the Barnegat and Bayocean post offices for the *Headlight-Herald*. Though unhappy with the cause, she said that Cape Meares residents were honored to have their own post office. But the Postal Service closed it down just ten months later, on January 31, 1954. The community made the best of it by claiming theirs was the "shortest lived post office in Oregon." Even that consolation prize was taken from them when

Tillamook County Pioneer Museum staff discovered other post offices with shorter durations.[8]

Port of Bayocean Morphs into Port of Tillamook Bay

After finishing their survey and considering alternatives, engineers with the Portland District recommended building a rock-filled breakwater across the south inlet. To close the Natatorium Gap, it would span 7,600 feet, from Pitcher (Biggs) Point to the hill behind Kaaren Ann Kottages. By their calculations, benefits exceeded costs with local participation factored in. However, the Port of Bayocean was the appropriate taxing authority, and its tax base was too small to contribute much of anything. The solution County Judge Effenberger, oysterman Jesse Hayes, and Colonel Lipscomb brainstormed during a meeting in Portland was to have the Port of Bayocean annex additional lands with a special election and then merge with the Port of Bay City. The date was set for May 15, 1953.[9]

On April 15th, the Corps held a public hearing at the Tillamook County Courthouse to hear from representatives of the oyster, timber, fishing, dairy, and transportation industries and answer questions about their proposed breakwater design. Since everything they owned would be lost if Bayocean remained an island for long, the Mitchells scampered across the south inlet at low tide and caught a ride into town. Francis had traced the breakwater route a week earlier to familiarize himself with it, but anything he might have said at the hearing was not reported.[10]

The *Headlight-Herald* published several articles and editorials promoting the Port of Bayocean expansion. They emphasized that the May 15th vote would not authorize taxes. Another election after the Corps determined a cost would deal with that. The strategy worked. By a vote of 752 to 521, the Port of Bayocean expanded to 227 square miles, a 1,335% increase. The tax base grew by an even higher percentage because the land annexed was more valuable and its population greater.[11]

After waiting to see if anyone sued, county commissioners changed its name to the Port of Tillamook Bay on November 4, 1953, to reflect its broader scope. Port commissioners George Bagley, Lewis Bennett, and Russell Hoover retained their positions, with two others joining them.

They served until January 3, 1955, when Gladys Hoover swore in an entirely new board elected in November 1954. Her old neighbor George Bagley graciously handed over the gavel.[12]

Bagley might not have been so courteous if he had known that in September 1955, Margaret Coates, the port's new secretary, would tell Senator Richard Neuberger's aid, Howard Morgan, "Without evident support, we have in mind that the south entrance to the Bay may be used and improved rather than blocked and stopped up." An "I" was penciled above the crossed-out "we," perhaps by Morgan. Having grown up in Tillamook, he would have known that a direct route to Tillamook through a south inlet would enhance its port at the expense of Bay City's, risking a new war between local ports. In any case, Neuberger did not take up Coats's suggestion.[13]

Francis Mitchell Forced to Leave When Ida Suffers a Stroke

On the afternoon of Sunday, October 18, 1953, Ida Mitchell suffered a stroke. Her neighbors lit the bonfires set up by the Coast Guard, but it was low tide, so no boat could get close enough to pick Ida up before dark. The next day, Warren Hinsdale and others from Cape Meares boated over, placed her on an improvised stretcher, and took her out to a Coast Guard cutter in Sturgeon Channel that sped down to the south end of the bay and over to the Tillamook County General Hospital.[14]

Francis stayed in Cape Meares for the next couple of weeks but spent his days in Tillamook. When not with Ida, he harangued folks with conspiracy theories on the sidewalk, in stores, at the newspaper office, and in the courthouse. They included accusations against Sheriff Birch and Judge Effenberger. As Ida deteriorated, Francis became increasingly agitated. On the morning of November 4th, deputies arrested him for threatening Birch verbally and physically.[15]

Mitchell's behavior called his sanity into question, so Judge Effenberger—who had legal jurisdiction over such matters—sent Francis to local physicians Clemens Hayes and George Lemery. They both deemed Mitchell mentally ill. Effenberger deferred his final decision until two o'clock that afternoon so that Lyman Latourette could drive over from Portland and represent Mitchell at the hearing. Francis's behavior made it impossible for Lyman to argue that he was sane, so Effenberger committed him to the Oregon State Hospital. It took a couple of days for Elizabeth Bagley to complete the appropriate forms and for Gladys Hoover to record them, during which Francis was allowed to visit Ida. He arrived in Salem on Saturday morning, November 7, 1953.[16]

Dr. Dean Brooks evaluated Mitchell when he checked in. The psychiatrist described Francis—who had calmed down by then—as neatly attired, polite, cooperative, intelligent, in good health, and appearing younger than his eighty-three years. He claimed to have never been sick enough to visit a doctor. As a devout member of the Tillamook Christian Church, he did not smoke or drink. Francis attributed his middle name to ancestor Sir Francis Drake.[17]

When their conversation turned to mental health, Mitchell admitted his sanity had been questioned in 1934, but he had "beat the crooks to the punch" by convincing a Tillamook physician otherwise. According to Francis, his enemies' accusations of beating Ida were a ploy to keep him from telling the world of their misdeeds. He referred to 310 pages he had prepared for the Department of Justice detailing every swindle and plot against him. Dr. Brooks added,

> [He] quite evidently enjoys talking [and was] preoccupied with thoughts surrounding what he feels to be misdoings and crooked dealings on the part of certain men in the development of his home community of Bayocean. He is litiganous [*sic*] and tells how many times he has gone to court - even as far as the U.S. Supreme Court - in trying to right these wrongs. Definitely feels that people are in league to frame him, to keep him from pressing his suit. He seems to feel himself to be the rightful crusader for others who have lost their holdings through what he believes crooked dealings. He tends to minimize the fact that the ocean actually isolated his community and therefore caused the prices of real estate to drop sharply.[18]

Dr. Brooks diagnosed Mitchell as paranoid, a personality disorder with delusions described as, "erroneous judgments not subject to correction by experience." Stressful events often initiate the psychosis. If left untreated, the condition becomes chronic, and the delusions become increasingly resistant to change.[19]

Not long after his initial interview, Dr. Brooks read editorials written by *Headlight-Herald* owner Elsie DeCook accusing Sheriff Birch and Judge

Effenberger of railroading Francis. So, he asked a hospital social worker, June Kelder, to investigate. She first interviewed State Senator Warren McMinimee because he had called several times asking about Mitchell. Initially, McMinimee said his calls were on behalf of fifteen concerned constituents, but he then went on to report several unpleasant personal encounters with Mitchell. During the last incident, in 1949, Francis had "squared off to strike" the senator when he refused to sign a petition before reading it. McMinimee slipped into a group of people walking by to escape. Later, he learned that the petition's purpose was to disbar a local attorney.[20]

Kelder next called Elizabeth Bagley to get details on the court proceedings, only to find out that she had known Mitchell since 1918:

> She said he had always been very paranoid and that it was his own fault that the community had not prospered since he kept people out of it "with his tongue." Whenever anyone moved in and wanted to take an interest in running the town, he would be so unpleasant they would leave. For years he paid taxes on land for other people to prevent tax foreclosure; actually these people had wanted to let the land go, so they were not being persecuted by the sheriff as the patient thought. Several years ago an injunction was placed against the patient because he was threatening people. Mrs. Bagley said that ever since she has known him, the patient has been more or less as he is now, but recently he has been getting worse. For years he has cornered people on the street or has blocked them in their cars in order to tell them about his problems. He has not been violent toward anyone except his wife, and he is known to have beaten up on her. When his wife had her stroke, he objected because others on the island signaled the coast guard. He wouldn't let the only other woman on the island touch his wife to clean her up since he was feuding with the woman's husband. For several hours, his wife lay on the floor covered with a rug until moved to Tillamook by the authorities. The patient objected to her transfer because he said one shouldn't move anyone who has had a stroke and with his training he could care for her.[21]

Sheriff Birch told Kelder the incident began when he refused to un-deputize a fellow islander. A deputy removed Mitchell from the courthouse when he started shaking Birch by the shoulders. But he sneaked in through another door, shouted profanities at the sheriff, and refused to let up after being warned that he would be locked up, saying that would make him a martyr and protect him from those who wished him harm. While in the cell, Francis became docile, so the sheriff released him. He then walked over to the Tillamook Post Office and threatened Mr. Doty of the Tillamook Christian Church, who had counseled Francis while in jail. That convinced Birch that "his removal from the island and his wife's illness have upset him to the degree he might become dangerous." Judge Effenberger agreed but tried finding a nursing home willing to take Mitchell in—unsuccessfully—before holding the insanity hearing.[22]

Kelder found Elsie DeCook's reasoning hard to follow and later learned that some of her statements were false. The editor's primary intent appeared to be removing Sheriff Birch from office. Reverend Aldis Webb, the pastor of the Tillamook Christian Church whom Effenberger had appointed as Mitchell's guardian, shared DeCook's angst with Birch: "the wrong guy went down there." The social worker came away from these two interviews concerned about the hospital becoming embroiled in a local political battle. She thought Francis "fortunate to avoid institutionalization as long as he had." That was good enough for Brooks.[23]

Neither Francis nor Ida Mitchell would return to Bayocean. Ida died on December 28, 1953. She was eighty-five. Gerald and Nellie Reeher, Salem residents who befriended the Mitchells and purchased a Bayocean Park lot when they owned a store in Tillamook, gave Francis a ride to her funeral on January 2, 1954.[24]

Engineers Design a Breakwater to Close the South Inlet

As Francis Mitchell was settling into his room at the Oregon State Hospital in late November and early December 1953, the Corps' Board of Engineers deliberated on the Portland District's breakwater plan. When finished, they asked Colonel Lipscomb to use sand dredged from the bay instead of rocks because it would cost less to build and maintain.[25]

The cost of the revised design, submitted by Lipscomb in December, was $1,775,000. Local ports would have to contribute $275,000. The

Portland District would deduct $20,000 if the owners of lots in the project area and oyster farmers signed easements giving the Corps free rein. Another $5,000 would be cut if Tillamook County agreed to build and maintain a road on top of the breakwater. The Board of Engineers approved the plan in January 1954.[26]

At an election held on May 21, 1954, the Ports of Bay City and Tillamook Bay—which had not merged—asked their constituents to approve taxes to pay interest on the bonds needed to raise $90,000 and $160,000, respectively. Port of Bay City voters approved the tax by a wide margin, but Port of Tillamook Bay voters voted 1,415 to 1,190 against it. Cape Meares residents voted forty-eight to zero in favor, but voters in districts far from the bay voted three to one against it. Tillamook leaders favored the breakwater, so they added a second tax vote to the general election on November 2nd. Their continued promotion and a larger turnout in districts closer to the bay resulted in a favorable vote of 1,699 to 1,593.[27]

Despite the first Port of Tillamook Bay tax measure failing, Tillamook's congressional delegation had convinced their colleagues to authorize the breakwater project in September 1954. They got $200,000 appropriated in July 1955 to get things started, with the remaining $1,300,000 added to the Rivers and Harbors Act in January 1956.[28]

Homes Deconstructed and Vandalized

By August 1953, the Gilkisons were so concerned about the expansion of the south inlet that they moved the rest of their furniture and belongings from Kaaren Ann Kottages to their Cape Meares rental. By February 1954, they knew the breakwater would run through their motel. So, they bought a house in Bay City that April and moved into it in August, after Del did some remodeling. He then took apart the cement blocks that had been mortared together seven years earlier and barged them across the bay.[29]

Birger Bugge had moved into a bungalow after his place collapsed in December 1952, but the isolation and primitive living conditions wore on him. In 1953, he stayed at the Tillamook Hotel a couple of times but kept returning to the spit, the last time in February 1954, because "sleepless nights, no appetite, nothing to do all day, too much fuss and clatter of life 'outside' upset his nerves." Richard and Nellie Walton also grew weary of the stark existence. Between July and October 1954, they bought six adjacent lots in Bay City and had a new house built there using materials salvaged from their Bayocean home.[30]

In late September 1954, the Goldmans emptied their cottage on High Terrace while George Bagley and his brother Clifford dismantled their father's house on the bay. When George returned with Elizabeth on Sunday, November 28th, Harvey Sandy was alone, Birger Bugge having made his final exit, destination unknown. The Bagleys reported the last remnants of the Gillham place, first enjoyed by Johan and Dora Poulsen, having fallen to the shore the night before. A tiny summer cottage Johnny Burton had built in 1936 at the corner of Bay and Stark Streets fell in mid-December. The Thomas house succumbed within a month. By the end of January 1955, every structure along the bay, south of the town center, was gone. The Goldman place was just seven feet from the dune's edge and soon fell. One of the first houses built (for Fannie Potter in 1911) was one of the last to go.[31]

On January 8, 1955, Lyman Latourette had written Francis Mitchell at the Oregon State Hospital to tell him The Mitchell and Bayside Inn were at risk because the dune behind Bayocean Cottages was nearly gone. High Terrace would soon become a new gap, with the town center at its bay end, so Harvey Sandy was also preparing to leave for Bay City.[32]

Once Sandy left, thieves and vandals had their way on Bayocean Island. Francis Mitchell, of course, had not been able to remove furniture, clothing, and other personal belongings nor board up The Mitchell and Bayside Inn to slow scavengers down. He asked Dr. Brooks for permission to do so but did not receive it. His guardian, Reverend Webb, did not arrange for the removal and safekeeping of his possessions. Nor did any of his friends. As a result, everything he owned was stolen or destroyed. Perry Reeder, then a teenager, was distressed when he visited the town he loved and saw it wantonly destroyed.[33]

Breakwater Revision Destroys Most of What Remains

Captain James Henshaw would supervise the breakwater construction. As soon as Congress appropriated the first $200,000 in July 1955, he traveled to the spit and immediately saw that its route and design had to be modified. Storm surges would soon pass down High Street and 12th Avenue to enter the bay at the pier. The new gap would eventually destroy the town center as it expanded because it was north of the original breakwater's endpoint. The south inlet had narrowed to four thousand feet, but the two lobes had grown to a half-mile in length and terminated far east of the original breakwater route. Waves now sped through a single, primary channel eight hundred feet wide at an average of over five feet per second. A sand-filled breakwater could not withstand such forces.[34]

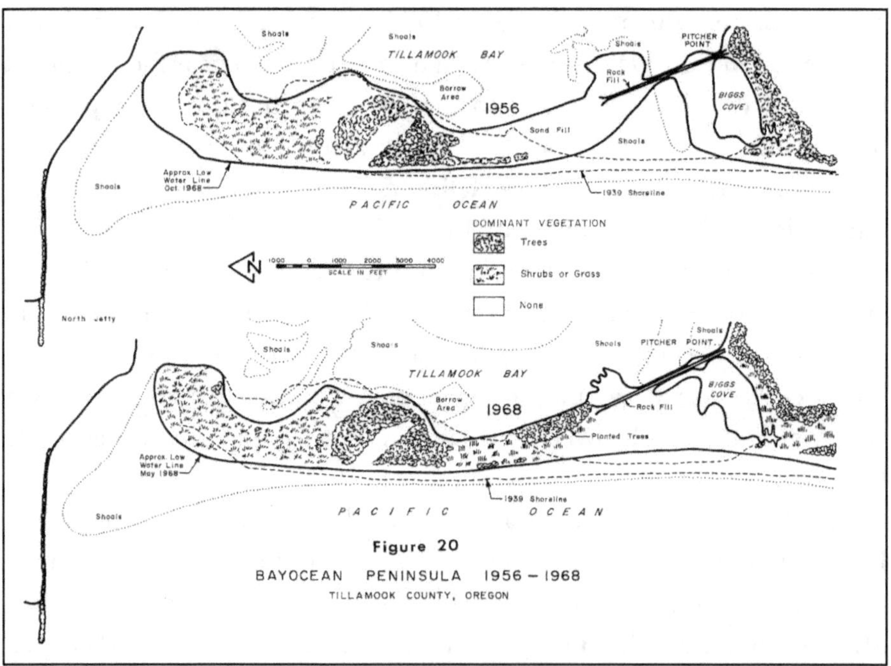

Breakwater design and aftermath. Figure 20, Appendix E, "Extension of Tillamook South Jetty, Tillamook Bay, Oregon: Final Environmental Impact Statement," (Portland District, Army Corps of Engineers, 1978).

Engineers from the district, divisional, and national levels of the Corps met in Portland on October 21st to redesign the breakwater. It would now be 9,600 feet long and terminate at Point Spruce, just south of the alcove where the worker's camp had been located. Sand gaps north of that were too high for waves ever to breach them. The first 4,200 feet, still starting at Pitcher Point, would be made entirely of rock. A wooden trestle across the 800-foot south inlet would allow trucks to cross over and dump rocks along the edge of the project out to Point Spruce. They would then work backward, dropping stones into the main channel below the trestle, which they would disassemble as they retreated. The top would be fifteen feet wide and twenty feet above sea level, with each side sloping steeply at one foot in every foot and a half. A crane would shape rocks dumped on the bay side of the main breakwater to form a lower berm twenty feet wide and twelve feet high to provide additional support.[35]

North of the south inlet, sand dredged from the bay would raise the entire project area to an elevation of at least twenty feet above sea level to match the breakwater and prevent future washovers when storm surges coincided with extreme high tides. Every structure below that elevation would be bulldozed, burned, and buried to enable it. The changes would cost an additional $129,000, but the Corps hoped to reduce that by using lower quality sandstone quarried along Bayocean Road. And they predicted that a new shoreline would soon form and protect the breakwater, reducing annual maintenance costs.[36]

After Congress approved funding in January 1956, Captain Henshaw started gathering signatures on leases from the oyster farmers whose beds the breakwater would cover and owners of the remaining lots and "approximately thirty-five buildings" that would be bulldozed, burned, and buried. They included the Bayside Inn, The Mitchell, the remains of the Locke home, and the fully intact houses of the Meyers, the Zimmermans, George Bauman and Cople Britton, the Haldums, and Elsie and Chester Nieland, the last owners of the Snyders' place. Four other cabins destroyed by the Corps, not mentioned earlier, were owned by E. C. and Lillian Bennett, Chester Stein, William and Inez Carey, and H. P. Long. Bungalows and outbuildings filled in the Corps tally. Only three houses and a few bungalows above the fill line remained standing after the contractor finished.[37]

The Corps found The Mitchell's silent owner, William George, but did not get a signature because he had died without heirs on January 7, 1952.

If the Corps had asked, Francis Mitchell certainly would not have signed, but Captain Henshaw explained why his guardian Reverend Aldis Webb and everyone else did: "all the houses and commercial buildings in the town had been wrecked by vandals." Photos taken on May 22nd confirmed that. Henshaw must have also explained that their homes would be lost as the new gap expanded and that their sacrifice would save the Tillamook Bay area by consolidating the sandspit and assuring its future integrity.[38]

Lyman Latourette signed his lease in April 1956 on the condition that doing so would not preclude his pursuit of a $9,000 claim filed against the Corps of Engineers in February for the loss of his bungalows. In March, he was told that such administrative settlements were limited to $1,000. On July 26th, a freak summer storm wiped out the few bungalows not already lost to the sea and Corps demolition. That prompted Latourette to file suit in federal court, saying the Corps' north jetty blocked replenishment of winter erosion from sand moved south by summer currents. The court acknowledged Latourette's reasoning but dismissed the case on February 15, 1957, saying,

> It is fundamental that riparian ownership is subject to the government's right in eminent domain to improve navigation…The government is not liable to compensate riparian owners for consequential damages caused by improvement made upon navigable waterways in aid of navigation [and] this Court is of the opinion that plaintiff had no vested right in the continuance of future accretions to his property by way of sands carried by the winds and in turn washed by the sea upon his lands.

Latourette did not appeal, and no other Bayocean landowner ever sued the Corps. On June 19, 1958, the county commissioners foreclosed on all seventy-one of his Bayocean Park lots. Lyman Latourette lost far more than any other individual landowner. He died at ninety on August 13, 1963.[39]

Captain Henshaw sent out invitations to bid on construction of the breakwater on March 1, 1956, but he waited to open those received until the 20th, the day after receiving checks for $250,000 from the two ports.

A week later, he awarded Portland's General Construction the contract for $1,163,686. By April 18th, men were busy blasting sandstone from the bluffs surrounding Flower Pot, a meadow one mile east of Pitcher Point. And trucks were soon dumping the rocks off Pitcher Point. The dredge *Washington* arrived on April 22nd but had to wait for Pacific Power and Light to lay submarine cables capable of delivering 11,000 volts. On May 4th, three crews began pumping sand in three shifts around the clock. Between June 5th and June 13th, every structure was bulldozed into piles and set ablaze. Dredged sand buried the remains and continued south.[40]

Building the trestle across the 800-foot-wide channel while water rushed through it presented the most significant challenge, made worse by dilapidated equipment. In a report filed after they finished, Henshaw said, "the contractor had, without a doubt, previously amortized his investment on all equipment used on the project with the exception of the five new items and the dredge… Breakdowns were the rule, rather than the exception. Mechanics were busy 24 hours per day…Spare parts were moving from Portland to Pitcher Point in an almost constant stream."[41]

Rocks being dumped between breakwater trestles to close the south inlet in September 1956. TB-333, Civil Works Project Photographs, 1839-1988, Box 64, POR-81, RG 77, NARA, Seattle, WA.

Absenteeism, high turnover, and the lack of construction skills among quarry workers were other significant problems. Twenty percent of the men were company employees. Eighty percent were local fishermen, sawyers, and loggers with a "cavalier attitude toward life and limb." One man suffered severe cuts when his coveralls got caught in a drill. Another wrenched his back when a rock fell on him. Corps inspectors forced General Construction's foremen to shut down equipment in the most egregious situations, preventing more severe casualties. Henshaw did compliment equipment operators and the dredge crew. He blamed the loss of a dump truck off the end of the trestle on the spotter and a design that forced massive trucks to operate on a fifteen-foot-wide surface. The captain also judged trestle removal impossible and unwise—he left it in place to provide additional support.[42]

Despite Henshaw's concerns, members of the Corps' Beach Erosion Board liked what they saw on October 10th. They were especially pleased to see sand accumulating on the seaward side of the breakwater. But a two-week-long storm hit soon after that, halting work, so Henshaw extended

Looking north, from a hill behind Pitcher Point, at the breakwater (now Dike Road) after it closed the south inlet. TB-379. Civil Works Project Photographs, 1839-1988, Box 64, POR-81, RG 77, NARA, Seattle, WA.

General Construction's deadline to November 16th. The company met it by repairing Bayocean Road and switching to smaller equipment to avoid tearing it up again. Then a sub-contractor leveled the sand and planted beach grass to stabilize it, finishing on December 22nd.[43]

Including the sub-contractor, the final tally was $1,262,000. Since the ports' share was $189,000, each got a refund. Captain Henshaw's supervisors must have appreciated his project coming in under budget as much as the ports did; not so his unsolicited opinion that the north jetty caused Bayocean's demise and that erosion was sure to continue.[44]

As predicted, after the breakwater was completed, the main channel of the north inlet flushed out and reached its previous width, allowing large ships to enter Tillamook Bay again. And backpressure caused by the obstruction slowed waves enough for the sand they carried to settle in line with the shores north and south of the break. By the middle of January 1957, people were enjoying a new beach, though it was 800 to 900 feet east of where it had been in 1939.[45]

A Tillamook County Road Department crew repaired Bayocean Road early in 1957 and laid a gravel road across the breakwater. Later, they would do the same on the lower bayside berm and convert the turnaround built by the Corps on the sand fill to a parking lot. Automobiles would then leave Pitcher Point on the bay side and return on the seaward side of Dike Road, as they do today.[46]

During the summer of 1957, Cape Meares residents took advantage of the warm, shallow waters trapped between the breakwater, the new shoreline, and the landfill to swim, go boating, fish for ocean perch, and picnic along its shores. They dubbed it Cape Meares Lake. Some started talking about ways to use the new landfill. In December, Francis Mitchell sent the Bagleys a cheerful Christmas card, complimenting Judge Effenberger and *Headlight-Herald* editor DeCook on their "support in carrying out the plans we Bayocean people have been working on since 1914." He planned to return soon and work towards getting a south jetty built. "Bayocean is bound to come back bigger and better than ever."[47]

Cape Meares Lake disappeared in April 1958 when a storm took out 150 feet of the new shoreline. The same occurred periodically over the next decade. In each instance, the beach returned. But as Henshaw had predicted, it kept moving east. In November and December of 1958, several Cape Meares residents pulled their homes back from the advancing dune cliff. Unlike those on the spit, they could continue doing so indefinitely. But the house last owned by the Houghs—who had rented it out after moving elsewhere when NAST shut down—was too big to move, so it sat abandoned, "deep in debris and rocks as the beach moves farther inland." It slowly crumbled in such an unspectacular fashion that no one recorded the day on which nothing of it remained.[48]

The Last Three Homes Fall

The three houses left standing along Bay Terrace by the Corps of Engineers in 1956 were gone within four years. Rainbow Girls House went first. Between May 5, 1957, and February 4, 1958, Lewis and Hilda Bennett and their son Harold took it apart, hauled the lumber down fifty steps to Bay Terrace, drove it to a barge, floated it across the bay, and stored it in a boatyard facility at Bay City. In the 1960s, Harold spent two-and-a-half years building a house for his family in his free time. From the location on Sandstone Point, they had a magnificent view of Bayocean. The Bennetts left their garage behind. Howard Sherwood Jr. (Buck) last observed a piece of it in the spring of 1972.[49]

The Currins' Dew Drop Inn went next. It was furthest from the sea, but a Garibaldi Boy Scout troop accidentally burned it down while playing with fire during an overnight stay. Their adult chaperone—who was sound asleep in a house just up the hill and oblivious to what was going on until it was too late—boated to town, aroused the boys' parents, and insisted they drive over to retrieve their delinquent sons. The local press said nothing of the incident.[50]

The last house was the one Jim O'Donnell had built and enjoyed for years. Its last owners were Portlanders Otto and Maldeena Notdurft. After hearing that the spit had become an island in November 1952, they drove to Cape Meares to check things out. When they saw the damage done, they were sure their cabin was gone and never returned. Burford Wilkerson took the last in a series of photographs of the Notdurft place hanging over the edge on February 15, 1960. Cape Meares resident Albert Kenney saw it still there on March 22nd. Wilkerson photographed a sandy patch where the house once stood on November 25th.[51]

The Notdurft cabin was the last of thirty taken by the sea. Eight were deconstructed. Six were sold at salvage prices and moved to Cape Meares to be enjoyed by others. Four burned down. The Army Corps of Engineers bulldozed and buried nine while building the breakwater in 1956. The fate of two of the fifty-nine homes built on Bayocean remains uncertain.[52]

The last photo of the last house. Burford Wilkerson Negative 2886, TCPM.

Bayocean is often referred to as a ghost town, but spirits would have been able to wander abandoned buildings only between January 1955, when Harvey Sandy left and, at best, when the Lewis and Hilda Bennett's garage fell in the spring of 1972.[53] Now that more than fifty years have passed, Bayocean does qualify as a cultural site. It did not, however, in the 1960s, 1970s, and 1980s when folks hunted for artifacts of the spit's white inhabitants as they once had the Tillamooks who preceded them. Authors Bert and Margie Webber were the most famous of them. They took their children there nearly every summer vacation to scour the spit. One of their sons grew so weary of it that he refused to return to Bayocean as an adult, but Dale Webber and his wife Sally persevered. The foursome discovered sections of narrow-gauge rail, chunks of pavement, and other items close to the surface. They kept track of the House of Hicks well pipe until it disappeared in April 1989.[54] Someday, archeologists may find a reason to unearth the sidewalks, streets, automobiles, appliances, and other incombustible objects not consumed by fire in 1956, but the first scientists to pay attention to Bayocean sought to understand what destroyed it.

University of Oregon Geographers Look for Reasons

As the Notdurft cabin hung precariously over the dune's edge in March 1960, Professor Samuel Dicken, head of the University of Oregon's Department of Geography, and two assistants were studying the impact of white settlement on Oregon's coastline. In November 1961, they concluded that the effect of "jetties at the mouths of the rivers, for the purpose of improving navigation…has been to deny sand to certain parts of the coast and to accumulate the sand in other parts; in other words, acceleration of erosion has occurred in some places and increased deposition has occurred in other places." Professor Dicken, who analyzed Bayocean, hypothesized that it suffered more erosion than elsewhere because Tillamook Bay's inlet was the only instance of a single jetty.[55]

Dicken considered the sand accumulating north of the jetty "good circumstantial evidence that the construction of the jetty also triggered erosion of the Bayocean Beach by denying sand to the beach. This is borne out by the fact that soundings made after the construction of the jetty revealed a loss of sand from the submerged portion of the beach, within the 10-fathom line. Furthermore, in similar situations in various parts of the world the construction of jetties or breakwaters has led to erosion of the adjacent beaches."[56]

Comparing 1939 and 1944 aerial photographs, Dicken estimated that Bayocean's shoreline recession averaged sixteen feet per year, close to the fifteen feet locals had reported then. Aerials taken in 1960 showed the rate of erosion increasing. And the end of Pacific Avenue in Cape Meares moved seventy-five feet east during the eighteen months of Dicken's study. Erosion varied along the spit: its northern extreme was longer and broader than when the Corps first measured it in 1939 whereas the southern seashore of 1960 was east of where the bay shoreline had been in 1939.[57]

In 1962, G. C. Hoare, a civilian engineer with the Corps of Engineers, used data collected at stations along the shore of the spit since 1939 to come up with similar erosion rates as Dicken. However, he attributed the cause to changes in offshore depths shown in hydrological charts. Between 1885 and 1927, the offshore gradient steepened sharply, which allowed storm surges to hit Bayocean's shoreline with greater force. Hoare thought the change was natural, having nothing to do with the north jetty, but offered no proof.[58] Both Dicken and Hoare added pieces to the puzzle but left others to complete it.

Meanwhile, the north jetty's root needed repairs again. As the Corps made plans for that, Tillamook leaders asked them to reconsider a south jetty—not to stop Bayocean erosion, because that no longer posed a threat, but to prevent shoals from shifting around the inlet unpredictably, creating a hazard for the most experienced pilots. The Corps agreed to do so after repairing the north jetty, for which Congress appropriated $500,000 in the spring of 1963. Umpqua River Navigation Company finished the work in August 1965 while Congressman Wendell Wyatt was "bird-dogging" fellow House Public Works Committee members to appropriate funding for the south jetty study.[59]

Francis Mitchell's Battles End

On July 25, 1965, Francis Mitchell died of congestive heart failure at the Oregon State Hospital. The plots imagined against him had grown more rigid and convoluted during his stay. The *Headlight-Heralds* Elsie DeCook sent Mitchell each week did not help. Though the letters from him that she published were always cheerful, what he read took his mind to a place where, as one caregiver noted, "revenge is all he lives for."[60]

Having nowhere else to direct it, Francis inflicted his angst on fellow inmates. No matter how many times someone listened to his rants, if they refused to listen again, his agitated response would create havoc in the ward for days. Mitchell was transferred six times during his twelve years at the hospital. Caregivers thought his fear of inmates plotting against him was a symptom of his paranoia, but it may have been true.[61]

Hospital administrators applied for Ida's postmaster survivorship pension. Some of it went towards Francis's care. Some of it paid the premiums on his $500 life insurance policy. He named Ida's brother-in-law, George Raddant, the beneficiary in return for having paid Ida's burial expenses, purchasing two adjacent lots at the Tillamook IOOF Cemetery and paying for Francis's funeral costs when the time came. In 1960, the hospital paid back taxes on six of the twelve parcels that Mitchell still owned in Cape Meares. Francis also received a monthly allowance that he spent on clothes and toiletries to keep himself looking sharp, and candy for staff and inmates willing to listen to his Bayocean tirades. Each Memorial Day, he bought flowers for Ida's grave.[62]

Francis attended church most Sundays and occasionally went on field trips. He received few letters and rarely had visitors, though he once spent a weekend with unidentified friends. Vance Mason recalled spending time with Mitchell during his commitment. They "watched the roofs and trees all get blowed [*sic*]to hell" during the Columbus Day Storm on October 12, 1962.[63]

On July 13, 1965, Francis told a nurse, "I knew I would come to the end sometime." Twelve days later, he did, at the age of ninety-five. With money from George Raddant, Nellie Reeher purchased a joint headstone. She arranged a funeral service on July 29th in Tillamook, after which Francis and Ida were reunited at the IOOF Cemetery.[64]

Finally, a South Jetty

Two days after Francis Mitchell died, Oregon Senators Wayne Morse and Maurine Neuberger (who succeeded Richard when he died) successfully added an amendment to the 1965 Omnibus Rivers and Harbors Act authorizing the construction of an 8,000-foot-long jetty on the south side of Tillamook Bay's entrance. Representative Wendell Wyatt got his bill passed by the House a couple of months later. President Lyndon Johnson signed the bill on October 27, 1965. Tillamook Bay's inlet would finally get a south jetty.[65]

Success this time around came from changes to both the numerator and denominator of the Corps' benefit-to-cost ratio. Harvesting the Tillamook Burn added lumber production to the benefits. The Port of Bay City, the Port of Tillamook Bay, and Tillamook County agreed to dredge Crab Harbor, prepare a staging area at Kincheloe Point, and maintain Dike Road once the contractor extended it, respectively. That lowered the costs enough that the Corps did not require cash contributions.[66]

An Umpqua crane setting stones on the South Jetty in 1973, as viewed from the west. Trucks delivering the stones can be seen in the background driving across the section built earlier. Photo taken by, and courtesy of, Dale Webber, Webber and Webber, *Maimed by the Sea*, 76.

Unlike the north jetty, the south jetty would have no wooden superstructure. A crane slowly moving seaward along its thirty-foot wide top would place massive twenty-to-thirty-ton stones in an interlocking pattern to withstand the pounding of the Pacific Ocean. The jetty's height would range from sixteen to eighteen feet above mean lower low water. Corps engineers thought that a 5,000-foot-long diagonal jetty, running from the northwest corner of the spit to a point 1,400 feet from about the midpoint of the north jetty, would keep the main channel clear of shoals. However, consultants hired by the two ports said the south jetty needed to be 3,000 feet longer and 200 feet closer to the north jetty to prevent shoaling, similar to the Corps' first design in 1911. After months of negotiations, the Corps agreed to seek congressional authorization for the ports' 8,000-foot design in exchange for the ports going along with funding and construction of the Corps' 5,000-foot design initially; the rest of the jetty would be funded and built later if deemed necessary.[67]

Though the purpose of the south jetty was to improve the inlet channel, Portland District Engineer Colonel Robert Bangert said,

> It is expected that sand will fill in south of the jetty from the northward littoral drift, causing accretion for a short distance south. It is further believed that the jetty will eliminate or greatly reduce the loss of material into the inlet, thus effecting a decrease in the rate of erosion within the area.[68]

Bangert's chief engineer, B. E. Wilcox, was more specific a year later in replying to Elizabeth Ryan: "It is expected that completion of this jetty will materially reduce the rate of erosion southward to Cape Meares."[69] Though careful not to say that the north jetty had caused the erosion, both men clearly believed that it had.

After Representative Wendell Wyatt and Senators Wayne Morse and Mark Hatfield shepherded an appropriations bill through Congress in 1968, Umpqua River Navigation Company won the contract to build the south jetty. They started work in early June 1969. Their ocean-going barges brought the stones to Crab Harbor, where a stationary crane off-loaded and stockpiled them at Kincheloe Point. Trucks capable of handling 30-ton rocks carried them across the north end of the spit to a pile behind the jetty's base at the apex of the curve at the spit's northwest extent. A loader took them out to a mobile crane—one of the largest on the Pacific Coast—at the end of the road built across previously-laid stones.[70]

Umpqua had completed 3,695 feet of the jetty before shutting down operations in the summer of 1971. Strong undercurrents had gouged a hole in front of the jetty during a winter storm surge. Filling it consumed all the boulders funded, leaving the first stage short. Sand immediately started accumulating south of the new jetty. Oregon's new senator, Bob Packwood, worked with Hatfield and Wyatt to secure more funds in 1971. Umpqua added 2,830 feet between 1972 and 1974 because the Corps agreed to add part of the parallel section. It reduced the distance between jetties to 1,200 feet at the same time, because it was apparent by then that the ports' consultants had been correct in saying that proximity was necessary to keep the channel clear of shoals. In 1977, they authorized another 1,475 feet to reach 8,000. Tillamook's new representative, Les Aucoin, joined Hatfield and Packwood for the final appropriation, and Umpqua started work on the first of May 1978.[71]

An Umpqua crane operator set the final stone of the south jetty on September 13, 1979. The company hosted a celebration at Kincheloe Point on October 19th. Fifty to a hundred people endured freezing rain to explore the construction site, examine the equipment, and listen to Senator Hatfield. The Oregon National Guard capped things off with a nineteen-gun salute. That evening, Congressman Aucoin spoke at a dinner where Umpqua's vice-president reported two million tons of rock having been hauled from Fisher Quarry (between Vancouver and Camas, Washington) on 630 trips. One of the enormous stones was left along Dike Road at Kincheloe Point to commemorate the event. A plaque cut into its face, stolen since then, pegged the final cost at $20,600,000.[72]

Oregon State University Academics Figure It Out

Before the final extension of the south jetty, the Corps distributed an environmental impact statement that included:

> Prior to jetty construction, erosion on Bayocean Peninsula occurred primarily during the winter as a result of the northward littoral drift, and accretion occurred during summer due to the southward littoral drift. Following construction of the north jetty in 1914 and its reconstruction and extension in 1932 and 1933,

> erosion of Bayocean Peninsula increased greatly. One study suggests that this erosion occurred as a result of the north jetty blocking the seasonally reversing littoral drift currents.

The study cited was a doctoral dissertation submitted to the Department of Geography at Oregon State University (OSU) by Tom Terich in August 1973.[73]

After arriving at OSU in 1971, Terich had asked John Byrne (Dean of OSU's College of Oceanography, later its president) to recommend a coastal investigation for his dissertation. Byrne referred him to Professor Paul Komar, whom he had recruited from California's Scripps Institute of Oceanography in 1970 because of his work on coastal processes. Komar suggested that Terich look at Bayocean because it "was unusual, and hence of special interest to coastal scientists and engineers." South jetty construction presented an ideal opportunity to track geomorphological changes in real-time. Though in different departments, the student and his advisor worked more closely than most over the next two years. When Terich received his doctorate in 1973, he found a tenured position at Western Washington State College and left Bayocean behind. But Komar expanded on their work with future oceanography graduate students. Their cumulative effort put OSU's College of Oceanography at the forefront of coastal dynamics research.[74]

Tom Terich began by reviewing past work, including a wave study by the National Marine Consultants in 1960 and 1961. It confirmed earlier anecdotal observations that high winds and waves hit the Oregon shoreline primarily from the southwest in winter whereas milder summer winds and waves approached from the northwest. He also discovered that in 1969, OSU oceanographers had tracked sand migrating north and offshore at Newport, Oregon in the fall and winter and returning south and back onshore during the spring and summer. If the same was true at Bayocean—as Corps of Engineers geologist Lloyd Ruff postulated in 1939—sand removed from the spit during winter was prevented from returning during the summer by the north jetty.[75]

To confirm that, Terich compared past and present offshore depth and onshore elevation changes working outward from both jetties in every direction. He then measured the sediment budgets of soil samples collected along Bayocean's shoreline by the Corps since 1939 to determine their source. His calculations led Terich to conclude that the Rockaway Littoral Cell (between Cape Meares and Cape Falcon) had "a reversing longshore sand transport with near zero net annual drift" and that "beach erosion can result from the construction of a jetty" even when such equilibrium exists.[76] These are principles taken for granted today, but in 1973, Tom Terich was challenging the assumptions held by the Corps of Engineers and others that littoral drift along the Oregon Coast was north to south and that jetties had no effect.

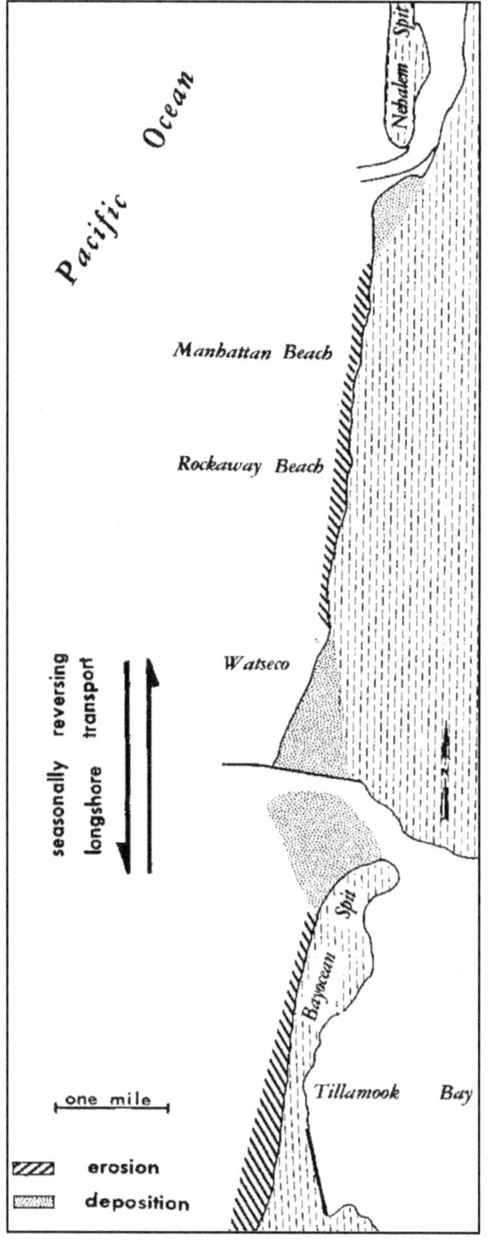

Figure 47, Terich, "Bayocean Spit."

When Geibisch and Joplin built the north jetty between 1914 and 1917, Terich explained, it interrupted the littoral equilibrium and created a new bay. The embayment was shaped like a barbed hook, with the jetty as its throat and the old shoreline curving northward to Rockaway Beach from its base at Barview as the barb. Sand drifting into the embayment during the summer remained there instead of returning north in the winter. By 1920, a shoreline running parallel to prevailing summer wave crests met the 5,400-foot-long jetty 2,500 feet from its base. Littoral sands then moved north and south each season along this new shoreline, having reached equilibrium.[77]

When deterioration of the north jetty let waves remove sand from the embayment at the end of the 1920s, the embayment receded. After the jetty was repaired and extended by three hundred feet in 1933, the shoreline expanded and reached the 3,200-foot point of the jetty in 1940. The Corps estimated that the embayment then held eight million cubic yards of sand and that it would have taken ten years to fill if not for jetty deterioration. If so, 800,000 cubic yards of sand was moving up and down Rockaway Beach each year. The erosion north of the jetty was not apparent because losses stretched across twelve miles of shoreline.[78]

As for Bayocean, sand moving north in winter would have created an embayment south of the north jetty if it were not the inlet to Tillamook Bay. But because it was, incoming tides carried the sand to Kincheloe Point, expanding it north and east. Outgoing tides pushed sand flowing into the main channel offshore. Sand ending up in other parts of the inlet became shoals. No matter which direction the sand moving north went, it could not return south to Bayocean during the summer as it had before.[79]

The spit continued losing sand until the south embayment filled, which was more expansive and shaped differently than the one above the north jetty. Terich estimated that 1,800,000 cubic yards of sand were entrapped during just its first three years.[80] The 600,000 annual average differed from the Corps' 800,000, though they should have been the same because the two embayments were part of the same littoral cell. However, the parties involved were both estimating and doing it over different periods and decades apart. Whatever the correct number was, Professor Komar later deemed the sand movement within the Rockway Littoral Cell "about the highest anywhere in the world."[81]

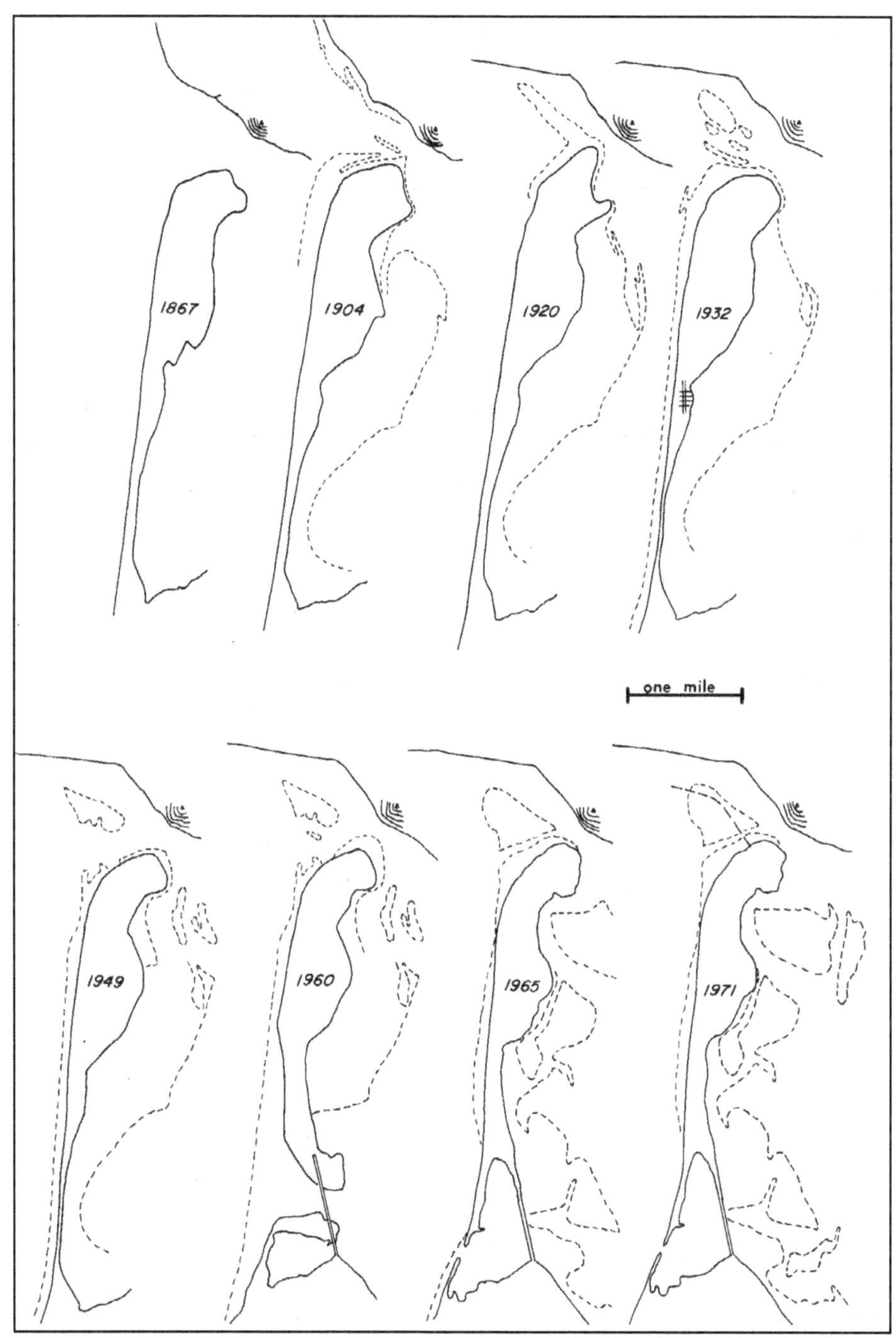

Coast and Geodetic Survey Charts showing the changing shape of Tillamook Spit over a century. Figure 35. Terich, "Bayocean Spit."

By 1973, the new Bayocean shoreline had reached 2,000 feet on the south jetty, running parallel to prevailing winter wave crests. Winter winds blew so much of the newly accumulated sand through Rabbit Hollow into Tillamook Bay that beach grass was planted to stabilize it in 1976. Salal and shore pine have since joined the grasses to leave little exposed sand. By the time Umpqua dropped the last boulder in 1979, the embayment had reached its greatest extent at the 4,700-foot point of the south jetty. The cycle of erosion begun sixty-five years earlier had finally come to a stop.[82]

Professor Komar's next graduate student was master's degree candidate Jose Roman Lizarraga-Arciniega. Applying the same techniques as Terich had to the other pairs of jetties along the Oregon Coast, Lizarraga-Arciniega confirmed that seasonally reversing net-zero littoral drift was the rule along the entire Oregon Coast. Despite that, and additional research by Komar and future students, a Corps engineer questioned north jetty causation of Bayocean erosion in 1984: "The cause-and-effect relationship there has been the subject of a lot of debate...there is some indication that at least some erosion was occurring even before that." Today, however, Corps engineers readily acknowledge north jetty causation, and internal jetty construction guidelines cite the work of Komar and his students.[83]

Though Terich and Komar figured things out too late to save Bayocean, their analysis helped others avoid the same fate. When Salishan Resort property owners consulted Komar about erosion threatening their summer cottage in 1971, he already knew enough to warn them against building a single jetty at the entrance to Siletz Bay. Some had proposed that as a solution, but it would have destroyed Salishan Spit just as it had Bayocean.[84]

One thing Professor Komar and his students did not question was the wisdom of building on sand. Those who do usually cite the parable Jesus told during his Sermon on the Mount, but the Nazarene was not a geologist. As it turns out, sand is as good a structural base as any so long as nothing removes it. Some of the largest cities in the world stand in the deserts of the Middle East. Atlantic City, Miami, and other great cities of the United States were built on sands along the East Coast. The Pacific

Ocean applies much greater forces than the Atlantic Ocean, resulting in an everchanging landscape; but that applies to capes as well as dunes.[85] If William Reynolds had dug a basement into the sandhill at the midpoint of Bayocean and built a regular house instead of a treehouse, it would still be standing.

Bayocean in the Twenty-First Century

As it turns out, even thirty-ton stones are no match for the Pacific Ocean. Waves bust apart and remove an average of twenty-eight feet of them from the end of the south jetty every year. By 2003, waves had ripped 666 feet from its end. The north jetty had shrunk by 384 feet, and the roots of both had failed in spots. This led to another study by Portland District engineers that concluded that shorter jetties could keep the inlet clear and maintain the prescribed depth. However, they recommended that each get caps of 25 to 50-ton stones, broader and taller than the rest of their respective jetties, to prevent future shrinkage.[86]

The north jetty's root was repaired in 2004. In 2010, a thousand interlocking stones took it back out to 5,213 feet and the cap was added. Since then, the cap has done its job, but during the spring of 2022, the Corps had to add another 34,000 tons of rock along 1,350 feet of its root. Meanwhile, the south jetty continued shrinking, to 6,880 feet by the end of 2021. Repair funding requests submitted each year were denied until the Infrastructure Investment and Jobs Act of 2022 secured the $62,000,000 needed from Congress. Repairs should begin in the spring of 2023, and the work should be completed by the end of 2025.[87]

Paul Komar and his students also discovered that extending a jetty beyond the end of its embayment caused no additional erosion. Logically, the reverse should be true. So, if the cap placed on the south jetty does not stop shrinkage, it would have to lose over 2,000 feet—where the shoreline meets it at 4,700 feet—before Bayocean's shores begin eroding again. And, counterintuitive as it might seem, the spit's foredune has risen as the jetty deteriorates. All seven stations set up by the Northwest Association of Networked Ocean Observing Systems in 1997 show average annual gains of between one and two feet, although a few have recorded intermittent drops.[88]

Another modern concern is global warming. It has not yet threatened Bayocean because the Juan de Fuca Plate has been rising at a rate of just eight inches per century less than sea rise along Tillamook County's coastline. However, in 2013, coastal experts—including Paul Komar and his former student Jonathan Allan—estimated that between 2010 and 2100, sea level will rise between 18.5 and 58 inches.[89]

The most immediate threat to Bayocean is a major subduction earthquake, which is long overdue. The Juan de Fuca Plate will drop by several feet along the Oregon Coast when it occurs, making it easier for storm surges to breach Bayocean's southern section again long-term. And the tsunami immediately following the earthquake will pass over the spit and take out Bay City. Hopefully, all of its residents will take refuge on the hill behind the town before it hits. Those caught on the spit will need to reach its hilly center or Cape Meares, whichever is closer.[90]

Whether Bayocean's dune rises or falls in the future, those who own lots there now will hang on to them. In 1973, Bert and Margie Webber were surprised to learn that the owners of fifty Bayocean Park lots located in the ocean or buried by the Corps of Engineers in 1956 were still paying county property taxes. The number had dropped by only two in 1982. Owners lived as far away as Virginia, but none were in the Mitchells' hometown of Kansas City. Curious as to why people continued to maintain ownership, Bert called a few:

> Some say their lot was willed to them "and it wouldn't be right to part with it." Others hold property in perpetual trust. Some law firms hold property as parts of unsettled estates. One woman said, "It belonged to my parents and as a child I grew up there. Our land was not totally taken by the ocean and someday I believe it will all come back. The taxes are minimal and I just want to keep it."

A few were upset enough by the implication of his asking that Bert quit calling.[91]

In January 1991, individuals still owned thirty-eight parcels. The Tillamook County Assessor appraised the twenty in the littoral zone at zero but valued the eighteen on land at $3,120. A few lots have changed hands since then, and the total has dropped to thirty-four, but neither is likely to change in the future because the assessor stopped charging taxes and mailing out bills after the spit was zoned Recreation Management at the end of the 1980s. Once the assessor stopped mailing tax bills, there was no mechanism to change ownership and addresses. As a result, the Elmer D. Allen Estate still owns one of the lots that Nellie bought from Harkness Chapin.[92]

Except for the federal land at its northwest corner, Tillamook County owns the rest of Bayocean. It was zoned Recreation Management because there are no streets or utilities. The lack of fire hydrants precludes permanent structures because they would burn to the ground—as they had in the past—before a fire truck arrived. County commissioners considered designating it as a county park in the 1980s but did not have enough money to develop or maintain that status. And they did not want to rule out Bayocean as a potential future source of funds. So, in 1991, they wrote Ordinance 42, which prohibits motor vehicles, camping, open fires, and other uses, and began managing Bayocean Spit as a day-use facility.[93]

In 2000, becoming increasingly concerned that his hometown would be forgotten because no evidence of it remained, Perry Reeder and his family started clearing trails and marking townsite locations. The following year, a group focused on preserving the spit's natural state asked county commissioners to rezone it Recreation Natural. The commissioners responded by establishing a Bayocean Task Force in 2002 and appointing fifteen people representing diverse user groups, Perry Reeder being one of them. After a year of sometimes contentious sessions, in May 2003, the task force recommended the status quo. Seven years later, in July 2013, the Reeder family started a process that led to their installing a ten-foot-high Bayocean Townsite sign above the spot where children caught the bus each morning on the north side of 12th Avenue, across from The Mitchell.[94]

In the spring of 2014, Bay Ocean LLC proposed the construction of an eco-resort with "25 seasonal luxury tents on temporary, wood decks sited below the ridgeline on the leeward side of the property." The name, location, and nature of the facility harkened back to the worker's camp Bertha (Weaver) Morgan described. Preservationists campaigned vigorously against the proposal while the Reeders and others who owned lots on the spit supported it. The Tillamook County Planning Commission rejected the eco-resort in January 2015, because of Recreation Management zoning restrictions. A few months later, the county commissioners asked them to consider rezoning the spit Recreation Natural to discourage similar proposals in the future. The planning commission recommended doing so that November, but the commissioners did not act.[95]

Perry Reeder's family did some minor excavating in October 2015. Using two crabapple trees recalled from his youth as reference points, Perry instructed his younger family members to dig a hole in the sand which revealed the sidewalk, curb, and pavement where his family parked in front of Cottage Park when they arrived in 1944. They only had to dig down a few feet because the location was uphill from the town center and had been buried by sand carried by sea winds rather than by General Construction's bulldozers in 1956. Sand quickly refilled the hole. But in 2019, Tillamook High School students installed a three-sided, historical kiosk north of the parking lot, along Dike Road.[96] This chronicle joins these and other past efforts in making sure Bayocean, and what happened to it, is not forgotten.

CONCLUSION

Who to Blame

In the summer of 1906, when T. Irving Potter stood on Tillamook Spit's one-hundred-foot-high ridgeline, he was sure urbanites would pay top dollar to enjoy cool summers and experience the spectacular view of bay and ocean. He convinced his father, T. Benton, that developing Bayocean would add to his wealth.

T. Benton and his partner, Harkness Chapin, wisely waited until Elmer Lytle assured them that his Pacific Railroad and Navigation Company trains would shortly be delivering passengers to Tillamook. But the plan then set in motion allowed for no contingencies. After years of uninterrupted success selling city subdivisions, the partners believed they could not fail. That assumption and the miscalculations that followed were the first of many that would eventually lead to the resort's financial—and the spit's physical—demise.

The resort failed financially because it was too hard to reach. Reasonable construction costs, lot sales, and profitable resort operations all depended on Lytle's railroad. The railroad baron had assumed that laying tracks across the Coast Range and along the Pacific Coast would be more no more difficult than it had been in the Willamette Valley and that his short-term financing would hold out. He was wrong in both cases. As a result, the urbanites Potter and Chapin had counted on to pay top dollar for lots could not reach Bayocean Park in sufficient numbers until the competitive advantage of being first had been lost. Neither Potter nor Chapin had anticipated competitors building coastal resorts alongside Lytle's tracks as they were laid. Their views and hotels were not as spectacular as what Bayocean Park promised, but they were cheaper, easier to get to, and immediately available. Potter and Chapin's marketing had made urbanites impatient to enjoy summer vacations on the beach. As a result, the fortunes they and Lytle spent did them little good while benefiting the businesses of Tillamook County and connecting it to the rest of the world.

Bayocean Road could have at least partially offset the delay in rail transportation by enabling the growing number of urban automobile owners to reach Bayocean Park. But its delay was even greater—decades rather than years—because Potter and Chapin had underestimated the difficulty of building a road along the south end of Tillamook Bay. The money they spent paving resort streets was wasted. T. Irving's idea to speed guests to the resort on *Bayocean* was innovative and provided additional publicity, but few urbanites were willing to endure two rough bar crossings each way. So, building and operating the ship needlessly drained cash reserves. Tillamook County worked with receiver Sydney Vincent to lay the first sections of Bayocean Road, but as Bayocean property taxes dwindled, so did the county's interest. By the time the commissioners made the deal with the Tillamook-Bayocean Company that enabled completion of the road in the late 1920s, it was too late to save the resort.

It is tempting to think lot buyers should have realized that the grand resort promised was too good to be true, but Potter and Chapin may very well have pulled it off if everything had gone as planned. Metropolitan dailies ran editorials and articles as well as ads assuring readers of the success of the venture. And not one Oregon newspaper questioned T. Benton about his Reis Tract water debacle. Given how things turned out, if skeptical media coverage had ended Bayocean Park before it started, that would have served the Potters and Chapin as much as their readers.

When some lot buyers did start questioning the resort's viability in 1911, others pushed back despite the fact that the grand hotel and other promised resort facilities had not been built. The thirty-one lot owners who put up cabins between 1911 and 1915 certainly thought spending summers on the spit worth the prices they had paid. They had no way to know erosion would start taking these homes a decade later. The people who bought and built homes in the 1940s were fully aware of erosion because they were taking advantage of the bargain prices that resulted from it. Some, like the Currins, could afford to treat the money spent as rent for enjoying extraordinary summer vacations for a few years. Others thought the cabins placed distant from dune gaps on the bay side would be safe. They were correct, in that none were lost during the 1952 blow-out. But the south inlet devoured them as it expanded north.

The working-class families and retirees who lived on Bayocean year-round could not afford to be as sanguine as summer visitors. They chose to live near the town center, where the spit was wider. Natatorium Gap seldom breached because it was higher in elevation that the others, which is why Del and Grace Gilkison built Kaaren Anne Kottages there. If a breakwater had been built sooner, they might all still be there. But by the time it went up four years later, looters and vandals had ravaged the vacant homes. And erosion of the gap north of the town center forced the Corps to bury what remained in order to prevent future breaches.

Like many others, Francis Mitchell believed Bayocean Park would eventually be built as promised. His mistake was betting his and Ida's life savings on it. The stress of dealing with construction delays, design changes, Harkness Chapin's survey error, and The Mitchell's failure to provide sufficient income would have been enough to cause Francis's mental breakdown. Whatever did, his paranoia grew worse without treatment. He imagined a succession of enemies conspiring to deny him the promised grand resort because that allowed him to deny the reality that it would never be built. Increasingly erratic behavior caused strife among neighbors and made it impossible for a nice enough resort to flourish. Francis Mitchell's story is a testament to the suffering caused by mental illness.

Ironically, if the grand resort promised had been built, erosion would have destroyed more than it did. The six-story Hotel Bayocean would have been deconstructed along with the Annex. The Coney Island-style amusement park would have dwarfed everything else destroyed by the Corps. Twenty-eight miles of perfectly paved streets would have motivated hundreds if not thousands of people to build homes instead of fifty-nine, and only those built north of 15th Avenue (where hills begin) would have survived.

Consequently, the only assumptions and miscalculations that really matter are those that caused the north jetty to be built without a south jetty to match. If both had been constructed at the same time, folks would still be enjoying bay and ocean views from their homes along Clarke Street, staying in their favorite bungalows, or renting rooms at Kaaren Ann Kottages, Bayside Inn, or the Annex. The Natatorium pool would be busy, especially on chilly days. And The Mitchell would be selling groceries and incidentals to resort guests.

Feuding among ports is partially to blame for Bayocean's physical demise. If they had worked cooperatively rather than competing and gaming port creation rules, they would have had enough money for two jetties. But the courts denied the Port of Tillamook's expansion and the first Port of Bayocean's right to exist, and the Port of Bay City did not have enough on its own. So, its commissioners asked the Corps if a single, north jetty might work. Later, the president of their successors, John Bozorth, reiterated their dependence on Corps engineers to answer that question in his letter to General Bixby, Chief of Engineers. By attaching that letter to his approval notice, Bixby accepted that responsibility.

Corps engineers would not have built a single jetty if they thought it could destroy the spit. They were career Army officers sworn to serve their country, and their internal deliberations show their intent to do the right thing. Pacific Division Engineer Lt. Colonel Biddle expressed reservations, but they had to do with whether a single jetty would *work*. If he had known that the north jetty would maintain the bay inlet channel as well as it did, he would have fully supported the north jetty. What no engineer brought up was the possibility of erosion because they believed jetties did not impact littoral drift. That was an assumption based on anecdotal reports that academic studies later showed to be incorrect.

The Corps should have reconsidered north jetty construction when Barview was wiped out in 1915, so soon after construction started. At the least, it meant that oceanographic processes were at play that they did not understand. Twenty years later, a few Corps engineers started suspecting the north jetty was causing Bayocean's erosion, but their commanding officers held firm on the natural forces theory. They could do nothing about the problem at that point anyway for, as they regularly pointed out, the Corps had no congressional mandate to protect private property, even if its own actions caused the threat.

Federal courts delivered the coup de grâce in pointing out that the law did not care if the Corps of Engineers caused Bayocean's physical destruction. In 1923, one judge rejected Southern Pacific Railroad's private takings approach after its tracks were ripped out by the storm that destroyed Barview. In 1956, another judge told Lyman Latourette that he had no legal claim to the return of sand trapped behind the north jetty. Whether the law cares or not, building the north jetty without a south jetty to match caused the erosion that destroyed Bayocean. The Corps of Engineers approved its construction because their engineers assumed they knew more about natural forces than they did. The sea destroyed Bayocean, but the hubris of man is to blame.

ACKNOWLEDGMENTS

I had no idea that Tillamook Spit once hosted a resort town called Bayocean, or that its landscape had changed dramatically over the last century, until I happened upon an exhibit at TCPM in the fall of 2014. Having seen no evidence of the streets, houses, and facilities depicted in the photos while hiking the spit in the past, I was non-plussed.

After returning home, I found Bayocean mentioned on several websites and then purchased a copy of Bert and Margie Webber's *Bayocean: The Oregon Town That Fell Into the Sea*, which they all cited. It was a fascinating read, but I came away with many questions. So, I drove an hour and a half back to the museum from my home in Portland. There, Ruby Fry-Matson showed me the Bayocean folders and boxes in her basement research library. What I read provided answers to some questions but raised more of them, so I kept returning. Eventually, Ruby allowed me to scour every cabinet, shelf, and drawer. If I could not find an item I learned of elsewhere, Ruby always did. When she casually mentioned uncurated boxes in the attic one day, I asked and got permission from Gary Albright (museum director at the time) to peruse them. TCPM's unpublished books, personal journals, family histories, recorded interviews, scrapbooks, subject files, Bayocean Park lot contracts, photographs, and albums provided many pieces to the Bayocean puzzle. They appear regularly in the notes that follow. I am indebted to Gary and Ruby for their trust and support. Tillamook County is lucky to have this institution and its staff safeguarding its memories.

Unlike the research I did (to complement that which my father, Art Sutherland, had already done) before writing *Calvin Tibbets: Oregon's First Pioneer*, I had no interest in authoring a book about Bayocean initially. However, I did want to share stories that were not covered or that contradicted what I had read elsewhere. So, I created and started posted articles to www.bayocean.net.

Tracking down every building moved from the spit before it became an island in 1952 was my first obsession. Not long after posting a story about locating the last of them, in the spring of 2015, Grant McOmie asked me to coordinate a day on the spit so he could produce a story for KGW-TV. Spending time with Grant, videographer Jeff Kastner, and surviving Bayocean residents energized me.[1] The broad interest generated by the program convinced me that the Bayocean story held appeal beyond Tillamook County and that additional research could serve a higher purpose than scratching my curiosity itch.

Interviewing individuals who had lived on Bayocean as children was the most interesting aspect of my research. Barbara (Schlegel) Bennett, Sue (Bagley) Barr, Perry Reeder Jr., Mike Watkins, Phyllis (Locke) Anderson, Jesse Vance Mason Jr., Jerry Schlegel, Donny Meyers, and Joann (Dolan) Steffey graciously shared their memories, photos, and memorabilia. Joann Steffey's nephew, Tom Williams, jumpstarted www.bayocean.net by promoting it on Tillamook County Facebook history groups. Interest and feedback from the groups' members motivated me to continue. Sadly, Barbara, Vance, Donny, Joann, and Tom have since died. Others who shared their photos and family archives were Bonnie (Reddekopp) Lawrence, Lorraine Eckhardt, Joyce (Sweger) Loftis, Dale Webber, and John Norrman Dobbins, Arleta Potter's grandson.

Hunting for every tidbit of information about Calvin Tibbets had taught me the value of county records and the critical role staff play in accessing and understanding them. All Tillamook County officials were helpful. They included County Clerk Tassie O'Neil, Chief Deputy Clerk Christy Biggs, Library Directors Sara Charlton (retired) and Sarah Beeler, retired Board of Commissioners Chief of Staff Paul Levesque, County Surveyors Dan McNutt (retired) and Mike Rice, County Assessor Denise Vandecoevering, Chief Deputy Assessor KaSandra Larson, and Geographic Information Services Analyst Wendy Schink.

Elsewhere in Oregon, reference services managers Scott Daniels at the Oregon Historical Society and Layne Sawyer (retired) at the Oregon State Archives and several coworkers exceeded their official duties in service and attitude. Karen Feickert, Multnomah County Circuit Court Records Supervisor, helped me find, retrieve, and attain copies of thousands of pages of archived legal records. Multnomah County Library staff always seemed eager to find and, if necessary, borrow the most esoteric of documents.

NARA holds historical records that are no longer needed by federal agencies. Locating those related to Bayocean led me to the iconic main building in Washington, DC, and branch offices in College Park, MD, Seattle, WA, and San Bruno, CA. Staff were consistently knowledgeable. Ken Hawkins (retired), who literally wrote the book on how to navigate NARA's collections, guided me through the labyrinth at times.[2]

In the fall of 2018, Jule Gilfillan asked for help with an Oregon Field Guide program she wanted to produce for Oregon Public Broadcasting TV. On our first day on the spit, I met Heidi Moritz, a coastal engineer with the Army Corps of Engineers. She answered my questions as well as Jule's and responded when I asked others later.[3] During the months that followed, Jule regularly called with "a quick question," as did OPB radio's Kristian Foden-Vencil later, when he later took an interest. Finding the answers to their questions usually required an extensive search of the twenty-five gigabytes of data I had collected by then. That forced me to admit that I had spent more time collecting than analyzing, and it led to a growing sense of obligation to share more of what I had learned. Bert and Margie Webber had published the last of their books in 1989, so an update was in order. I felt that a chronological structure would tell the Bayocean story better than a topical one, but I knew that would make writing it more difficult, so I procrastinated.

In March 2019, three-time OSU Press author and retired journalist Greg Nokes introduced me to Associate Director Tom Booth. He was interested enough to introduce me to Acquisitions Editor Kim Hogeland. Previously, I had received contract offers from other publishers, but the prospect of spending a year writing seemed too daunting. The possibility of being published by OSU Press—whose books I had enjoyed reading for decades—was enough to get me started. If I had known that it would take three years and three drafts to pass muster with Kim, I probably would not have, but I am glad I did. Though we parted ways before the end, I will always appreciate Tom having lit the spark that got me writing and Kim's guidance.

Jonathan Allan, Paul Komar, John Byrne, and Thomas Terich—all affiliated with OSU's School of Oceanography at some point in their careers—helped me better understand the geomorphological processes that created and destroyed Tillamook Spit. I also asked Komar, Byrne, and Terich about the roles they played in figuring out what happened. David Gene Lewis, anthropologist, and assistant professor at OSU, shared his Native American perspective on the spit's prehistory and pre-Bayocean Park history.[4]

Professionals who provided content feedback, in addition to Kim Hogeland, were her anonymous reviewers, Greg Nokes, poet and senior editor at *Bear Deluxe* Casey Bush, and OPB producer Jule Gilfillan. I considered every comment whether I liked them or not and implemented consensus views. But when their recommendations conflicted, which seemed more often than not, I followed Ricky Nelson's "Garden Party" advice and pleased myself.

Late in this process, I was fortunate to meet Lisa Jensen, a writer working on a novel about Bayocean. Her copyediting skills and keen interest in the subject matter complemented the work previously done by Jaya Chatterjee of Reedsy. Bill Sullivan and Steve Forrester, who have both published and authored books, gave me tips on preparing mine for print and distribution.

Lastly, I am grateful to the friends and family whose words of encouragement helped me get through difficult periods: my neighbor Diane Holland, my brothers Dean and Bryan Sutherland, my sister-in-law Roxane Sutherland, my friend Eleanor Culhane, my mother Vi Sutherland and—until his death in December 2020—my father Art Sutherland. In the days before he died, I thanked my father for introducing me to historical research via Calvin Tibbets in 2012 and let him how much I had enjoyed sharing that part of our lives.

NOTES

My notes section is longer and my bibliography shorter than is typical because I used mostly primary sources. In some instances, no secondary sources were available. And too many of those I did find relied on anecdotes and—given the fickle nature of memory and personal agendas—conflicted in discussing the same event citing different individuals. When secondary sources did agree, it was often because they were repeating falsehoods that had become accepted as truth by repetition. Obsessed as I was with understanding exactly what happened to Bayocean, I looked to court and government records to resolve discrepancies between multiple sources when they were available. With each pass through the draft, I became more familiar with each person, place, and event, so I was better able to parse things out.

As problematic as newspaper articles are, for the reasons just mentioned, they were often the only source of information available. So, I used them extensively. Though it is now acceptable to omit newspaper section and page numbers, I included them because my eyes have spent too many hours squinting at deteriorating microfilms looking for a story cited only by date to inflict that on others. NARA citations may seem labyrinthine, but anyone who has looked for one of its holdings, or does so in the future, will appreciate them. On the other hand, to limit the word count—which nearly every reviewer recommended—I provided less information on sources I knew readers could find easily; the best example being web pages. Ephemeral as they are, I saw no reason to provide the date each was last viewed or updated. If a hyperlink becomes dysfunctional, or a reader wants to see exactly what a web page looked like when this book was published, it should be available on the Wayback Machine at https://archive.org.

Most reviewers also wanted me to get to the Bayocean story more quickly. As interesting as Tillamook Spit's prehistory was to me, working through an entire first chapter was frustrating for them. So, I transferred Tillamook Indian tales of how South Wind created the spit and an entire village moved there after taking revenge on Wild Woman to articles at www.bayocean.net and cited them where appropriate. The same is true of the first encounter between Tillamook Indians and white sailors, early American land and water surveys, and white settlement.

My first draft included too many numbers and decimal places for many reviewers, so I removed some and rounded off others. Dollar figures ending in multiple zeros should be considered approximate regardless of whether *about* or other modifiers precede them. I provided inflation-adjusted numbers only so often as necessary to provide context during each era of Bayocean's history. Unless stated otherwise, I used the Consumer Price Index calculator at https://www.measuringworth.com because readers are most familiar with it and the valuations are conservative relative to other calculators offered there. The most recent numbers available were for 2022.

NOTES

During the late nineteenth and early twentieth centuries men were often referred to by their first two initials. I went along with that for individuals who appear once or twice. However, for those who appear more often, I used their first or nick names if I could find them—the first initial and middle names in the case of the Thomas Potters. I did this to help readers feel some sense of familiarity with the Bayocean players I came to know so well over the years. Married women were almost always referred to then as *Mrs.* followed by their husbands' first and last names with their first names left out. If I was able to determine a woman's first name, I used it even if she only appears once. I set maiden names in parentheses.

I dealt with the problem of Bayocean facility name changes by bringing them together in the index. What to call Bayocean's main hotel presented a bigger dilemma. When the Potters dropped plans to build Hotel Bayocean and refitted the Annex to serve guests rather than employees, they began advertising the latter as the former. Receivers continued the practice, as evidenced by a postcard in the Bayocean Miscellaneous folder at TCPM stamped August 18, 1918. Newspaper coverage vacillated, suggesting that editors were conflicted on how to deal with this. Eventually, they resolved the problem by referring to the Annex as "the Bayocean hotel," which morphed into "Bayocean Hotel." Bert and Margie Webber used the latter, but I was not comfortable calling the building something its proprietors never did. I settled on the use of Annex because that is the natural truncation of the original name. When referring to it and other Bayocean resort facilities, I capitalized their names whether preceding them with Bayocean or not.

Except for widely known acronyms and initials, I used them sparingly in the main text but extensively in the notes. They include: BNC for the Bayocean Natatorium Company, FERA for the Federal Emergency Relief Administration, NARA for the National Archives and Records Administration, OSRC for the Oregon State Relief Committee, OSU for Oregon State University, PCRC for the Potter-Chapin Realty Company, PRNC for the Pacific Railway and Navigation Company, TBC for the Tillamook-Bayocean Company, TBPRC for the T. B. Potter Realty Company, TCPM for Tillamook County Pioneer Museum, and WPA for the Works Progress Administration. The United States, Oregon, and Tillamook are the federal, state, and local governments mentioned, respectively, unless noted otherwise.

While Bayocean existed as a resort, the Tillamook County Board of Commissioners operated differently than today. Two commissioners served purely administrative roles, as all three do today. The third member was referred to back then as the Tillamook County Judge because he had some legal duties. That is why some sources cited refer to them as the Tillamook County Court in To avoid confusing them with the Tillamook County Circuit Court, which deals with criminal and most civil cases on behalf of the state of Oregon, I chose to call them commissioners.

NOTES

Introduction

1. "Heavy Seas Do Damage at Bayocean," *Tillamook Headlight-Herald*, December 18, 1941, 1; Russell Hoover to Bert Webber, March 2, 1973, Bayocean Gov. Doc. box, Webber Research Archives, Tillamook County Library (TCL).
2. William R. Coats testimony, Bayocean Preliminary Exams & Survey, File 7250, Box 175, Civil Works Project Files, 1902-1968, POR-81, RG 77, NARA, Seattle, WA; the Coatses' 1940 Christmas card, Bayocean Miscellaneous folder, TCPM; "Attractive Beach Home Completed on Tillamook Coast," photo caption, *Oregonian*, May 22, 1932, sec. 2, 2; 1933 and later Tillamook County Assessment Rolls Vol. 3, Tillamook County Courthouse, Basement Tax Vault (county and location assumed hereafter).The Fo'c's'le was located on Lot 43 in Block 45. The *Oregonian* article reported $9,000 as its cost; Coats told the Corps it was $10,000.
3. Dorthea Hahn Mills, "Bayocean," *Oregon Coast Magazine*, November/ December 1994, 40. Though Dorthea does not mention it, the newspaper sketch shows a room above the garage.
4. W. R. Coats testimony, NARA 7250.
5. Hoover to Webber, March 2, 1973; 1940 Census, Bayocean Precinct, Tillamook, Oregon; "Ocean on Rampage," *Oregon Journal*, December 18, 1941, 14; "Marcellus Cottage Torn Down," *Tillamook Headlight-Herald*, December 25, 1941, 3.
6. Jerry Sutherland, "Bayocean Homes and Their Fate," https://www.bayocean.net/2022/10/bayocean-homes-and-their-fate.html. My tally does not include residences built on the Cape Meares section of Bayocean Park. Some of them will be mentioned in the text, as will all of those built on the spit.
7. Jerry Sutherland, "The Tillamook Indians and Bayocean," https://www.bayocean. net/2015/03/the-tillamook-indians-and-bayocean.html.
8. For a list of previous works on Bayocean, see: Jerry Sutherland, "Outside Reading," https://www.bayocean.net/p/outside-reading.html.

Chapter 1

1. "Thomas Irving Potter in His Variety," *Spectator*, May 18, 1912, 10.
2. 1900 Census, Los Angeles Ward 3, Los Angeles, California; California Death Index, 1940-1997, https://familysearch.org/ark:/61903/1:1:VGTV-3KH. Portland City Directories (Portland: R.L. Polk and Company, 1901 to 1914); Carl Abbott, *The Great Extravaganza: Portland and the Lewis and Clark Exposition* (Portland: Oregon Historical Society Press, 2004), 59; 1900 Census, Ward 1, Duluth, Minnesota.
3. Plat Book 271, 29; Plat Book 308, 27; Plat Book 308, 29; and Plat Book 326, 11; all Multnomah County. The first Arleta Park is in North Portland. The other three are in the Arleta Neighborhood of Southeast Portland. Arleta's descendants said she disliked her father naming things after her so much that

she changed her name to Natalia as an adult. Indeed, that is how she signed her name to deeds after marrying John Dobbins. However, Natalia is the name on her birth certificate, so she was rejecting a childhood nickname. But to avoid confusion, I will always refer to her as Arleta: Bert Webber and Margie Webber, *Bayocean: The Oregon Town That Fell into the Sea* (Medford, OR: Webb Research Group, 1989), 194; California Birth and Death Records, 1800-1994, https://www.familysearch.org/ark:/ 61903/1:1:QGLW-8QM6.

4. Articles of Incorporation of Reis Tract Real Estate Company, File No. 39277, California State Archives; Real Estate—City—For Sale, *San Francisco Call*, February 21, 1904, 38; Jerry Sutherland, "T. B. Potter's Success Before Bayocean," https://www.bayocean.net/2016/10/t-b-potters-success-before-bayocean.html; Petition to Change Name to T. B. Potter Realty Company, September 30, 1904, File No. 39277, California State Archives; "Plan Gigantic Resort," *Oregonian*, June 29, 1907, 10.
5. *Salinas Daily Index*, March 1, 1905, 1, 3; Map Book K, 13, Santa Clara County; Arleta Park, Map Book 4, 5; Addition to Arleta Park, Map Book 4, 17; Map Book 4, 30, Map Book 4, 36, Map Book 6, 37, and Map Book 7, 6; all San Mateo County; Plat Book 14, 41, Kansas City.
6. "Thomas Irving Potter in His Variety"; The Yacht 'Bayocean' Arrived Sunday," *Tillamook Headlight*, June 22, 1911, 6.
7. Joseph E. Taylor III, *Persistent Callings* (Corvallis: Oregon State University Press, 2019), 25; Paul Michael Clock, *The Saga of Pacific Railway & Navigation Co.: Punk Rotten & Nasty* (Portland: Corbett Press, 2000), 25. With the help of Clock's map on page 15, Tillamook native John Chaix, and Google Maps, I learned that, east of Milepost 28, the Wilson River Highway follows a completely different route than the old wagon trail did. In March 2020, after driving and hiking it in stages, I can understand why it was such a challenge to navigate.
8. Clock, *Punk Rotten & Nasty*, 25, 26, 45. By 1905, Lytle had purchased lines run from Portland to Hillsboro in 1871 from the Southern Pacific Railroad: "Railroad History of Portland, Or," Pacific Railroad Preservation Association, http://www.sps700.org/gallery/essays/portlandrailroadhistory.shtml.
9. Caroline C. Dobbs, *Men of Champoeg: A Record of the Lives of the Pioneers Who Founded the Oregon Government* (Portland: Metropolitan Press, 1932), 17-23; Webley and Mary Hauxhurst family folder, TCPM.
10. Ada M. Orcutt, *Tillamook: Land of Many Waters* (Portland: Binfords & Mort, 1951), 22-27; David G. Lewis (assistant professor, Oregon State University, and author of *Quartux: Journal of Critical Indigenous Anthropology*, https://ndnhistoryresearch.com) e-mail to author, November 23, 2019; Sauter and Johnson, *Tillamook Indians of the Oregon Coast*, 173.
11. Hauxhurst Homestead Serial Patent #843, https://glorecords.blm.gov/details/cdi/default.aspx?doc_id=1445208&sid=jx1215tz.ioe; Tillamook County Deed Record 6, 240, Tillamook County Courthouse, Clerk's Record

Room (county and location assumed hereafter); Hauxhurst family folder. For more on the Hauxhursts, other homesteaders, their land grants, and the community of Barnegat they established, see: Jerry Sutherland, "Barnegat Before Bayocean," https://www.bayocean.net/2015/04/barnaget-before-bayocean.html.

12. Homestead File No. 5474, Absalom B. Hallock, April 20, 1888, Oregon City Land Office, Records of the Bureau of Land Management, RG 49, NARA, Washington, DC; Betty Watkins, "Bayocean Post Office Gives Up Name Following Transfer to Cape Meares," *Oregonian,* April 5, 1953, 22.
13. Patricia Failing, "Absalom Barrett Hallock (C. 1822-1892)," https://oregon encyclopedia.org/articles/hallock_absalom; William John Hawkins, "Absalom B. Hallock. Architect, Engineer, Surveyor (1826-1892)," *Portland Friends of Cast-Iron Architecture Newsletter* 18 (1981); *Oregon Statesman*, May 12, 1855, 3; *Oregon Statesman*, September 1, 1862, 3; *Oregon Statesman*, March 23, 1863, 2; "Common Council," *Oregonian*, July 10, 1878, 3.
14. A. B. Hallock Journal, December 15, 1880–July 6, 1882, A 035, University of Oregon Special Collections and University Archives (SCUA); Absalom Hallock Journal, May 1, 1890–August 6, 1890, Absalom Hallock Papers, Mss 92, OHS; Paul D. Komar, *The Pacific Northwest Coast: Living with the Shores of Oregon and Washington* (Durham, NC: Duke University Press, 1997), 73; Harry Cotter to Absalom Hallock, September 16, 1892, Mss 92; Minutes of January 11, 1891, Tillamook County Court Journal A, OSA.
15. *Tillamook Headlight*, June 12, 1891; Barnegat Post Office Applications, Reports of Site Locations and Completed Geographical Information Forms, 1837-1950, Records of the Post Office Department, RG 28, NARA, Washington, DC; Watkins, "Bayocean Post Office"; "Another Pioneer Gone," *Tillamook Headlight*, November 3, 1892; John A. Biggs Pioneer Dies," *Tillamook Headlight-Herald*, January 15, 1942, 5; Lewis A. McArthur and Lewis L. McArthur, *Oregon Geographic Names*, 7th ed. (Portland: Oregon Historical Society Press, 2003), 767.
16. Jerry Sutherland, "Cape Meares Landslides," https://www.bayocean.net/2015/05/cape-meares-landslides.html.
17. Edward Hallock Probate Case File 738, Tillamook County, OSA; Deed Record 6, 308.
18. Deed Record 6, 313-314; George W. Elliott v. Scott Bozorth and John Waterman, Oregon State Supreme Court Case No. 6805, OSA; Bozorth family folder, TCPM.
19. Sutherland, "The Tillamook Indians and Bayocean"; Jerry Sutherland, "Kincheloe Point," https://www.bayocean.net/2015/04/ kincheloe-point.html. Deed Record 6, 376. Historical nautical charts can be found by searching "Tillamook Bay" at https://historicalcharts.noaa.gov.

20. "Withdrawal for Tillamook Bay Jetties," Secretary of War E. A. Hitchcock, Serial No. OR-21738, filed with Oregon State Bureau of Land Management January 28, 1901; "Tillamook Bay and Bar, Oregon," House Document #185, 50th Congress, 1st Session, 1888.
21. The Kansas City sales office was open through 1911 because of a 1908 addition: *Kansas City, Missouri City Directory*, (St. Louis, MO: Hoye City Directory Company, 1907); Plat Book 15, 8, Kansas City. Though using *salesmen* is considered sexist today, they were always referred to as such by sources and I found no mention of a female salesperson. Bert and Margie Webber present evidence suggesting T. Benton acquired his own Pullman to facilitate rail travel across his empire, but I am not convinced. He was such an aggressive marketer, I am sure he would have painted *Bayocean Park* in huge letters on the sides of the Pullman and featured photos of it in promotional material: Webber and Webber, *Bayocean*, 189-191.
22. "Plan Gigantic Resort"; "Right Up Next to Del Monte," *Oregon Journal*, June 18, 1907, 9; Water Rights Appropriation by H. L. Chapin, Water Rights Book 1-1, 56-61, Tillamook County Clerk; Jerry Sutherland, "Rewitness Card # 56," https://www.bayocean.net/2015/02/rewitness-card-56.html. Pacific Oyster Company now operates on land covering the old pier. The *Oregon Journal* article is the first instance of *Bayocean Park* being mentioned in the press. It was attributed to "Journal Special Services—Bay City," which was most likely Scott Bozorth. He had managed the *Oregon Journal* before moving to Portland, and the article highlighted the many ways in which Bay City would benefit from Bayocean Park promotion and construction.
23. Potter-Chapin Realty Company Articles of Incorporation, File No. 11918, OSA; Deed of Dedication of Bayocean Park, Bayocean Park subdivision packet, Tillamook County Surveyor. The Tillamook County Clerk's copy of the dedication on pages 21 to 22 of Deed Record 9 incorrectly labels it "Bay Ocean Park," whereas the original at the surveyor's office labels it "Bayocean Park." Incorrect spelling of the subdivision was evident from the start.
24. "Plan Gigantic Resort."
25. William Eastman et al. v. Potter-Chapin Realty Company et al., Multnomah County Circuit Court Case No. 46258; "Bayocean Park," advertisement, *Oregonian*, July 28, 1907, sec. 3, 7; "Scenic Views at Bay Ocean," Accession Number 99.106, TCPM. I have print and digital copies of twelve brochures produced through 1911. I am sure there were more.
26. *Bayocean Park* (Portland: Potter-Chapin Realty Company, 1907), https://digital.osl.state.or.us/islandora/object/osl:33339; "Right Up Next to Del Monte"; "Fine Hostelry for Bayocean," *Oregon Journal*, August 4, 1907, 20. Hotel Del Monte continues to flourish as Hermann Hall, part of the Naval Postgraduate School. See: "Historic Hotel Del Monte Tour Guide," https://libguides.nps.edu/hoteldelmontetour/architecture. Hotel Del Monte

now hosts the Naval Postgraduate School: Dudley Knox Library, "Naval Postgraduate School," https://library.nps.edu/hotel-del-monte.

27. *Bayocean Park*; "Right Up Next to Del Monte"; "Fine Hostelry for Bayocean."
28. Deed Record 7, 473; Jerry Sutherland, "Bayocean Park's First Sale," https://www.bayocean.net/2015/09/bayocean-parks-first-sale.html; "P" Direct and Indirect Indexes to Deeds; Register for Contract 631, Bay Ocean Lot Contracts, Accession No. 79.210, TCPM. R. L. Durham paid $6 per month at six percent interest on $450 for Lot 29 in Block 44 from September 3, 1907, to January 18, 1916. His deed was recorded on March 7, 1916.
29. "Reality Sold on 'Show Me' Plan," *Oregon Journal*, September 29, 1907, 23; "Put Your Finder on the Lot You Want!" *Oregon Journal*, September 22, 1907, sec. 5, 54; "$1,000 Reward Will Be Paid to Anyone Proving That the Descriptions of Bayocean Park Published by Us Are Not Correct," advertisement, *Oregonian*, September 5, 1907, 5; "The Time Has Passed for Argument as to the Absolute and Natural Fitness of Bayocean Park as the Greatest Resort of the Pacific Coast," advertisement, *Oregon Journal*, September 12, 1907, 18.
30. "Encouraging Report," *Oregon Journal*, November 3, 1907, sec. 3, 10.
31. *Eastman v. Potter*; Jon R. Moen and Ellis W. Tallman, "The Panic of 1907," https://www.federalreservehistory.org/essays/panic-of-1907; Clock, Punk, Rotten & Nasty, 26, 46.
32. Brevities, *Chemawa American*, November 15, 1907, 7; "Skyscraper Is Rapidly Filling Up with Tenants," *Oregon Journal*, February 2, 1908, sec. 5, 5; "$150 Found at Bayocean Park," *Oregon Journal*, February 23, 1908, sec. 5, 8; "Bayocean Park's Outlook," *Oregonian*, September 27, 1908, 11.
33. "Buy in Bayocean Park," *Spokesman Review* (Spokane, WA), January 28, 1908, 9; "Prominent Men of Spokane and Portland in Tillamook," *Tillamook Herald*, March 24, 1908, 1; Personal Mention, *East Oregonian*, July 24, 1908, 5. PCRC did not discuss lots repossessed publicly; they were accounted for in net sales.
34. Clock, *Punk, Rotten & Nasty*, 45, 57, 91. Having hiked through and across some of the PCRC tunnels and trestles of the Oregon Coast Range, I am amazed it took only two and a half years to get the job done. It was Lytle's fault for making promises impossible to keep.
35. "Views of Bayocean at Tillamook Bay Oregon" (Potter-Chapin Realty Company, 1909).
36. "$742,840 Worth of Property in Bayocean Has Already Been Sold at the Present Low Prices," advertisement, *Oregonian*, May 30, 1909, sec. 4, 10.
37. "Gearhart Park," advertisement, *Oregonian*, May 2, 1909, sec. 4, 13; "Ocean View," advertisement, *Tillamook Herald*, October 7, 1909, 2; Jerry Sutherland, "Bayocean Park, Oceanview, and Cape Meares, https://www.bayocean.net/2015/03/cape-meares-and-bayocean.html. Higgins, like the Potters, had

trouble keeping his subdivisions' syllables joined. Oceanview is not to be confused with Oceanside, a community on the south side of Cape Meares.

38. "Hotel Bayocean: A Hotel Del Monte Brought to the Oregon Beach," advertisement, *Oregonian,* October 4, 1909, 10; "Real Accommodations for Surf Bathers-The Ocean Natatorium at Bayocean," *Oregonian*, October 5, 1909, 4; Jerry Sutherland, "Competition for Bayocean's Natatorium," https://www.bayocean.net/2015/05/competition-for-bayoceans-natatorium.html.
39. "Bayocean Park," *Tillamook Herald*, October 8, 1908, 5.
40. *Tillamook Herald*, June 17, 1909, 1, 4.
41. "Autoists Return from Tillamook," *Oregonian,* August 27, 1907, 7; "Bad Roads Held Men From Home," *Oregon Journal*, July 12, 1909, 2; "Oregon Legislators and Staff Guide," Oregon Secretary of State, http://sos.oregon. gov.
42. "What Bayocean Will Pay You," advertisement, *Oregon Journal*, July 4, 1909, 20; "Bayocean from a Woman's Viewpoint," advertisement, *Oregon Journal,* July 25, 1909, 9; "Oregon Beach Will Draw Many Guests," *Oregon Journal,* November 21, 1909, sec. 6, 8.
43. Elmer Allen, *The Diaries of Elmer Allen* (Tillamook: TCPM Publishing, 2018), 53-54, 301-30; "$742,840 Worth of Property"; Nellie's lots were numbers 2 and 3 in Block 33. 2.
44. "A Real Beach Resort for The Northwest at Last"; NARA M841, Roll 106.
45. "Bayocean Park Goes Ahead," *Oregonian,* November 3, 1907, sec. 3, 10.
46. "Bayocean Park," *Tillamook Herald*, October 8, 1908, 1.
47. Barnegat Precinct, Tillamook County, Official Register of Electors, 1908, OSA; Charles Oluf Olsen, "'Coney Island' for Clams," *Oregon Journal*, May 8, 1949, 1, 4, 5; "Logs Drift Out to Sea," *Tillamook Herald*, June 10, 1909, 1. Petition for Intervention of February 2, 1915, R. J. Marsh et al. v. T. B. Potter Realty Company et al., Multnomah County Circuit Court Case No. 35700A. The receivership case was referred to as Register Number E-2452 until it closed on May 25, 1931. I had all 2,758 microfilmed pages of it printed and digitized. It took a week to read, but I felt compelled to do so because there was so little news about Bayocean during those seventeen years.
48. Potter to Beebe, December 31, 1910, Bayocean Miscellaneous folder, TCPM; H. L. Chapin testimony, Folder 2, T. B. Potter Realty Company v. George S. Breitling, Oregon State Supreme Court Case No. 8739, OSA; Bertha Morgan family folder, TCPM; Deed Record 7, 534-535; Deed Record 9, 369. T. Benton bought another 265 tideland acres in 1910 and 1912: Deed Record 12, 536; Deed Record 23, 420-421.
49. Morgan family folder; Brevities, *Tillamook Headlight*, April 12, 1894. The federal government granted Barnegat School District No. 40 a piece of land at the foot of the cape where locals built a one-room schoolhouse in April 1894: Brevities, *Tillamook Headlight*, April 12, 1894. Land movement on the

northern slopes of Cape Meares is constant but so negligible for years at a time that people kept building roads, houses, and other structures in its path. Today, precise instruments track the slide's movement: Mike Rice (Tillamook County Surveyor) in discussion with the author, November 21, 2019.

50. Morgan family folder. Bertha does not give the year, but the building could not have been destroyed the following winter because crews would not have had time to start over and finish before May 1910: T. Benton Potter to Charles Beebe, May 6, 1910, Bayocean Miscellaneous folder, TCPM.

51. "Good Times! Fine Weather! Rapid Progress!" *Oregonian* , November 11, 1908, sec.3, 9; Round About Town, *Tillamook Herald*, August 5, 1909, 5; Photos 888 and 890, Album 1, TCPM; "A Thousand Wonders At Bayocean," *Oregon Journal*, June 11, 1911, sec. 7, 3; NARA M841, Roll 106; "Fourth Class Not Money-Order Office," *Daily Bulletin of Orders Affecting the Postal Service* 30 no. 8921 (1909).

52. Potter to Beebe, December 31, 1910, TCPM; T. B. Potter Realty Company v. Axel Anderson, Tillamook County Circuit Case No. 1502; "Good Times! Fine Weather! Rapid Progress!"; Morgan family folder. Sturgeon Channel was also called South Channel because it ran south along the bay side of Bayocean before angling east and across the south end of the bay to Tillamook. Potter and Chapin planned to convert the camp to a second tent city for guests when the workers left, which is why it was labeled as such on some maps. On April 19, 1910, the Weavers resided in Bayocean, but they had not registered as voters as of September 15, 1910: 1910 Census, Barnegat Precinct, Tillamook, Oregon; Barnegat Precinct, Tillamook County Official Register of Electors, 1908, 1910, OSA.

53. "Cargo of Equipment," *Oregon Journal*, August 15, 1909, 15; "Big Machines on Way to Bayocean," *Tillamook Herald*, August 19, 1; *Surf*, July 1912, 5; *Tillamook Herald*, September 9, 1909, 5; *$100,000 Worth of Machinery and What It Is Doing at Bayocean* (Portland: Potter-Chapin Realty Company, 1909), author's collection.

54. *Bayocean: The Resort Perfect* (Portland: T. B. Potter Realty Company, 1910), TCPM. A note in the brochure said, "the main hotel will not be finished until the development work of the resort would justify its completion."

55. "A Real Beach Resort for The Northwest at Last"; *Views of Bayocean*; "Bayocean's Improvements," advertisement, *Oregon Journal*, May 29, 1910, sec. 4, 12.

56. Water Appropriations, Bayocean Park Folder, Tillamook County Surveyor. For Coleman Creek's location, see: Jerry Sutherland, "Cape Meares Landslides," https://www.bayocean.net/2015/05/cape-meares-landslides.html

57. "Alleged 'Water Trust' Is Called to Explain," *San Francisco Call*, December 29, 1907, 64; "Reis Tract's Water Is Cut Off in Revenge," *San Francisco Call*, January 6, 1908, 4; "Reis Tract Now Is at Mercy of Fire," *San Francisco Call*, April 2, 1908, 5.

58. "Reis Tract Water Suit Is Defective," *San Francisco Call*, May 10, 1908, 19; Journal of Proceedings Board of Supervisors, *Recorder*, November 27, 1909, sec. 2, 7.
59. "City Lures T. B. Potter," *Oregonian*, January 20, 1910, 20; 1910 Census, 8th Precinct, Portland, Oregon. The house belonged to James McCracken. Its address changed from 819 Johnson to 2447 NW Johnson in 1931. In 2018, it was a three-unit condominium with 4,187 square feet plus 1,350 in the basement valued at $1,500,000: https://multcoproptax.com.
60. "City Lures T. B. Potter,"; Potter to Beebe, May 6, 1910; Reply filed June 5, 1916, Frances L. Potter, Trustee v. T. B. Potter Realty Company, et al., Judgement Role No. 11096, NARA, Seattle, WA; "Engineers Come to Improve Bayocean," *Oregon Journal*, January 30, 17; T. B. Potter Realty Company Articles of Incorporation, File No. 14444, OSA; Deed Record 16, 258-261; PCRC Articles of Incorporation.
61. Classifieds, *Oregonian*, February 9, 1910, 2; In Society, *Oregon Journal*, June 6, 1910, 4. The Chapin mansion was at 623 (later 1615) NE Wasco Street. In the 1950s, it served as the Battleship Oregon Museum, but was razed to build Holladay Park Plaza in 1968: Craig Addams's post and comments by Michael Long and Robert Mercer, September 6, 2016, Dead Memories Portland, https://www.facebook.com/groups/deadmemoriesportland/permalink/1369873023041515.
62. Map showing lots for sale, sold, and withdrawn as of February 1910, Folder 3, *TBPRC v. Breitling*; "What Bayocean Will Pay You," advertisement, *Oregon Journal*, July 4, 1909, 20; Deed Record 212, 602; "Bayocean to Halt Sand," *Oregonian*, April 1, 1912, 1.
63. "Time Flies," advertisement, *Oregon Journal*, June 26, 1910, 11; *Views of Bayocean*; *Eastman v. Potter*. "Says Bayocean Will Eclipse All," *Oregon Journal*, June 26, 1910, 19.
64. "Run to Ocean Did Much for Cause of Better Auto Roads," *Oregon Journal*, July 10, 1910, sec. 4, 8; "Tillamook County Celebrates," *Tillamook Herald*, July 8, 1910, 1; "Happy Auto Party Off for Coast," *Oregon Journal*, July 3, 1910, sec. 4, 9.
65. "Run to Ocean Did Much for Cause of Better Auto Roads"; "Tillamook County Celebrates." T. Irving would not have shown guests the large pipe run below and to the end of the pier that automatically discharged sewage into Tillamook Bay at high tide: Jerry Sutherland, "Bayocean Park Plumbing," https://www.bayocean.net/2015/06/bayocean-park-plumbing.html. Because Bayocean Park was completed in stages, and the grandest facilities promised were never built, it did not have a grand opening as such. Facility and seasonal openings were often called that for publicity purposes. However, it can be said that the resort first opened to the public on July 1, 1910.
66. Society, *Oregonian*, July 3, 1910, sec. 3, 8; A. G. Beals, "History of Bayocean for 63 Years," TCPM; Reply to Complaint of June 5, 1916, Frances L. Potter v. T. B. Potter Realty Company, Judgement Roll 10535, NARA, Seattle, WA;

Deed Record 15, 527. Fannie signed the deed *F. L. Potter, Vice-President* on July 18, 1910. It was for two lots Harkness bought for $900, so he was not completely estranged.

67. "'Best Trip Ever' Opinion of Party on Bayocean Run," *Oregon Journal*, July 6, 1910, 5; "Bayocean Tent City," advertisement, *Oregon Journal*, July 24, 1910, 9.
68. "Announce 1911 Bayocean Plans," advertisement, *Oregon Journal*, December 3, 1910, sec. 2, 10; Chapin testimony, Folder 2, *TBPRC v. Breitling*; *Hotel Bayocean* (Portland: J. O. Wrenn, Architect, n.d.), Folder 3, *TBPRC v. Breitling.*
69. Tillamook Bay Railway and Navigation Company Articles of Incorporation, File No. 15763, OSA; "Proposed Summer Travel Line Will Follow Shore for Nine Miles," *Oregon Journal,* March 7, 1911, 6; "New Railroad for Bay City," *Statesman Journal*, March 5, 1911, 1.
70. "3-Screw Vessel to Be Built Here," *Oregonian* , February 24, 1911, 12; *Eastman v. Potter;* Fritz Timmen, *Blow for the Landing: A Hundred Years of Steam Navigation on the Waters of the West* (Caldwell, Idaho: Caxton Printers, 1973), 189; US Department of Commerce, "Forty-Third Annual List of Merchant Vessels of the United States, with Official Numbers and Signal Letters, and Lists of Vessels Belonging to the United States Government, with Distinguishing Signals, for the Year Ended June 30, 1911," (1911): Part II, 137. "Yacht Bayocean Makes First Dip," *Oregonian* , May 25, 1911, sec. 2, 18. The *Oregonian* quoted the yacht's cost as $50,000, but court documents later provided the correct amount.
71. "Bayocean Makes Fast Trial Trip," *Oregonian,* June 13, 1911, 6; Marine Notes, *Oregonian,* June 16, 1911, 20; "Bayocean to Tillamook," *Oregon Journal*, June 19, 1911, 10; "Fast Swimmers from Over Coast Will Race Friday," *Oregon Journal*, June 5, 1911, 42.
72. E. C. Sammons, "Bayocean on Way," *Oregonian,* June 25, 1911, 18. The Bayocean channel was completed sometime after March 5th because the only channel then deep enough for seagoing ships led to the Bay City pier: "New Railroad for Bay City." The first ship to dock there was the *Toledo*: "Scenic Views at Bay Ocean."
73. "The Yacht 'Bayocean' Arrived Sunday"; "Newest of Resorts Awakens," *Oregonian,* July 9, 1911, sec. 3, 9; "A Thousand Wonders at Bayocean," *Oregon Journal*, June 11, 1911, sec. 7, 3.
74. "The Yacht 'Bayocean' Arrived Sunday"; "Newest of Resorts Awakens"; "A Thousand Wonders at Bayocean."
75. E. C. Sammons, "Bayocean on Way," *Oregonian,* June 25, 1911, 18.
76. "Exclusively Passenger Yacht Bayocean," advertisement, *Oregonian,* June 25, 1911, 12; Marine Notes, June 25, 1911, 20; Marine Notes, June 27, 1911, 18; "Contract Signed for Yacht", *Oregonian,* February 26, 1911, sec. 3, 14; Marine Notes, *Oregonian,* July 2, 1911, sec. 2, 18; "Newest of Resorts Awakens."

77. "The Realm of Music, *Oregon Journal*, June 18, 1911; "Newest of Resorts Awakens," *Oregonian*, July 9, 1911, sec. 3, 9; "A Thousand Wonders at Bayocean"; *Timely Hints for a Summer Vacation*, (Portland: Potter-Chapin Realty Company, 1911), TCPM. For more on Arthur Cavill, see: Gary Osmond, "Portland's 'Aquatic Pied Pinter'," *Oregon Historical Quarterly* 123, no. 2 (2022): 170-193.
78. A. G. Beals Lumber Co. Journal, July 3 - 5, 1927, TCPM; "Hotel Bayocean Annex Schematic," Photo Number 344, TCPM; T. B. Potter Realty Company v. Schmitt and Schmitt, Multnomah County Circuit Court Case No. 60385. TCPM's caption is incorrect. Wording on the "schematic" says, "T. B. Potter Realty Company Administrative Building." Its dimensions are 125 feet by 26 feet, so TBPRC made it larger than planned, but the number of rooms stayed the same: Francis D. Mitchell, File No. 20848, Oregon State Hospital (OSH).

Chapter 2

1. "Ask Receiver for Big Realty Co.," *Oregon Journal*, July 6, 1911, 10.
2. "Plaintiffs All Salem Men," *Oregonian*, July 7, 1911, 12; "Bayocean Buyers Ask for Receiver," *Oregonian*, July 7, 1911, 12; Arthur B. Emmons, II, *The Profession of Medicine: A Collection of Letters from Graduates of the Harvard Medical School* (Harvard Medical School, 1915), 165. This pay rate was for a graduate of 1907 with four years of experience.
3. "Bayocean Step Stamped as Plot," *Oregonian*, July 9, 1911, sec. 2, 8; *Eastman v. Potter.*
4. "Bayocean Suit Ousted as Unfair," *Oregonian*, July 23, 1911, sec. 2, 18.
5. "Over Sunday at Bayocean," advertisement, *Oregonian*, July 13, 1911, 3; "Music Galore at Bayocean," *Oregonian*, July 23, 1911, sec. 3, 9; "Bayocean Suit Ousted as Unfair."
6. "Crawford Is Blamed," *Oregonian*, July 20, 1911; "Bayocean Suit Ousted as Unfair."
7. Eastman v. Potter.
8. "Music Galore at Bayocean"; *Surf*, December 1911, 3; Alameda Personals, *Oakland Tribune*, April 8, 1911, 14; Bayocean Items, *Tillamook Headlight*, October 19, 1911, 5; *Surf*, January 1912, 1. On May 24, 1915, Harold Bennett identified Fannie Potter's cabin (owned by TBPRC), pictured in the *Surf* and elsewhere, as having been owned by Dr. Jack Goldman when he lived there in the 1940s. It was located on Lot 13 in Block 57: 1951 Tillamook County Assessment Roll, Vol. 3, 56.
9. Harold Bennett, in discussion with the author, September 29, 2021.
10. "Bayocean's Hospitality," *Tillamook Headlight*, March 23, 1911, 1; *Surf*, December 1911, 1; Driftwood Lodge Bayocean, Oregon–Paradise of the Beach (fourfold postcard, n.d.), Bayocean Miscellaneous folder, TCPM; Watkins interview by Hysmith; Deed Record 7, 533; "For Rent–An Ideal Summer Home," *Surf*, May 1912, 4; "Music Galore at Bayocean"; Caption,

Surf, May 1912, 2; "Bayocean Project Committee Named," *Oregon Journal*, April 23, 1915, 5. The Driftwood Lodge sat on Lots 14 to 16 in Block 26. Jones's cabin was on Lot 18 of Block 42. Fouch's lot was number 15 in Block 38: 1912 Assessment Roll, Vol. 5, 1-105 (Bayocean Park is the only subdivision in this volume).

11. I have not found a copy of the November 1911 *Surf*, but the December edition was Issue No. 2, and it refers to the earlier one.
12. Paul Levesque, "History of Port Districts on Tillamook Bay, Oregon," (2010), 11-17, https://www.bayocean.net/2015/06/paul-levesque.html; "Tillamook Bay and Bar, Oregon," House Document #349, 62nd Congress, 2nd Session, 1911.
13. "Tillamook Bay and Bar" 1911.
14. Ibid.
15. Ibid.
16. Ibid.
17. "Bayocean Will Start Work on South Jetty," *Tillamook Headlight*, September 21, 1911, 1; "Bayocean Port Turned Down," *Oregonian*, September 6, 1911, 6; "First Election Results in Favor of Organization"; *Surf*, December 1911, 1; State ex rel. Blum v. Port of Bayocean, 65 Ore. 506, 133 P. 85 (1913). The *Headlight* coverage of T. Irving's (whom they referred to as T. Benton) proposal to use Port of Bayocean funds to start work on a south jetty made it sound like a single north jetty was a bad idea proposed by Corps engineers.
18. State v. Port of Bayocean.
19. Levesque, "History of Port Districts," 11-14.
20. State v. Port of Bayocean.
21. Levesque, "History of Port Districts," 19-20, 24, 27-28.
22. "To City at Last," *Surf*, December 1911, 1, 4; Clock, *Punk, Rotten & Nasty*, 88, 91; "Working on the Railroad," Tillamook Forest Center placard; "More Comfort for Bayocean Guests Who De-Train at Bay City," *Surf*, January 1912, 3.
23. "Life in New Hands," *Oregonian*, January 4, 1912, 18; Clock, *Punk, Rotten & Nasty*, 46, 91. Brian McCamish, "Port of Tillamook Bay Railroad," http://www.brian894x4.com/POTBrailroad.html; Gail Wells, *The Tillamook: A Created Forest Comes of Age* (Corvallis: Oregon State University Press, 2003), 36.
24. "A Strong Factor," *Surf*, May 1912, 2; "Bayocean: Playground of the Pacific Northwest," State Library of Oregon, https://digital.osl.state.or.us/islandora/object/osl:84375; Jerry Sutherland, "Southern Pacific Railroad Brochures," https://www.bayocean.net/2016/04/southern-pacific-railroad-brochures.html.
25. "First to Entertain in the Open-Air Plunge," *Surf*, January 1912, 3; M. J. O'Donnell testimony, State ex rel. Blum v. Port of Bayocean, Oregon Supreme Court Case No. 7974, OSA; *Surf*, December 1911, 2.
26. "Miles Completed," *Surf*, April 1912, 1; "Building A Home?" advertisement, *Surf*, April 1912, 4; *Surf*, April 1, 1912, 4, 8; "What Did Things Cost in 1914?" https://www.reference.com/history/did-things-cost-

1914-b0182b0c72964792; "Bayocean Building is Active," *Oregonian*, March 5, 1912, 8.

27. "Bayocean Is Still Active," *Oregonian*, September 1, 1912, sec. 3, 9; "Road Work, Street Grading," *Oregon Journal*, December 29, 1912, sec. 7, 8; "Exciting Meeting at Court House," *Tillamook Herald*, March 4, 1913, 1, 4; Editorial, *Tillamook Herald*, July 11, 1913, 2; Editorial, *Tillamook Headlight*, August 12, 1913, 2.
28. Mitchell File, OSH; "Annual Calendar and Catalogue of the State Agricultural College of Oregon," ed. State Agricultural College of Oregon (Salem, Oregon: Frank C. Baker, State Printer, 1888-1889, 1889-1890, 1890-1891, 1891-1892). 1890-1891, 1891-1892 #82; "Twenty-six New Druggists," *Kansas City Times*, March 23, 1895, 2.
29. "Mrs. F. D. Mitchell Passes Away," *Tillamook Headlight-Herald*, December 31, 1953; Marriage License No. 15652, Office of Recorder of Deeds for Jackson County, Kansas City, Missouri. I was unable to find Ida's middle name.
30. *Meyers Brothers Druggist* 26, no. 1 (1905): 47, 221; For Sale–Real Estate, *Kansas City Star*, March 3, 1906, 11.
31. "Mrs. F. D. Mitchell Passes Away"; T. B. Potter Realty Company v. F. D. Mitchell, Tillamook County Circuit Court Case No. 1503, OSA. Initially, Francis and TBPRC give conflicting dates for his purchase of Lot A in Block 59, but they eventually agreed on July 30, 1907.
32. "Buildings Go Up on Every Side," *Oregonian*, March 23, 1908, 13; Olsen, "'Coney Island' for Clams." Francis arrived in Portland in 1907, not Bayocean Park. The pier he told Olsen his boat docked at was not completed until the spring of 1908. Jim O'Donnell testified to Mitchell's arriving in 1908: Folder 2, *TBPRC v. Breitling.*
33. John T. Medcalf Bayocean Diary (September 6, 1948, to January 20, 1949), Jack Medcalf Box, Accession No. 98.135, TCPM; "Whale Creates Excitement," *Oregon Journal*, November 1, 1908, sec. 2, 6.
34. Dr. George S. Breitling testimony, Folder 2, *TBPRC v. Breitling*; F. D. Mitchell testimony, Folder 2, *TBPRC v. Breitling;* 1910 Census, Barnegat Precinct, Tillamook, Oregon. I found no record of the Mitchells living anywhere but Bayocean Park between 1908 and 1912.
35. Breitling testimony, Folder 2, *TBPRC v. Breitling*; Mitchell testimony, Folder 2, *TBPRC v. Breitling;* 1910 Census, Barnegat Precinct, Tillamook, Oregon.; "$742,840 Worth of Property in Bayocean Has Already Been Sold at the Present Low Prices," advertisement, *Oregonian*, May 30, 1909, sec. 4, 10. The Mitchell lot was number 44 in Block 54. Francis must have moved The Mitchell during the first half of 1910 because he testified that he complained about it to T. Benton during a visit to Kansas City that year.
36. "Leaders Wanted," *Surf*, April 1912, 2; Classified Column, *Surf*, April 1912, 6; "Bay Drug Company," advertisement, *Surf*, July 1912, 4; Mitchell File, OSH.

37. "Will Erect New Hotel," *Surf*, May 1912, 1; Caption, *Surf*, May 1912, 2. Deed Record 23, 504-506; Deed Record 23, 559-561; Deed Record 24, 27-28. The lots were numbers 11 to 14 in Block 29.
38. Charles Carson to Tillamook County Historical Society, October 21, 1970, Charles Carson family folder, TCPM; Dean Collins, Among Our Neighbors, *Oregon Journal*, April 2, 1940, 8; postcard captioned "W. H. Baker and Bros, Bayocean, Ore" by H. R. Gregg in the possession of John Chaix, who said Gregg was a Bay City photographer between 1909 and 1915 in a Messenger exchange August 11, 2015; "The Amusement Pavilion," *Surf*, May 1912, 4.
39. "The Commercial Club," *Surf*, May 1912, 1; Classified Column, *Surf*, May 1912, 4; "In Readiness for Sport," *Surf*, May 1912, 1; Webber and Webber, *Bayocean*, 39; "Ripples," *Surf*, May 1912, 4; "District Boundary Board Minutes 1906-1921," 98-99, TCPM; 1917 Assessment Roll, Vol. 4, 115. Bayocean Scholl District No. 58's first schoolhouse was on Lot 16 in Block 30. For details on the Tillamook Indian village and the Wild Woman myth explaining it, their summer camps on the spit, and their first—deadly—encounter with whites, see: Sutherland, "The Tillamook Indians and Bayocean."
40. Caption, *Surf*, July 1912, 5; Ripples, *Surf*, July 1912, 5; The Personal Notes, *Surf*, July 1912, 9; Ben Trasher Contract No. 2193, July 15, 1909, TCPM; "Tennis," *Surf*, July 1912, 8. Completion of Lytle Road had ended the need for yacht *Bayocean* to deliver guests from Portland, and it was too large to haul rail passengers across the shallow bay from Garibaldi or Bay City: "Bayocean Hotels Crowded," *Oregonian*, July 28, 1912, sec. 3, 9.
41. Personal Mention, *Oregonian*, July 27, 1912, 4; "Thomas Irving Potter in His Variety," *Spectator*, May 18, 1912. Coin Manufacturing Machine Company Corporation, File No. 14936, Oregon State Corporate Division; Amended Complaint filed January 20, 1915, *Marsh v. TBPRC*; Deed Record 20, 487. Though relatively unknown then, Don Lee later gained notoriety for his work on Portland's Great Light Way: Dan Haneckow (Portland historian) Messenger exchanges with the author, June 5 and August 19, 2019.
42. "Elks Attract Bayoceaners," *Oregonian*, July 14, 1912, sec. 3, 5; Deed Record 27, 155. The treehouse lot was number 37 in Block 81.
43. Bayocean News, *Tillamook Headlight-Herald*, June 16, 1938, 7.
44. "Bayocean Is Still Active," *Oregonian*, September 1, 1912, sec. 3, 9; "Many Improvements At Bayocean," *Tillamook Herald*, August 12, 1913, 1; At The Seashore, *Oregon Journal*, August 9, 1913, 10; News Of The Beaches, *Oregon Journal*, July 19, 1914, sec. 5, 7; Beals, "History of Bayocean."
45. "Bitulithic O.K. Says Hyland," *Oregonian*, May 24, 1912, 4; "Bayocean to Fix Up," *Oregonian*, July 26, 1912, 7; "Bayocean Is Still Active"; Chapin testimony, Folder 2, *TBPRC v. Breitling*; Bayocean, *Oregon Journal*, July 20, 1912, 7; Deed Record 24, 128-130; Deed Record 30, 459-460; "Snug Harbor," *Surf*, May 1912, 2; "Ripples," *Surf*, May 1912, 4; Jerry Sutherland, "The First House to Go,"

https://www.bayocean.net/2016/04/the-first-house-to-go.html. Hyland's place was on Lot 47 in Block 61: Deed Record 25, 306. Clemens's house was on Lot 29 in Block 39. The Lockwood place was on Lot 29 of Block 43: 1913 Assessment Roll, Vol. 4, 111. Captain Hirsch never received a deed, so his place was built and sold while the lot was being purchased on a contract. It had to be the house that Jim O'Donnell bought from TBPRC because no other house was built on Bay Terrace for over twenty years. It was on Lot 26 in Block 57. The Burns cabin was on Lot 7 in Block 61: 1915 Assessment Roll, Vol. 4, 138. The *Surf* called it a "splendid cottage overlooking the sea."

46. *Bayocean* (Portland: Bayer's Clever Printing, 1912), Folder 3, *TBPRC v. Breitling*. Adding larger tents reduced the total number to fifty.
47. "Bay Ocean Well Patronized," *Oregonian,* August 5, 1913, sec. 5, 5." Conversion of the Administration Building explains why Mortimer Fouch never built the Hotel Sea Crest. He transferred the lots from the company to himself on July 1, 1915, and built a summer cottage there: Deed Record 44, 123; C. R. Moore, "Report on Beach Erosion Studies, Tillamook Bay, Oregon: With Reference to Bay Ocean," (Portland, OR: U.S. Army Corps of Engineers, 1940), Plate XIV.
48. *Tillamook Herald,* June 13, 1913, 2; Mike Arenaeult, "The Majestic Lake Lytle Hotel Was Ahead of its Time," Rockaway Beach Oregon Memories and History, March 21, 2021, https://www.facebook.com/groups/RockawayBeachOregonMemoriesandHistory/permalink/4048781805152547.
49. 1914 Assessment Roll, Vol. 4, 137, 139; 1918 Assessment Roll, Vol. 4, 122; Montagu Colmer and Charles Erskine Scott Wood, *History of the Bench and Bar of Oregon* (Portland: Historical Publishing Company, 1910), 236-237; "Bayocean News Items," *Tillamook Herald,* June 13, 1913; Swan Hawkinson testimony, Folder 2, *TBPRC v. Breitling*; "Mrs. Swan Hawkinson," *Tillamook Headlight-Herald,* August 23, 1956, 8; Swan Hawkinson, Oregon Death Index, 1903-1998, OSA; 1914 Assessment Roll, Vol. 4, 120; 1916 Assessment Roll Vol. 5, 127; "Tent City Attracts Throngs," *Oregonian,* July 27, 1913, 4. The Turner house was on Lot 49 in Block 61. The Hawkinson lot was number 10 in Block 44: Deed Record 26, 193-194. Arthur Smith's place was on Lot 10 in Block 42. The improvement value shifted to lot 11—owned by Eva DePeel—in 1917, which she and Arthur alternated paying taxes on until the improvement value dropped to zero in 1925: 1914 through 1926 Assessment Rolls Vol. 4. Assessment rolls similarly switch ownership of Lots 10 and 11 in Block 61 between the Mallorys and DeWitt, though there were two cabins in this case. The Hughson lot was number 4 in Block 67: Deed Record 31, 417-418.
50. "Bayocean May Change Hands," *Oregonian,* January 21, 1913, 8; "Bayocean Sunday Events," advertisement, *Oregon Journal,* August 24, 1911, 4; "Yacht Bayocean to be Overhauled," *Oregonian,* May 26, 1912, 12. "Thru Service

Without Change of Cars to Bayocean Via S. P. and P. R. & N.," advertisement, *Surf*, July 1912, 6.

51. "Yacht Bayocean to Be Overhauled," *Oregonian*, May 25, 1912, 12; "Water Pageant Most Brilliant," *Oregon Journal*, June 10, 1912, 1; Helen Parker Alexander, "Memories of Bayocean," Bayocean Miscellaneous folder, TCPM.
52. "Bayocean Will Be Excursion Craft," *Oregonian*, March 22, 1913, 17; Amended Answer of June 10, 1919, *Potter v. TBPRC*; "Yacht Bayocean Sails," *Oregonian*, April 7, 1913, 1; *Naval Investigation: Hearings Before the Subcommittee of the Committee on Naval Affairs, US Senate, Sixty-sixth Congress, Second Session* (1921), https://books.google.com/books?id= vFITAAAAIAAJ&hl=en; Robert J. Cressman, "Bayocean," http://public2. nhhcaws.local/content/history/nhhc/research/histories/ship-histories/ danfs/b/bayocean-i.html; US Department of Commerce, "Seagoing Vessels of the United States Part VI" (1924): 24; "North Pacific Gales Damage Shipping Along Coast of California," *Stockton Independent*, October 30, 1924, 1.
53. "Gearhart Park," advertisement, *Oregonian*, May 22, 1910, sec. 4, 6; Bayocean Natatorium Company Articles of Incorporation, File No. 18298, OSA; "Attention," advertisement, *Oregonian*, August 10, 1913, 13; "Man Wanted," advertisement, *Oregonian*, October 9, 1913, 6.
54. *Tillamook Herald*, January 2, 1914, 1; "Feeney & Bremer Co. Completes Big Job," *Tillamook Herald*, April 7, 1914, 1; Chapin testimony, Folder 2, *TBPRC v. Breitling*; "Seaside Natatorium," advertisement, *Oregon Journal*, June 3, 1914, 14; "Booster Band at Bayocean Sunday," *Tillamook Herald*, July 21, 1914, 1; "Business Men's Sports at Beach Big Attraction on Excursion," *Oregonian* , July 12, 1914, 11; "Summer Resort Busy," *Oregonian*, April 19, 1914, sec. 4, 2. The *Herald* and the *Oregonian* reported the natatorium costing $75,000, but Chapin testified to the smaller amount in court.
55. *TBPRC v. Schmitt and Schmitt*; "Feeney & Bremer Co. Completes Big Job," *Tillamook Herald*, April 7, 1914, 1; "Oregon's Finest Beach Resort Bayocean," *Oregonian*, June 3, 1917, sec. 3, 9; T. Irving Potter to T. J. Cronise, June 24, 1914, Bayocean Box 4, TCPM; "Summer Resort Busy," *Oregonian* , April 19, 1914, sec. 4, 2. The press reported incorrect dimensions of the natatorium, like they did its cost and that of other facilities and the *Bayocean*, which is why I use those provided by court records. TBPRC abandoned the rock crusher when storms left sufficient gravel on the beach to make concrete.
56. "Booster Band at Bayocean Sunday," *Tillamook Herald*, July 21, 1914, 1; *TBPRC v. Schmitt and Schmitt*; "Bayocean Popularity Grows," *Oregonian*, July 11, 1915, sec. 4, 8; Petition for Intervention. Workers then moved the generator to the natatorium to heat the pool and power streetlights, after which it was often referred to as the *light plant*. The company transferred ownership of the electrical utility the following year: Chapin testimony,

Folder 2, *TBPRC v. Breitling*; Certificate of Title No. 527, Register of Titles Vol. 2, 53, TCPM.

57. "Many Deep-Sea Diversions Thrill Visitors at Beaches," *Oregonian,* July 12, 1914, 8; H. L. Chapin testimony, *TBRPC v. Breitling*; Petition for Intervention; "Bungalow City," advertisement, *Oregon Journal*, September 6, 1914, sec. 3, 1; *Bayocean; Beautiful Ocean Resort; Tillamook Bay* (T. B. Potter Realty Company, 1914), author's collection. Some remaining tents cost $8.50 per week and $24.00 for four weeks. The brochure said there were forty bungalows and ten tents. The *Oregonian* said there were forty-three bungalows. Harkness Chapin testified there were forty-two, as did others consistently in the years ahead.
58. "Booster Band at Bayocean Sunday," *Tillamook Herald*, July 21, 1914, 1; "Many Deep-Sea Diversions Thrill Visitors at Beaches," *Oregonian,* July 12, 1914, 8; "Bay Ocean Has Excursions," *Oregonian,* August 9, 4.
59. Swan Hawkinson testimony, Folder 2, *TBPRC v. Breitling*; "Many Deep-Sea Diversions Thrill Visitors at Beaches"; "Bay Ocean Has Excursions," *Oregonian,* August 9, 1914, 4; "First Piling in Tillamook Jetty," *Oregon Journal*, April 26, 1914, 8; "Barview Season at Zenith," *Oregonian,* August 16, 1914, sec. 3, 5.
60. "Booster Band at Bayocean Sunday"; "Bay Ocean Has Excursions," *Oregonian*; High School Notes, *Tillamook Herald*, May 1, 1914, 3; Bayocean News Notes, *Tillamook Herald*, June 26, 1914, 6. The reference to a ghost was likely the editor's way of expressing his displeasure with the Oregon Supreme Court decision on *Elliott v. Bozorth.*
61. Breitling testimony, Folder 2, *TBPRC v. Breitling;* "Sea Lions Seen at Bayocean," *Oregonian*, August 23, 1914, sec. 3, 4; 1915 Assessment Roll, Vol. 4, 125; "Bayocean Notes," *Tillamook Herald*, April 3, 1914, 2; "Bayocean News Notes," *Tillamook Herald*, June 26, 1914, 6; 1915 Assessment Roll, Vol. 4, 133, 135, 132; Potter to Cronise. Burckhard's cabin was on Lot 19 in Block 44: Deed Record 42, 626. The Clack house was on Lot 11 in Block 46. King's places were on Lot 1 in Block 57 and Lot 6 in Block 59. He probably rented out the second and lived in the first because it was on the east side of High Street. Dick's place was on Lot 42 of Block 54. In 1932, for unknown reasons, the improvement value dropped to that of an outbuilding, which locals recalled being unused in the 1950s: 1932 Assessment Roll, 68.
62. Deed Record 29, 280-281; Deed Record 87, 338-344; "Season at Bayocean Opens," *Oregonian* 1916-6.25 sec. 3, 9; "Bayocean Project Committee Named," *Oregon Journal*, April 23, 1915, 5; Deed Record 27, 184; Deed Record 29, 303. Assessment rolls, maps, and aerial photos suggest that Johan and Dora's cabin straddled Lots 48 and 49, Agnete's cabin straddled Lots 2 and 3, and Thora's cabin straddled Lots 1 and 51, all at the south end of Block 60. Schwerdtmann's house was on Lot A in Block 62. The Woodhouse cabin was on Lot 22 in Block 67.

63. "Death Takes Physician," *Oregonian*, January 2, 1965, 11; Deed Record 28, 307; 1915 Assessment Roll, Vol. 4, 121; "Bayocean Society is Gay," *Oregonian*, July 18, 1915, 11. Lockwood's second house was on Lot 26 in Block 43. Resort coverage in metropolitan press society pages mention several homeowners in 1914, and a few in earlier and later years, that I leave out because I found no other record of them in local or metropolitan newspapers, deed indexes, assessment rolls, government documents, Bayocean alumni interviews, and the like.

Chapter 3

1. *T. B. Potter Realty Company. v. F. N. Derby*, Oregon State Supreme Court Case No. 8492, OSA.
2. Ibid.
3. Breitling testimony, Folder 2, *TBPRC v. Breitling.* Jones told Breitling that the lots were repurchased rather than repossessed.
4. Breitling testimony, Folder 2, and plat map with notes, Folder 3, *TBPRC v. Breitling*; David Baker testimony, Folder 2, *TBPRC v. Breitling.* The plunge must have already filled in and the bathhouse deconstructed as a result.
5. P. D. Hance testimony, Folder 2, *TBPRC v. Breitling*; Hawkinson testimony, Folder 2, *TBPRC v. Breitling*; Baker testimony, Folder 2, *TBPRC v. Breitling.* Problems with T. Irving's wave generating machine may be the reason he found no buyers elsewhere: "Stockholders of Bayocean Co. to Meet Wednesday," *Oregon Journal*, March 3, 1919, 4. In "Memories of Bayocean," Helen (Parker) Alexander said it was "rough paving filled with goose-egg cobbels [*sic*]. As a result, we all brought strong walking shoes."
6. Chapin testimony, Folder 2, *TBPRC v. Breitling*; W. J. Clemens testimony, Folder 2, *TBPRC v. Breitling.* I found no lots in assessment rolls owned by Hance or Baker that might have been a commercial building. They must have been built while the lots were on contract and sold to others who then used them as houses. A high-resolution version of the plat map with roads is available at https://drive.google.com/file/d/1Gtx2WtRX2DsQ1KXM_Tz2SFg1jP-z_biC/views=sharing.
7. Chapin testimony, Folder 2, *TBPRC v. Breitling*; M. J. O'Donnell testimony, *TBRPC v. Breitling.*
8. Chapin testimony, Folder 2, *TBPRC v. Breitling.*
9. Mitchell testimony, Folder 2, *TBPRC v. Breitling.*
10. Ibid.
11. Ibid.
12. "Launch Henrietta No. 2 Sold," *Oregonian,* May 7, 1913, 13; Exhibit "A", November 25, 1916, *Marsh v. TBPRC*; "News of Oregon Ports," *Oregonian,* March 26, 1914, 14. Charles Carson, October 21, 1970. This Axel Anderson is not the man who piloted the Morning Star II in 1959: Floyd Price, Old

Tillamook Times, January 31, 2022, https://www.facebook.com/groups/242715339171621/permalink/4631901586919619.

13. "Bayocean Suit Filed," advertisement, *Tillamook Herald,* July 21, 1914, 4; "Steamboat Service Established: Oregon," *Daily Bulletin of Orders Affecting the Postal Service* 35 no. 10450a (1914).
14. "Bayocean Suit Filed"; "Bayocean Company Sues Lot Owner," *Oregon Journal,* July 30, 1914, 2. Though Mitchell is not attributed, the writing style matches other papers written later, and Charles Carson recalled Axel Anderson and Carl Shagren ending up on opposite side of "the war waged by Mr. Mitchell": Charles Carson, October 21, 1970. Francis must have gotten the lot owner list from Christian Lauritzen.
15. "Potter Realty Co. Loses Suit Against Anderson," *Tillamook Herald,* July 31, 1914, 2; "Booster Band at Bayocean Sunday," advertisement, *Tillamook Herald,* July 21, 1914, 1.
16. T. B. Potter Realty Company v. Axel Anderson, Tillamook County Circuit Court Case No. 1527, OSA.
17. *TBPRC v. Mitchell*; Mitchell testimony, Folder 2, *TBPRC v. Breitling*; Circuit Court Cases, *Tillamook Herald,* October 5, 1916, 4; Portland City Directory (Portland: 1916), 854.
18. Jerry Sutherland, "William George Owned Mitchell's General Store," https://www.bayocean.net/2016/07/william-george-owned-mitchells-general.html; Mitchell testimony, Folder 2, *TBPRC v. Breitling.* The Mitchell was on Lot 44 in Block 54. In his testimony, Francis did not say where he and Ida lived from October 1912 to January 1914, but Tillamook County Bank would not have risked a second loan unless they were local and at least one of them was employed.
19. Sutherland, "William George Owned Mitchell's General Store"; Society, *Oregonian,* August 18, 1912, sec. 3, 3; *Tillamook County and City Directory,* (Tillamook: W.W. Woodbeck, 1916), 47; Portland City Directory (Portland: 1916), 854.
20. "To All Property Owners at Bayocean," *Tillamook Herald,* October 9, 2.
21. "Bayocean Park Lot Owners Would Have Receiver Appointed," *Oregon Journal,* November 26, 1914, 16. Gatens must not have thought his recent visit to Bayocean Park prejudiced him: "Sea Lions Seen at Bayocean," *Oregonian,* August 23, 1914, sec. 3, 4; R. J. Marsh et al. v. T. B. Potter Realty Company et al., Multnomah County Circuit Court Case No. 35700A.
22. "Bayocean Park Lot Owners Would Have Receiver Appointed."
23. "Affidavits Declare Potter-Chapin Co. Perfectly Solvent," *Oregon Journal,* December 11, 1914, 13; "Bayocean Plea Fought," *Oregonian,* December 11, 1914, 13.
24. "Affidavits Declare Potter-Chapin Co. Perfectly Solvent."

25. "Sum of $50,000 Is Asked Because of Alleged Slander," *Oregon Journal*, December 22, 1914, 17. Small ads featuring the bungalows and the annex ran a dozen times in the *Oregonian* and *Oregon Journal* during the summer of 1914.
26. Amended Complaint, filed January 20, 1915, *Marsh v. TBPRC;* Motion for Dismissal filed February 2, 1915, *Marsh v. TBPRC.*
27. Petition for Intervention; Answer filed February 26, 1915, *Marsh v. TBPRC*; Counter Claims filed March 2, 1915, *Marsh v. TBPRC;* "Buyers Foil Peace Plan," *Oregonian,* March 1, 1915, 9. The *Oregonian* reported thirty-six counter claims, but one more came in after their article.
28. Frank C. McNurlen v. Potter-Chapin Realty Company et al., Multnomah County Circuit Court Case No. 60147.
29. "Bayocean Buyer Recovers in Full," *Oregonian,* February 11, 1915, 8; *McNurlen v. PCRC.* Chapin later revised his mileage numbers to match Vincent's: "Affidavits Declare Potter-Chapin Co. Perfectly Solvent," *Oregon Journal*, December 11, 1914, 13.
30. L. E. Latourette, F. D. Mitchell, Fred Haldeman, Thomas Muir, and Charles J. Soderberg circular, September 9, 1915, Affidavit filed June 16, 1916, *Marsh v. TBPRC.*
31. *McNurlen v. PCRC*; "Bayocean Buyer Recovers in Full."
32. Minnie Schmidt v. Potter-Chapin Realty Company and T. B. Potter Realty Company, Multnomah County Circuit Court Case No. 60482.
33. "Buyers Foil Peace Plan"; Stipulation filed March 23, 1915, *Marsh v. TBPRC.*
34. Motion to Vacate Restraining Order and Affidavits filed May 8, 1915, *Marsh v. TBPRC*; "Lays Troubles to Judge's Actions," *Evening Telegraph* (Portland), October 31, 1916, 16; *Capitol's State Who's Who Combined with Who's Who for the Western States,* (Portland: Capitol Pub. Co., 1953), 314.
35. "S. B. Vincent Resigns," *Oregonian*, March 24, 1915, 6; "S. B. Vincent Gets Important Place," June 13, 1913, 2; "Bayocean Project Committee Named," *Oregon Journal*, April 23, 1915, 5.
36. "Bayocean Project Committee Named," *Oregon Journal*, April 23, 1915, 5.
37. Motion and Affidavits filed May 4, 1915, *Marsh v. TBPRC.* Order filed May 19, 1915, *Marsh v. TBPRC.*
38. Order filed March 1, 1916, *Marsh v. TBPRC*; Geoff Williams, "A Glimpse at Your Expenses 100 Years Ago," https://money.usnews.com/money/personal-finance/articles/2015/01/02/a-glimpse-at-your-expenses-100-years-ago; Motion filed December 7, 1916, *Marsh v. TBPRC*; Order filed April 22, 1915, *Marsh v. TBPRC*; Order filed July 31, 1915, *Marsh v. TBPRC.*
39. Latourette et al. circular filed September 9, 1915, *Marsh v. TBPRC.*
40. "Tillamook Pioneer Succumbs to Heart," *Oregon Journal*, July 26, 1915, 9; "Bayocean Society is Gay"; "Two Men Drown Off Tillamook Bar," *Tillamook Herald*, August 3, 1915, 1; "Bayocean Season is Early," *Oregonian*, July 4, 1915, 9; "Bayocean Popularity Grows"; Bayocean, *Oregon Journal*, June 25, 1916, sec. 4, 4.

41. "Bayocean Season is Early," *Oregonian*, July 4, 1915"; "71 Leave St. John's School," *Oregonian*, January 26, 1918, 7; "Bayocean Society is Gay," *Oregonian*, July 18, 1915, 11; "Bayocean Social Life Gay," *Oregonian*, August 18, 1915, 9; "1874-Yes-Osteopathy is New," advertisement, *Oregonian*, April 11, 1902, 7. Van Tine's cottage was on Lot 20 of Block 43: Deed Record 30, 638-639. Swank's place was on Lot 10 of Block 40: Deed Record 41, 465. The Pagoda was on Lot 29 of Block 42: Deed Record 30:440.
42. Alexander, "Memories of Bayocean."
43. "Bayocean Society is Gay"; Becky Jensen, "Seaside Promenade," https://www.seasideor.com/seaside-stories/seaside-or-promenade; Objections to Reports of S. B. Vincent of April 15, 1920, *March v. Potter*; Tillamook County Road Contract #2668.
44. Tillamook County Road Record Journal 3, 384-389.
45. Tillamook County Court Journal H, 261-262, Tillamook County Clerk's office; "About Us," *Tillamook Headlight-Herald*, https://www.tillamookheadlightherald.com/site/about_us.html; Road Record Journal 3, Map of Bayocean County Road, January 1912, Sheet No. 1, Tillamook County Surveyor; Tillamook County Road Contract #2668. TBPRC had submitted the lowest bid in the spring of 1913, but it was more than budgeted, so the county commissioners revised their specifications.
46. Folder 1, Bayocean Road #781, Tillamook County Public Works Department; Tillamook County Court Journal I, 119-121.
47. Latourette Affidavit filed August 17, 1918, *Marsh v. Potter*; Bayocean, *Oregon Journal*, July 9, 1916, sec. 4, 8; "Bayocean Season Under Way," *Oregonian*, July 15, 1917, sec. 3, 9; Charles Carson, October 21, 1970.
48. "The Tillamook Bay Jetty," *Tillamook Herald*, August 24, 1915, 2; "Bar View Badly Hit by Storm," *Tillamook Herald*, November 23, 1915, 1; Southern Pacific Co. v. United States, 58 Ct. Cl. 428, 1923 U.S. Ct. Cl. LEXIS 297 (US Court of Claims June 4, 1923, Decided).
49. *Southern Pacific Co. v. United States*. An appellate court confirmed the decision: Southern Pacific Co. v. United States, 58 Ct. Cl. 428, 1923 U.S. Ct. Cl. LEXIS 297 (US Court of Claims June 4, 1923, Decided).
50. Complaint filed January 3, 1916, *Potter v. TBPRC*; Reply of Complainant filed 1916, *Potter v. TBPRC*. "Mrs. T. B. Potter Is Suing to Foreclose Bayocean Mortgage," *Oregon Journal*, January 3, 1916, 1.
51. Order filed February 14, 1916, *Marsh v. TBPRC*; TBPRC to Frances L. Potter, Trustee, Mortgage No. 22964, Tillamook County Mortgage Book 1, 188–193.
52. Reply filed June 5, 1916, *Potter v. TBPRC*. The plaintiff's figure of $100,000 cited at the beginning of *Marsh v. TBPRC* must have been an approximation.
53. "Bayocean Purchasers Take Notice," *Oregon Journal*, January 5, 1916, 14. "Bayocean Lot Buyers Form Association to Fight Mrs. Potter," *Oregon Journal*,

January 6, 1916, 15; Order filed March 1, 1916, *Marsh v. TBPRC*; Order filed April 12, 1916, *Marsh v. TBPRC*.

54. Motion filed June 16, 1916, *Marsh v. TBPRC*; Motion filed December 7, 1916, *Marsh v. TBPRC*; Order filed January 12, 1917. *Marsh v. TBPRC*; Statement of Receivers filed March 18, 1919, *Marsh v. TBPRC*. My cash balance comes not from a balance sheet but from my subtracting disbursements of $28,268.20 from receipts (which included the starting balance) of $29,047.41. Besides Vincent's annual $3,600 salary, his secretary Reardon and bookkeeper Strahl were paid a total of $3,063.30. Jim O'Donnell's salary probably took most of the $6,193.34 construction costs.
55. "The Bayocean Road," *Tillamook Herald*, August 4, 1916, 3; Map of Bay Ocean Road, January 1917, F41-055, Tillamook County Surveyor; "Suit Filed Against Delinquent Buyers of Bayocean Realty," *Oregon Journal*, December 24, 1916; "Contract for Bayocean Road Let," *Tillamook Herald*, May 15, 1917, 1; Notice Of Delinquent Taxes of Real Property in Tillamook County Oregon for The Year 1914, *Tillamook Herald*, February 18, 1916, 2, 6, 7.
56. S. B. Vincent, Receiver for T. B. Potter Realty Company and Potter-Chapin Realty Company v. Pearl Alkire, et al., Tillamook County Circuit Court Case No. 1918, OSA; "Suit Filed against Delinquent Buyers of Bayocean Realty," *Oregon Journal*, December 24, 1916; Motion filed February 18, 1918, *Marsh v. TBPRC*; Stipulation filed April 16, 1919, *Marsh v. TBPRC*. Mailing addresses of the delinquent contract holders ranged from New York down to California and up into British Columbia.
57. Bayocean, *Oregon Journal*, July 29, 1917, sec. 4, 7; "Lays Troubles to Judge's Actions," *Portland Evening Telegram*, October 31, 1916, 16; "Bayocean Receiver Says Hands Are Tied by Court Decisions," *Oregon Journal*, October 9, 1917, 12.
58. "Bayocean Receiver Says Hands Are Tied by Court Decisions."
59. Order filed October 9, 1915, *Marsh v. TBPRC*. Order filed May 27, 1916, *Marsh v. TBPRC*.
60. Bayocean Natatorium Company v. T. B. Potter Realty Company, Multnomah County Circuit Court Case No. 71185.
61. Ibid; "Accounting Is Sought," *Oregonian*, December 20, 1917, 11.
62. Thomas Anthony Terich, "Bayocean Spit, Tillamook, Oregon; Early Economic Development and Erosion History" (doctoral dissertation, Oregon State University, 1973), 40.
63. "Two Receivers Named," *Oregonian*, March 17, 1918, 10; "School Principal Dies," *Oregonian*, May 25, 1929, 10; Oath Of Receivers filed May 23, 1918, *Marsh v. TBPRC*; "Veteran Educator Dies From Injuries," *Park Record* (Park City, Utah), December 30, 1943, 8; "Bayocean," *Oregon Journal*, June 22, 1920, sec. 5, 5.

64. Petition filed May 18,1918, *Marsh v. TBPRC;* Supplemental Report filed May 22, 1918, *Marsh v. TBPRC*; "Sydney B. Vincent Dies," *Oregonian,* December 10, 1926, 9.
65. "T. B. Potter, 51, Is Dead," *Oregonian,* May 2, 1916, 22; Webber and Webber, *Bayocean*, 53; Thomas Benton Potter, Probate Packet No. 23016-23073, California Superior Court (Alameda County), California, Wills and Probate Records, 1850-1953; 1917 San Francisco Voter Registration, California State Library; Lewis B. Thomas Draft Registration, May 22, 1917; "Feminine Divers to Compete Here," *Oregonian,* May 13, 1917, sec. 2, 3.
66. T. Benton Potter Probate; "Mrs. T. B. Potter Buys Campbell Home," *Evening Times-Star* (Alameda, CA), December 6, 1911, 1; Webber and Webber, *Bayocean*, 53; "Pebble Beach Society Colony Grows Rapidly," *San Francisco Examiner,* September 28, 1919, Society, 4.
67. Craig Addams, Dead Memories Portland; Deed Record 42, 510; Deed Record 61, 582; Oregon Death Index, 1903-1998, OSA; Cape Meares News, *Tillamook Headlight-Herald*, August 17, 1950, sec. 2, 2.
68. "O. K. Jeffery Home in Alameda Park Is Sold For $30,000," *Oregon Journal*, January 13, 1918, 23; "Nothing the Matter With Portland," *Oregon Journal*, March 19, 1918, 10; Deed Record 37, 626; "New Type of Refrigerator Made," *Oregonian*, March 17, 1929, 20; "Divorce Filed," *Oregon Journal*, March 30, 1934, 17; "T. Irving Potter, Inventor, 76, Dies," *New York Times,* December 18, 1963, 37; "Who We Are," http://muracream.com/WhoWeAre.

Chapter 4

1. Order filed July 3, 1918, *Marsh v. TBPRC*; Affidavit filed August 17, 1918, *Marsh v. TBPRC.* Sources always refer to John Albert Biggs Sr. by his nickname. His obituary connects them: "John A. Biggs Pioneer Dies," *Tillamook Headlight-Herald*, January 15, 1942, 5.
2. Petition filed September 9, 1918, *Marsh v. TBPRC*; *Tillamook Headlight*, February 14, 1918, sec. 2, 2; "The Bedloe is Launched," *Tillamook Headlight*, January 9, 1919; Fred White, "Oregon America's Banner Shipbuilding District, With Proud War Record," *Oregonian,* January 1, 1920, sec. 3, 22; David Laine, October 20, 2015. The first *Headlight* article said Arstill would continue working on the mile and a quarter section between Dick Point and Flower Pot, but he did not do so until 1921: "Heavy Work on Bayocean Line," *Tillamook Headlight*, September 29, 1921, 1.
3. Petition filed September 9, 1918, *Marsh v. TBPRC.*
4. "The Mitchell," advertisement, *Oregonian*, July 7, 1918, sec. 2, 14. Though Francis Mitchell always claimed ownership of The Mitchell publicly, he told census takers the truth.

5. NARA M841, Roll 106; "Sealions Seen at Bayocean," *Oregonian,* August 23, 1914, sec. 3, 4; "Bay Ocean Hotel Now Open," *Oregonian,* July 14, 1918, sec. 3, 8.
6. "Bay Ocean Popular Spot," *Oregonian,* August 4, 1918, sec. 3, 8; "W. J. Clemens Improving," *Oregonian,* May 16, 1918, 11; Funeral Notices, *Oregonian,* October 31, 1918, 13.
7. Order filed February 7, 1921, *Marsh v. TBPRC*; TBPRC Articles of Incorporation.
8. Amended Answer filed June 10, 1919, *Potter v. TBPRC.*
9. Petition filed June 20, 1920, *Marsh v. TBPRC;* Alexander, "Memories of Bayocean."
10. Webber and Webber, *Bayocean*, 39. Others said that erosion destroyed this dance hall, but that cannot be true because it would have been a slow process recorded in photographs and newspaper articles, of which there are none. The destruction, regardless of cause, is another event missed by the press.
11. First Report of Receivers filed December 9, 1919, *Marsh v. TBPRC.*
12. Objections To Reports filed April 15, 1920, *March v. Potter*; First Report of Receivers.
13. First Report of Receivers; Order filed February 7, 1921, *Marsh v. TBPRC.*
14. Ibid.
15. Petition filed June 30, 1920, *Marsh v. TBPRC*; "Bayocean," advertisement, *Oregonian,* June 20, 1920, sec. 4, 7; Bayocean, *Oregon Journal*, June 22, 1920, sec. 5, 5; "Hundreds Throng Bayocean," *Oregonian,* July 11, 1920, sec. 4, 5.
16. Order of August 20, 1919, *Marsh v. TPBRC*; US District Court Civil (Equity) Docket, Volume 19, 158, NARA, Seattle, WA; Bayocean, *Oregon Journal*, June 22, 1920, sec. 5, 5
17. Second Report of Receivers filed April 16, 1923, *Marsh v. TBPRC*; Report filed September 23, 1920, *Marsh v. TBPRC.*
18. Petition filed June 30, 1920, *Marsh v. TBPRC*; "Dredge to Build Road," *Oregonian,* January 16, 1920, 6.
19. Petition filed June 21, 1921, *Marsh v. TBPRC*; "Reed College Men Operate Bayocean Resort This Year," *Oregon Journal*, July 3, 1921, 6; "Students Back Bayocean," *Oregonian,* August 7, 1921, sec. 4, 5; James Hamilton letter, June 22, 1921, author's collection; "Summes [*sic*] Resort Run by Students," *Tillamook Headlight*, June 30, 8.
20. "Summes [*sic*] Resort Run by Students"; Robert Osborne, "College Boys Manage Summer Resort," *Oregon Journal*, September 4, 1921, sec. 6, 6; Reed College, *Griffin* (Portland, Oregon: 1923), 36. The Reedies must have taken down the dance hall when they left because it was never mentioned again, and dances were held in the Annex and Bayside Inn. The boilers must have been retrofitted to burn wood during World War I.
21. "College Boys Manage Summer Resort"; "Death Takes Physician," *Oregonian,* January 2, 1965, 11; *Reed College Bulletin* (Volume 15, No. 2) April 1936, 45.

22. Second Report of Receivers; Reed College Notes, *Oregon Journal*, December 4, 1921, sec. 2, 5.
23. "Heavy Work on Bayocean Line."
24. Stipulation of June 10, 1922, *Potter v. TBPRC*; Deed Record 44, 612-615.
25. Ibid; "Bayocean," advertisement, *Oregonian,* August 25, 1922, 7; "Bay Ocean Is Filling Up," *Oregon Journal*, July 23, 1922, sec. 3, 10.
26. Petition filed July 17, 1922, *Marsh v. TBPRC*; Deed Record 45, 222.
27. Ida S. Harvey v. Frances Potter-Thomas, Tillamook County Circuit Court Case No. 2938, OSA; "A Glimpse at Your Expenses 100 Years Ago"; Ida S. Harvey v. Frances Potter-Thomas, Tillamook County Circuit Court Case No. 3049, OSA.
28. Deed Record 51, 21; Deed Record 55, 325-326; Latourette v. United States, 150 F. Supp. 123, 1957 U.S. Dist. LEXIS 3672, (US District Court for the District of Oregon, February 15, 1957). Oregon and California are community property states, so Arleta automatically co-owned the property.
29. *Harvey 3049*; "Proposed Resort at Bayocean," *Oregon Journal*, November 9, 1921, 11.
30. Harvey 3049.
31. Ida S. Harvey v. Frances Potter-Thomas and J. S. Dobbins, Tillamook County Circuit Court Case No. 3468, OSA.
32. Judgements, *Recorder* (San Francisco), May 16, 1928, 1; Deaths, *Oakland Tribune*, December 7, 1952, 50; 1940 Census, A. D. 22, Block Nos. 4-5; San Francisco, California; Webber and Webber, *Bayocean, 26*; Tillamook Circuit Court Journal 37, 440; Funeral Notices, *Berkeley Daily Gazette*, December 11, 1973.
33. Petition of October 21, 1922, *Marsh v. TBPRC*; "Tillamook County Builds Many Roads," *Oregonian,* December 3, 1922, 18.
34. Order filed February 10, 1923, *Marsh v. TBPRC*; Order filed August 5, 1924, *Marsh v. TBPRC*; Petition filed October 29, 1924, *Marsh v. TBPRC*; The Bayocean Company Incorporation Papers, File No. 28304, Oregon State Corporation Division.
35. Second Report of Receivers; Petition filed July 9, 1923, *Marsh v. TBPRC*; Third Report of Receivers filed May 19, 1925, *Marsh v. TBPRC*; Petition and Order filed June 14, 1924, *Marsh v. TBPRC.*
36. "Tillamook County District Boundary Board, 1904 & 1905, 1921 to 1927, Volume 1," 142, 157, TCPM; "School Directories 1913, 1914–1950, 1951," Records at the Old Wilson School Building, Education Service District Old Gym Storage Area; Robert and Barbara Watkins, interview by Gerry Hysmith, October 8, 1988, transcript, Watkins family folder, TCPM.
37. Petition For Sale of Assets.
38. Order filed May 4, 1926, *Marsh v. TBPRC.*
39. Offer filed May 18, 1926, *Marsh v. TBPRC.*
40. Objections filed May 29, 1926, *Marsh v. TBPRC*; Petition filed June 1, 1926.
41. "Bayocean Assets Sold," *Oregonian,* June 3, 1926, 7; Decision of The Court signed June 2, 1926, *Marsh v. TBPRC.*

42. Scott Morrison and Paul Morin, "History of State Highways in Oregon," (Salem: RW Engineering Group for the Oregon Department of Transporation, 1917), 14; Acceptance of Terms filed June 2, 1926, *Marsh v. TBPRC.* Harkness Chapin mistakenly spelled the street "Mears" instead of "Meares" on the Bayocean Park plat. He was not the first or last to do so.
43. Acceptance of Terms; Order filed July 9, 1926, *Marsh v. TBPRC*; Notice of Transfer filed July 13, 1926, *Marsh v. TBPRC.*
44. Decree on Final Report filed May 27, 1931, *Marsh v. TBPRC.*

Chapter 5

1. Ackley family folder, TCPM; "Change of Ownership," advertisement, *Tillamook Herald,* March 2, 1922, 7; Everett Morse and Minnie M. Condit family folder, TCPM; "Connie Lee Dye Esteemed Citizen Dies On Sunday," *Tillamook Headlight-Herald,* May 30, 1940, 1; Webber and Webber, *Bayocean,* 74; Colmer and Wood, *History of the Bench and Bar of Oregon,* 93.
2. "Arthur Glenn Beals Pioneer Dies After Long Illness," *Tillamook Headlight-Herald,* December 11, 1958, 1, 8.
3. "Bayocean District Will Be Developed," *Oregonian,* August 8, 1926, sec. 2, 2.
4. Report and Petitions approved June 29, 1929, *Marsh v. TBPRC*; Deed Record 73, 197.
5. Deed Record 144, 225; "Bayocean Bungalettes," advertisement, *Oregonian,* June 27, 1926, sec. 4, 7.
6. "New Bayocean Road Now Open to Automobiles," *Oregon Journal,* July 11, 1926, sec. 5, 10; "Road Reaches Bayocean, *Oregonian,* July 18, 1926, sec. 6, 12.
7. "New Bayocean Road Now Open to Automobiles"; "Road Reaches Bayocean."
8. F. D. Mitchell, "Warning", Bayocean Miscellaneous folder, TCPM; "Travel to Bayocean Gains–Road Is Open," *Tillamook Herald,* August 4, 1927; "Right-of-Way into Bayocean Bought," *Tillamook Herald,* July 28, 1927, 1. John Albert Biggs Jr.'s nickname comes from Deed Record 78, 514-515 and Deed Record 90, 193-194. James Allen Biggs, his father Bert's twin brother, was known as Al. Since Al, Albert, and Bert lived in the same area, things got confusing enough that the caption of James's obituary misnamed him: "John Allen Biggs Pioneer Resident Called by Death," *Tillamook Headlight-Herald,* January 7, 1943, 1. Fortunately, he was properly named in the text. The route through Cape Meares and southern part of Bayocean Park can be seen at: Jerry Sutherland, "Cape Meares and Bayocean," https://www.bayocean.net/2015/03/cape-meares-and-bayocean.html.
9. "Bayocean District Will Be Developed," *Oregonian,* August 8, 1926, sec. 2, 2; "Road Reaches Bayocean"; A. G. Beals Scrapbook, Accession No. 11,106.91, TCPM.
10. J. H. Jordon, "To Tillamook and Netarts," *Hillsboro Independent,* August 25, 1893, 3; "Declares Toll Roads Should Be Condemned by The State," *Oregon Journal,* August 19, 1906, 7.
11. "Portland Men Buy Bayocean Section," *Tillamook Herald,* August 12, 1926, 1.

12. Ibid; "Bayocean to Have Golf Course," *Tillamook Headlight*, August 11, 1926, 1; "Bayocean Golf Course Started," *Oregon Journal*, October 10, 1926, sec.2, 2.
13. "Wilson River Road Bill Is Vetoed by Governor Patterson," *Tillamook Herald*, February 17, 1927, 1.
14. Bayocean, *Tillamook Headlight*, February 25, 1927; "Orin Pierce Brigham," *Oregon Journal*, June 22, 1949, 5; Deed Record, 56, 114-115. Brigham's house was on Lot 9 in Block 35.
15. Alexander, "Memories of Bayocean"; Deed Record 56, 108-109; Watkins, interview by Hysmith; Deed Record 58, 355; "Bayocean Now Open," *Oregonian*, July 14, 1918, sec. 3, 8; "Department Heads for School Named," *Spokane Chronicle*, September 6, 1915, 3. The Hawkinson's new house was on Lot 11, Crook's on Lot 14, both in Block 44: 1927 Assessment Roll, 129, 68. The square footage of this and other houses moved to Cape Meares come from the Tillamook County Assessor's web site. To protect the privacy of current owners, I will not provide links to their accounts.
16. Application for Release filed January 12, 1928, *Marsh v. TBPRC*; Don Best, "Best of History: Famed Journalist, Writer Paul Pintarich Shared Memories of Rockaway's Natatorium," Tillamook County Pioneer, April 3, 2020, https://www.tillamookcountypioneer.net/best-of-history-famed-journalist-writer-paul-pintarich-shared-memories-of-rockaways-natatorium.
17. Application for Release.
18. "Denial of Reduction of Delinquent Taxes Is Urged in Petition," *Tillamook Herald*, May 19, 1927, 1; "Bayocean Petition Presented to Court," *Tillamook Headlight*, July 1, 1927, 1.
19. "Settlement Made on Bayocean Tax," *Tillamook Headlight*, July 15, 1927, 1; Tillamook County Court Journal M, 153-159; "Bayocean Back Tax Situation Cleared," *Tillamook Headlight*, July 29, 1927, 1; "Bayocean Come Back Celebrated," *Tillamook Headlight*, August 5, 1927, 1.
20. "Bayocean is Coming Back," advertisement, *Tillamook Headlight*, August 12, 1927, 3; *Tillamook Herald*, August 4, 1927; "Bayocean Dance," advertisement, *Tillamook Herald*, August 18, 1927, 3; *Tillamook Herald*, September 15, 1927, 1; *Tillamook Herald*, November 24, 1927, 5; Webber and Webber, *Bayocean*, 61-62; "BOP21," TCPM. The photo of the gas pump is undated, but on June 21, 2020, my father, Art Sutherland, said it was taken in the latter part of the 1920s based on the style of pump, automobiles, and clothing worn.
21. "Work To Start Soon on Bridge on Wilson River," *Tillamook Herald*, May 3, 1928, 1; "Wilson River Bridge Is Finished by Tillamook Men; Is 142 Feet Long," *Tillamook Herald*, May 31, 1928, 1.
22. "Stripped Down Ford Crosses Wilson Route," *Tillamook Herald*, June 21, 1928, 1; "Car Plunges Over Bank of Wilson River Sunday Occupants Only Bruised," *Tillamook Herald*, June 28, 1928, 1.

23. "Wilson River Road Sees Many Motors," *Tillamook Headlight*, August 17, 1928, 1; Peter J. Edwards, *Forest Grove: A Historical Context* (1993), 25, https://digital.osl.state.or.us/islandora/object/osl:941864. Stanley Coates and his sister Margaret, mentioned later, were not related to Bill and Betty Coats. Frequent misspelling of their last names by the press made it appear as though they might be.
24. A. G. Beals Lumber Co. Journal.
25. "Bayocean Will Get Military Academy," *Tillamook Headlight*, May 8, 1928.
26. A. G. Beals Lumber Co. Journal.
27. Resorts, *Oregonian*, June 20, 1928, 13; "Portland Boys Head for Camp; Dog Also Along," *Oregon Journal*, June 21, 1928, 8; A. G. Beals Lumber Co. Journal; "Dr. Harroun Dies, Age 83," *Oregonian*, November 17, 1953, 15.
28. "Dr. Harroun Dies, Age 83"; "Dr. Harroun Plans Call on President," *Oregon Journal,* November 9, 1948, 2; "Club Awaits Primary," *Oregonian*, May 12, 1936, 4.
29. A. G. Beals Lumber Co. Journal; 1940 Census, Bayocean Precinct, Tillamook, Oregon; Announcements, *Tillamook Herald*, August 23, 1928, 5; "Campfire Girls Invited to Gather at Bayocean," *Tillamook Herald*, August 16, 1928, 3; "Camp Fire Girls Entertained at Bayside Inn, September 20, 1928, 2.
30. Watkins, interview by Hysmith; Webber and Webber, *Bayocean*, 62.
31. Watkins, interview by Hysmith; Acting Postmasters Appointed Fourth Class, *The Postal Bulletin*, May 8, 1928, 1; Mike Watkins, in discussion with the author, June 19, 1915.
32. "County Road Work in Full Swing Now," *Tillamook Headlight*, July 13, 1928, 1; A. G. Beals Lumber Co. Journal.
33. "Thousands Visit Bayocean Sunday," *Tillamook Headlight*," August 14, 1928, 1; Bayocean Host to Visitors at Big Celebration," *Tillamook Herald*, August 16, 1.
34. "Thousands Visit Bayocean Sunday"; "Bayocean Host to Visitors at Big Celebration."
35. A. G. Beals Lumber Co. Journal; "Great Northern Investment Co. Offers 50 of the Choicest Lots in Bayocean to the Home Folks," advertisement, *Tillamook Herald*, August 16, 1928, 8; "Bayocean Homesites," advertisement, *Tillamook Herald*, August 16, 1928, 8.
36. Contract between Ralph Ackley and TBC, June 21, 1930, Bayocean Miscellaneous folder, TCPM; "Camp Ground," advertisement, *Oregonian,* June 29, 1930, sec. 2, 6; Wanted, *Oregonian,* June 29, 1930, sec. 2, 9.
37. "Bayocean Scene of Labor Day Affair," *Tillamook Headlight*, August 31, 1928, 1; "Bayocean Calls Many on Labor Day," *Tillamook Headlight*, September 4, 1928, 1; "Bayocean to Welcome Labor Day Vacationists," *Oregon Journal*, September 2, 1928, sec. 3, 1-2.
38. "Bayocean To Welcome Labor Day Vacationists."
39. Ibid.

40. A. G. Beals Personal Journal, 1924-1928, TCPM. This ledger kept track of all personal checks written. My total includes all items related to Bayocean, not just "investments."
41. Application For Release of Bond filed October 5, 1928, *Marsh v. TBPRC*; Objections to Release of Bond served December 6, 1928, *Marsh v. TBPRC.*
42. Objections to Release of Bond.
43. Ibid.
44. Application For Release of Bond; Objections to Release of Bond. Francis Mitchell submitted no comments, which is unlike him.
45. Reply To Objections filed December 12, 1918, *Marsh v. TBPRC*; Order of November 28, 1929, *Marsh v. TBPRC.*
46. Bayocean Natatorium Company Incorporation Papers, File No. 32143, Oregon State Corporation Division; Tillamook County Register of Titles Volumes 4, 53 and Volume 7, 64, TCPM (county and location assumed hereafter).
47. Tillamook County Commissioners to Senator Charles McNary, January 12, 1939, Folder 8, Box 3, Charles Linza McNary Papers, Ax 049, SCUA; "Bayocean Road to be Finished by November 1," *Tillamook Herald*, May 30, 1929, 1; "Bayocean Picnic Attracts 7,500," *Tillamook Headlight*, August 2, 1929, 1, 8.
48. "The First House to Go."
49. "Improvements At Bayocean Made," *Tillamook Headlight*, August 16, 1929, 1; Order signed June 29, 1929, *Marsh v. TBPRC*; Order signed November 13, 1929, *Marsh v. TBPRC.*
50. D. C. Baker testimony, NARA 7250; Bayocean, *Oregonian*, July 28, 1929, sec. 6, 10; "Bayocean People Busy Due to Road Contract," *Tillamook Herald*, June 13, 1929, 1; "Road Completion Brings Rejoicing," *Tillamook Herald*, October 11, 1929, 1, 5. Charles Carson said "Bayocean was dead" when his family stayed in a bungalow after the Bakers returned. Business later improved, but Carson took his family to Netarts after that: Charles Carson, October 21, 1970.
51. "Bayocean to Have School," *Tillamook Herald*, August 29, 1929, 1; Watkins, interview by Hysmith; 1930 Census, Bayocean Precinct, Tillamook, Oregon; Record of Superintendents Annual Reports, Education Service District Storage Area, Old Wilson School Gymnasium; Medcalf Diary.
52. Deed Record 64, 328; Record of Superintendents Annual Reports; Charles Ansorge (Cape Meares resident), e-mail to the author, April 11, 2020; Barbara Bennett, "From the Old School," *Tillamook Headlight-Herald*, July 3, 2002, Community, 1. The school lots were numbers 7, 8, 21, and 22 in Block 32.
53. "From the Old School"; Perry Reeder Jr., in discussion with the author, April 21, 2020; School Directories 1913 to 1951, Education Service District Storage Area, Old Wilson School Gymnasium; Deed Record 78, 514-515. To

see the school's location on today's landscape, see: Jerry Sutherland, "Locating Bayocean School," https://www.bayocean.net/2015/08/locating-bayocean-school.html.

54. D. C. Baker and Jennie E. Baker v. F. D. Mitchell and Ida Mitchell, Tillamook County Circuit Court Case No. 5153; Bayocean, *Oregonian*, August 10, 1930, sec. 4, 6. Stevenson bought Lots 12 and 13 in Block 3 in 1930. The house was completed sometime before 1937: Deed Record 63, 626; 1937 Assessment Roll Vol. 3, 76.
55. Bakers v. Mitchells.
56. O. D. Swanson and D. C. Baker v. F. D. Mitchell and Ida Mitchell, Tillamook County Circuit Court Case No. 5138.
57. Field Notes Of 4-H Clubs, *Oregonian,* February 8, 1931, Motor, 10; "New Club in Tillamook," *Oregonian,* January 3, 1932, sec. 5, 2; "Crews Working on Slide," *Oregonian,* December 28, 1931, 3.
58. "High Tides Damage Natatorium," *Oregonian* , April 25, 1932, 16; Samuel Newton Dicken, Carl L. Johannessen, and Bill Hanneson, *Some Recent Physical Changes of the Oregon Coast* (Eugene: Reprinted by *Eugene Register-Guard* and the Lane County Geographical Society, 1976), 62; Bayocean, *Oregonian*, June 26, 1932, sec. 5, 9; Webber and Webber, *Bayocean*, 85.
59. Funeral Notices, *Oregonian,* January 22, 1932, 10; Deed Record 67, 561; Deed Record 71, 623. Stevenson's lots were 12 and 13 in Block 3.
60. "Voting Place Changed," *Oregonian,* August 20, 1932, 4; "Judge Bagley Takes Outing," *Oregonian,* August 23, 1932, 9; Deed Record 67, 388; Geo. R. Bagley testimony, NARA 7250. Schwerdtmann stopped paying taxes in 1917, while he was transitioning from receiver Sydney Vincent's advisory committee to the board of BNC. He is the only person I know of who gave up their cabin for non-payment of taxes. It was the furthest north of any place built along High Street and the only one on the east side. Perhaps he saw the writing on the wall and gave up. The cabin was on lot A in Block 62. The neighboring lots Bagley bought were 13-16.
61. "Traffic Tied Up on Coast Roads," *Oregonian,* December 3, 1932, 1; "Contract Haulers Scored," *Oregonian,* September 4, 1932, sec. 3, 5.
62. Deed Record 67, 452–457, Deed Record 67, 587-589, Deed Record 72, 252-253, Deed Record 73, 203.
63. Beals, "History of Bayocean"; "T" Direct Index to Deeds; H. T. and Nettie Botts family folder, TCPM. I deduced the cause of the 1932 increase in deeds from the company's having granted no deeds from September 9, 1932, until it was dissolved on January 6, 1936, after which there was no one to make payments to or grant a deed: Tillamook-Bayocean Company Incorporation Papers, File No. 24486, Oregon State Corporation Division.
64. "Arthur Glenn Beals Pioneer Dies After Long Illness."

65. William E. Minshall, *Guide to Historical Markers of Tillamook County* (Wilsonville Lazerquick: Tillamook County Historical Society, 2004), 52; "Tough Times, Rough Work," Charles Sprague Memorial Wayside, Oregon Department of Forestry.
66. Geo. D. Riechers testimony, NARA 7250; Deed Record 67, 454–457; Deed Record 72, 252-253; Deed Record 73, 203; Deed Record 67, 587-589.

Chapter 6

1. "Tillamook Bay and Bar, Oregon," Report of the Chief of Engineers, US Army, 1933, Part 1, (Washington: US Government Printing Office), 1135-1138.
2. "Would Deepen Bar At Mouth Of Bay," *Tillamook Headlight*, November 18, 1927, 1; "Tillamook Bay and Bar, Oregon," Report of the Chief of Engineers, US Army, 1930, Part 1, (Washington: US Government Printing Office), 1838-1843.
3. "Would Deepen Bar At Mouth Of Bay"; *Tillamook Headlight*, November 18, 1927, 1; "Work on South Jetty is Favored by Committee," *Tillamook Herald*, February 23, 1933, 1; "Why Ban Tillamook?" *Oregon Journal*, May 15, 1933, 6.
4. Deed Record 32, 535; Maurine Coffin (granddaughter of David S. and Vesta Ellen Townsend Williams), in discussion with the author, July 11, 1917.
5. Maurine Coffin, July 11, 1917; Swan Hawkinson testimony, NARA 7250; Dicken, Johannessen, and Hanneson, *Some Recent Physical Changes of the Oregon Coast*, 58.
6. Dicken, Johannessen, and Hanneson, *Some Recent Physical Changes of the Oregon Coast*, 58; Maurine Coffin, July 11, 1917; G. A. Jones testimony, NARA 7250.
7. Portland City Directories; *1916-1917 Tillamook County and City Directory*, inside cover; George Jones testimony, NARA 7250.
8. Deed Record 36, 235; Sherwood House history handwritten by Buck Sherwood on September 1990, Bayocean School Scrapbook, Barbara Bennett Community Center, Cape Meares, Oregon. George and Rilly Jones's house was on Lot 15 in Block 12 of Oceanview.
9. Bayocean Water Company Incorporation Papers, File No. 32731, filed April 22, 1929, Oregon State Corporation Division; "Start Bayocean Inquiry," *Bend Bulletin*, July 12, 1933, 2.
10. "Y Campers Meet Gun Totin' Women, Say," *Oregon Statesman*, August 5, 1933, 3.
11. "Water Users' Complaint Heard," *Oregonian*, August 21, 1933, 2; Howard W. Shirley, "The Citizen Veteran," *Oregonian*, September 3, 1933, sec. 5, 4; Mitchell File, OSH; "Public Utility Defined," *Oregon Journal*, May 15, 1936, 4; Deed Record 73, 123-130.
12. Deed Record 68, 540; Deed Record 66, 117; Gertrude L. Gates, D. O. testimony, NARA 7250; Marius B. Marcellus testimony, NARA 7250; Deed Record 88, 340-341; Bayocean News, *Tillamook Headlight-Herald*, April 8, 1937, 3; Watkins, interview by Hysmith; Lena V. Brownell testimony, NARA

7250; "Lutie E. Cake," *Oregonian*, December 27, 1962, 16. Both Pagodas were on Lot 8 in Block 44: 1936 Assessment Roll, Vol. 3, 43.

13. "Bay Ocean Co-op Colony Is Happy in Self-Chosen Work," *Oregon Journal*, June 3, 1934, sec. 2, 11; Bayocean, Ore. Artisans' Cooperative Community, Oregon Grants, Folder 13-34, State Project Reports and Research Publications, 1933–1943, Records of the Work Projects Administration, 1922–1944, RG 69, NARA, College Park, MD. Swanson and Walter must have fallen behind on contract payments and let the Bayside Inn go back to Dye, who received it as part of his TBC settlement.
14. "Bay Ocean Co-op Colony Is Happy in Self-Chosen Work"; R. J. Hendricks, Bits for Breakfast, *Oregon Statesman*, May 26, 1934, 4.
15. "Bay Ocean Co-op Colony Is Happy in Self-Chosen Work"; R. J. Hendricks, Bits for Breakfast, *Oregon Statesman*, May 26, 1934, 4; "Beach Colony Growing," *Oregonian*, June 8, 1934, 5.
16. Bayocean Social Register No. 3, Box labeled "Bayocean Gov. Doc. Maps. News Clips," Webber Research Archives.
17. 1934 Diary of Blanche Marie Parrish, Joyce Loftis's collection; Deed Record 66, 229; Bayocean News, *Tillamook Headlight-Herald*, October 21, 1937, 9. Loftis is the daughter of Blanche Parrish and Alvin Sweger, who met while Artisans.
18. Parrish Diary.
19. Ibid.
20. Oregon Grants, Folder 13-34; "Self-Help Program of the Federal Emergency Relief Administration: Summary of Federal Aid to Self-Help Cooperatives in the United States, July 1, 1933–December 31, 1935," US Federal Emergency Relief Administration, Washington, DC, June 20, 1936, Table 1; West Salem News, *Oregon Statesman*, May 16, 1935.
21. "Cooperative Community at Bayocean Commended," *Tillamook Headlight-Herald*, August 8, 1935; 4Oregon Grants, Folder 13-34; Carl Victor Sanchez, "The Development of the Emergency Relief Program in Oregon: June 1932 to January 1936" (master's thesis, University of Washington, 1942), 72; Oral history interview with Elmer R. Goudy, April 5, 1978, SR 9458, OHS.
22. "State Relief Men Back Job Finders," *Oregon Journal*, October 1, 1935, 4; Oregon Grants, Folder 13-34; *Oregon Journal*, October 7, 1935, 8; Oregon Grants, Folder 13-34.
23. Ralph Stuller, "They Licked the Panic," *Oregonian*, October 6, 1935, 11; Joyce Loftis, in discussion with the author, October 1, 2015.
24. Oregon Grants, Folder 13-34; Port Angeles, Wash. Artisans' Cooperative Community, Washington Grants, Folder 14-35, State Project Reports and Research Publications, 1933–1943, Records of the Division of Self-Help Cooperatives, Records of the Work Projects Administration, 1922–1944, RG 69, NARA, College Park, MD.

25. Oregon Grants, Folder 13-34; Washington Grants, Folder 14-35; Washington Progress Reports, Folder 30-42.
26. Washington Progress Reports, Folder 30-42; Deed Record 80, 8; Charles Carson, October 21, 1970. For more on the Artisans, see: Jerry Sutherland, "Artisans' Co-operative Community," https://www.bayocean.net/2015/09/artisans-co-operative-community.html.
27. "County Court Secures Approval of $25,000 WPA Project for County," *Tillamook Headlight-Herald*, January 30, 1936, 1; Works Progress Administration, July 1936, OHS; Jerry Sutherland, "Bayocean Road Hard to Build and Keep Open," https://www.bayocean.net/2015/12/storms-close-bayocean-road.html. Because of continuing landslides, Cape Meares Loop Road became impassable many times since its construction in the 1960s. Since being closed in 2013, sections have moved another fifteen feet. After years of study and public input, Tillamook County handed rerouting 1.7 miles of the loop over to the Federal Highway Administration. Work began in January 2022 and should be completed by October 2023: Mallory Gruben, *Tillamook Headlight-Herald*, "County, Federal Highways to Restore Cape Meares Loop Realignment," January 6, 2022, https://www.tillamookheadlightherald. com/news/county-federal-highways-to-restore-cape-meares-loop/article_51e5fd74-6d8c-11ec-9d81-0f407659696d.html.
28. "$52,265.73 Spent on WPA Projects in Tillamook Co. Since October 1, 1935, *Tillamook Headlight-Herald*, May 15, 1936, 1, 10; "WPA Projects Completed," *Tillamook Headlight-Herald*, December 3, 1936, 1; Bayocean News, *Tillamook Headlight-Herald*, November 19, 1936, 3; Beals, "History of Bayocean." For more on Beals's dike, see: Sutherland, "Locating Bayocean School."
29. Bayocean News, *Tillamook Headlight-Herald*, April 8, 1937, 3; Beals, "History of Bayocean"; Deed Record 9, 2-3; 1932 Assessment Roll Vol. 4, 47; Deed Record 68, 500; Howard "Buck" Pierce Sherwood folder, TCPM. The house Baker sold to Beals was on Lot 7 in Block 31. The Sherwoods lived in the Buggy Knot Inn for fifty years, which is why it is still known as the "Sherwood House." The buggy and natatorium columns are long gone: Jerry Sutherland, "Sherwood House," https://www.bayocean.net/2017/06/sherwood-house.html.
30. "2 Newspapers Published Many Years, Merged," *Tillamook Headlight-Herald*, April 5, 1934, 1, 4, 7.
31. Bayocean News, *Tillamook Headlight-Herald*, December 3, 1936, 3; Bayocean News, *Tillamook Headlight-Herald*, December 17, 1936, 6. The Richardson cabin was on Lot 33 in Block 44: Deed Record 74, 244.
32. Dr. Peter Reid testimony, NARA 7250; *Spokane Daily Chronicle*, August 27, 1928, Sports Edition, 2; Jerry Sutherland, "Moving It Didn't Save the

Muellers' Cabin," https://www.bayocean.net/2017/06/moving-it-didnt-save-muellers-cabin.html. The Reid house was on Lot 24 in Block 34: 1940 Assessment Roll, Vol 3, 54. The Muellers' lot on High Street was number 52 in Block 67. The lot on Bay Terrace was number 29 in Block 57.

33. "Hearing Held on Ocean Erosion at Bayocean," *Tillamook-Headlight Herald*, September 29, 1938, 1, 8; "Paul C. Bates Funeral Set," *Oregonian*, February 6, 1943, 6; Folder 1 (Bay Ocean), File 7402, Box 96, Civil Works Project Files, 1902-1968; POR-81, RG 77, NARA, Seattle, WA.
34. Paul C. Bates, testimony, NARA File 7250; Riechers testimony, NARA File 7250; Map TM-1-212/2; Bayocean News, *Tillamook Headlight-Herald*, June 30, 1938, 6. I do not know the fate of the Amusement Pavilion. It last appears in an aerial photo taken by Joe Bell on July 22, 1932: Mike Watkins's collection.
35. R. H. Baldock testimony, NARA File 7402; Marcellus testimony, NARA File 7250.
36. Beals, "History of Bayocean;" Perry C. Reeder Jr. and Sarah (Reeder) MacDonald *Bayocean Memories Beneath the Sand* (Xlibris Corp, 2017), 41-42.
37. Baker testimony, NARA File 7250; Hawkinson testimony, NARA File 7250; Deed Record 70, 239; Bayocean News, *Tillamook Headlight-Herald*, July 21, 1938, 3; Certificate of Marriage No. 4917, June 5, 1937, Skamania County, Washington. Green Gables's new location was Lot 18 in Block 43.
38. Jones testimony, NARA File 7250; Coats testimony, NARA File 7250. Buck
39. "Hearing Held on Ocean Erosion at Bayocean."
40. Ralph Stuller, "An Oregon 'Ghost City' Stirs in Its Grave," *Oregonian*, October 2, 1938, NW, 4.
41. "Pounding Ocean Washes Out Spit," *Oregonian*, October 27, 1938, 1; "Bayocean Seeks U.S. Aid on Jetty," *Oregonian*, October 30, 1938, 8; "Army Engineers Inspection," *Tillamook Headlight-Herald*, November 3, 1; Robert E. Hickson Papers, Box 1, Folder 7, Mss 1707, OHS. "Work On Bayocean," *Tillamook Headlight-Herald*, November 27, 1938, 4.
42. "Highest Tide and Wind In 30 Years Strikes Rockaway. Property Badly Damaged," *Tillamook Headlight-Herald*, January 5, 1939, 1, 4; "Wave Sweeps Ten Men Out to Sea at Barview," *Tillamook Headlight-Herald*, January 5, 1939, 1.
43. Moore, "Report on Beach Erosion Studies," 19; Jerry Sutherland, "Bayocean Spit Breached in 1700," https://www.bayocean.net/2015/10/bayocean-spit-was-first-breached-in-1700.html.
44. "Bayocean Town Faces Threat of Being Destroyed, *Tillamook Headlight-Herald*, January 5, 1939, 1, 4.
45. Jerry Sutherland, "The House at Jackson Gap," https://www.bayocean.net/2016/03/the-house-at-jackson-gap.html.
46. "The Bayocean Hazard," *Tillamook Headlight-Herald*, January 5, 1939, 4; Bayocean News, *Tillamook Headlight-Herald*, January 5, 1939, 1; "Road Being Cleared," *Tillamook Headlight-Herald*, January 5, 1939, 1.

47. "Coast Thronged with Sightseers," *Oregonian*, January 10, 1939, 3; Bayocean News, *Tillamook Headlight-Herald*, April 4, 1939, 8; Bayocean News, *Tillamook Headlight-Herald*, January 12, 1939, 6.
48. Map K-7-113, Bayocean Folder, TCL; Commissioners to McNary, January 12, 1939. I found no rebuttal from the Corps regarding sand accumulation south of the Columbia and Nehalem River south jetties, but in the case of the latter, the low profile and porous design let sand through, negating much of the effect by 1939: Jose Roman Lizarraga-Arciniega, "Shoreline Changes Due to Jetty Construction on the Oregon Coast" (master's thesis, Oregon State University, 1975), 12.
49. NARA 7402; C. R. Moore, "Data on Jetties and Changes at Oregon Coast Ports," (Portland District, Army Corps of Engineers, 1938), 22-23; Berkeley Blackman, "Report on Jetties to Shore Protection Board," August 15, 1938, 28-29, Box 8, General Administration Files, 1917-1941, DIV-02, RG 77, NARA, Seattle, WA.
50. "Coast Community Feared in Danger," *Oregonian*, February 4, 1939, 12; 1940 Assessment Roll, Vol. 3, 60; Sue (Bagley) Barr, "The Bagleys of Bayocean,", https://drive.google.com/file/d/1LHlj5JDznCBGopqOCeUMM2ISz4UlDGmO/view, 22-24, 31; Deed Record 70, 39-40; Bayocean News, *Tillamook Headlight-Herald*, April 27, 1939, 7; Bayocean News, *Tillamook Headlight-Herald*, May 12, 1938, 9; Obituaries, "David C. Baker," *Oregonian*, March 19, 1975, sec A, 37.
51. Obituaries, "David C. Baker, Oregonian, March 19, 1975, sec A, 37; Deed Record 40, 601; 1930 Census, Bayocean Precinct, Tillamook, Oregon; "New Gale Devours More of Bayocean," *Oregonian*, February 7, 1939, 4; "High Tides Roll onto Coastline," *Oregonian*, February 5, 1939, 12; "Help at Once," *Oregonian*, February 10, 1939, 10. Baker's was the house on Lot 6 of Block 59.
52. Herman Edwards, "Bayocean Peninsula Yielding to the Pacific," *Oregonian*, February 19, 1939, NW 8.
53. Ibid; Jerry Sutherland, "Sandbags Couldn't Save E.H. Roberts's House," https://www.bayocean.net/2016/06/sandbags-couldnt-save-eh-roberts-house.html. Moore's map showed the middle two washes in different locations than Edwards's, but more detailed maps created by the Corps later agreed with Edwards. Based on reports from other sources, the reason for the discrepancy is that the first two washes were so close together that they quickly merged, and waves first washed through 7th Avenue after Moore left. I used Corps maps to delineate South Gap because Edwards's was not precise.
54. "Bayocean Peninsula Yielding to the Pacific."
55. "Bayocean Relief Being Promoted by Officials," *Tillamook Headlight-Herald*, January 19, 1939, 1, 8; "Army Engineers Lack Cash to Aid Bay Ocean Work," *Oregonian*, January 19, 1939, 1; Dr. Marcellus letters and telegrams in

Bayocean Miscellaneous folder, TCPM. Laws now require the Corps to share planning documents with the public, but this was not the case during Bayocean's time.

56. Terich, "Bayocean Spit," 133; "High Tides Roll onto Coastline"; "Bayocean," *Oregonian,* May 18, 1939, 14; "$27,363,000 Projects for Northwest Delayed," *Oregonian,* July 26, 1939, 1. James Mott's father was Dr. W. S. Mott, one of the three *Eastman v. Potter* plaintiffs T. Irving wined and dined in July 1911. He either stopped making payments and let TBPRC take back his lot or sold it to someone else who later got the deed because he never received one: "M" Indirect Index to Deeds.

Chapter 7

1. Bayocean News, *Tillamook Headlight-Herald*, April 27, 1939, 7; "U.S. Engineers Making Survey of Coast Area," *Tillamook Headlight-Herald*, April 27, 1939, 1; Bayocean News, *Tillamook Headlight-Herald*, May 25, 1939, 6; Paul Bates to Congressman Walter Pierce, January 13, 1941, Oregon River and Harbor Projects (Bayocean, Willamette Valley), 1933, 1937-1941, Folder 7, Box 25, Walter M. Pierce papers, Coll 068, SCUA. The Sanderses' house was on Lot 1 in Block 38, purchased from Henry King in 1934: 1940 Assessment Roll, 56; Deed Record 73, 167.
2. Webber and Webber, *Bayocean*, 86-91.
3. Ibid. By the end of the 1930s, photos of The Mitchell show no gas pump.
4. Webber and Webber, *Bayocean*, 86-91.
5. Ibid.
6. "Bayocean is Celebrating Fine Road Improvement," *Tillamook Headlight-Herald*, July 13, 1939, 1; Bayocean News, *Tillamook Headlight-Herald*, August 24, 1939; Bayocean News, *Tillamook Headlight-Herald*, September 14, 1939, 6; Bayocean News, November 16, 1939, 6; 1941 Assessment Roll, 59; "Sea Batters Bayocean," *Oregonian,* January 6, 1940, 8; Bayocean News, *Tillamook Headlight-Herald*, December 21, 3; Lyman E Latourette, "Latourette Annals in America" (1954), 119; "Death Calls G. R. Bagley," *Oregon Journal*, December 26, 1939, 1.
7. "Sea Batters Bayocean"; "Dr. Marcellus Buys New Home," *Oregon Journal*, April 12, 1940, 15; Caption of house sketch, *Spectator*, July 13, 1912, 14.
8. "High Water Halts Travel," *Tillamook Headlight-Herald*, January 30, 1940; Deed Record 50, 220-221; Bayocean News, *Tillamook Headlight-Herald*, February 1, 1940, 7.
9. Tillamook County Court Journal P, 105, May 24, 1940.
10. "Road at Bayocean Open Despite Seas," *Tillamook Headlight-Herald*, January 16, 1941, 1; Deed Record 83, 501-502; Deed Record 79, 554; Reeder and MacDonald, *Bayocean Memories Beneath the Sand*, 34;.

11. "Sanders Home Destroyed by Slide Friday," *Tillamook Headlight-Herald*, February 29, 1941, 1; "Home Topples Off Sea Cliff," *Oregonian*, February 16, 1941; "Mott Asks Repair," *Oregonian*, January 12, 1941, 4; "Holman Notifies Bayocean People of Act for Land," *Oregon Journal*, March 6, 1941, 2. "Bayocean Spit Repairs Denied," *Oregon Journal*, March 31, 1941, sec. 2, 8.
12. "Bayocean Spit Repairs Denied"; "Reports Read on Bayocean Work Progress," *Tillamook Headlight-Herald*, June 12, 1941, 1; "McNary Requests Revetment Work for Bay Ocean," *Oregon Journal*, June 30, 1941, 30.
13. Moore, "Report on Beach Erosion Studies," 1; Lloyd L. Ruff Jr., "Preliminary Notes on the Geology of Bayocean Peninsula" (Portland District, Army Corps of Engineers, 1939), 5-9; Doug Decker, "Tillamook Burn," https://www.oregon encyclopedia.org/articles/tillamook_burn. *Littoral* is roughly the equivalent of *shoreline*, but it is defined as the entire coastal zone impacted by wave action. For the Tillamook Indian version of how the spit was created, see: Sutherland, "The Tillamook Indians and Bayocean." William Skinner Cooper, who visited the spit in 1928, published a study in 1958 confirming it was in decline, saying it had once stood 246 feet high. See more about that and Ruff's explanation of how Tillamook Spit had originally formed at: Jerry Sutherland, "Prehistoric Geomorphology of Bayocean Peninsula," https://www.bayocean.net/ 2015/02/the-shrinking-of-bayocean-peninsula.html.
14. Caption of O-382, RH-Box 170, RG 77, NARA, College Park, MD; Moore, "Report on Beach Erosion Studies," 13, 47-48; Bayocean photos 1924-1956, Box 1B, Historic Photos, 1903-1953, POR-57, RG 77, NARA, Seattle, WA.
15. Moore, "Report on Beach Erosion Studies," 46, 50-51; Cape Meares News, *Tillamook Headlight-Herald*, May 25, 1939, 6.
16. NARA 7250; Moore, "Report on Beach Erosion Studies," 3, 49, 50. Seven of the forty-two bungalows must have been in such bad shape by 1939 that Moore did not count them.
17. NARA 7250; Moore, "Report on Beach Erosion Studies," 57.
18. Moore, "Report on Beach Erosion Studies," 1; "Shore Protection Board Report on Tillamook Bay, Oregon," December 17, 1940, Beach Erosion Studies (Entry 514, 1, 6), Box 48, RG 77, NARA, Washington, DC.
19. Webber and Webber, *Bayocean*, 96-97.
20. Henry King, Cremains File No. 14167, OSA; "T" Direct and Indirect Indexes of Deeds; The Bayocean Company Incorporation Papers; Deed Record 78, 6; Certificate of Title No. 1294, Register of Titles Vol. 7, 222, TCPM. The first stage of the 1925 Social Security Act granted Old-Age Assistance grants through the state: "Historical Background and Development of Social Security–Pre-Social Security Period," https://www.ssa.gov/history/briefhistory3.html.

21. "Ocean On Rampage," *Oregon Journal*, December 18, 1941, 14; Russell Hoover to Bert Webber, March 2, 1973, Bayocean Gov. Doc. box, Webber Research Archives; "Marcellus Cottage Torn Down," *Tillamook Headlight-Herald*, December 25, 1941, 3.
22. A Bayocean News column did appear, after a four-year absence, on June 28, 1951, but it could have been written by the *Tillamook Headlight-Herald* editor, as had been the case during the *Headlight* and *Herald* years.
23. Brian James Trimmer, "Defenders of the West: The History of Naval Air Station Tillamook" (Pepperdine University, 1997), 20, 25, 9. I could find no evidence of the Tillamook Guerillas—a short-lived, private militia that formed at the start of World War II—having anything to do with Bayocean. To read about them, see: Cain Allen, "Tillamook Guerrillas, 1942," https://www.oregonhistory project.org/articles/historical-records/tillamook-guerrillas-1942.
24. "Reflects Increase In Population," *Tillamook Headlight-Herald*, July 15, 1943; Harold Bennett, in discussion with the author, September 28, 2021.
25. Donny Meyers, in discussion with the author, October 24, 2020; Deed Record 110, 407-408; Deed Record 66, 26; Reeder and MacDonald, *Bayocean Memories Beneath the Sand*, 7.
26. "Bayocean Gets Gift from Sea," *Oregonian,* March 13, 1943, 6.
27. "Erosion at Bayocean," *Tillamook Headlight-Herald*, October 15, 1942, 1; Tillamook County Court Journal Q, 55; "Watch Bayocean Grow," advertisement, *Tillamook Headlight-Herald*, August 24, 1944, 3. The county must have considered the lots north of 22nd Avenue unavailable because two-thirds of 2,800 is 1,867.
28. Deed Record 89, 185-186; Nellie Walton to Cheryl Adamschuck, November 4, 1967, Michael Watkins's collection. The Waltons' lot was number 28 in Block 57.
29. Eleanor C. Bishop, *Prints in the Sand: The U.S. Coast Guard Beach Patrol in World War II* (Missoula: Pictorial Histories Pub. Co., 1989), ix-1.; Jerry Sutherland, "The War Dog Beach Patrol of Bayocean," https://www.bay ocean.net/2016/02/the-war-dog-beach-patrol-of-bayocean.html.
30. Bishop, *Prints in the Sand*, 16, 53-57. Entry 186, Boxes 20-23, Ship and Unit War Diaries, 1942-45, 13th Naval District, Records of the Surface Facilities Branch, RG 26, NARA, Washington, D. C.; Jerry Sutherland, "The War Dog Beach Patrol of Bayocean."
31. Bishop, *Prints in the Sand*, 16; Donny Meyers, in discussion with the author, February 9, 2016; April 1943 to September 1944 Beach Patrol Station Logs, Bay Ocean, Oregon, Entry 159E, Boxes 3303–3304, Entry 159F Boxes 2932–2934, RG 26, NARA, Washington, D. C.
32. Bayocean Patrol Logs; Garibaldi Scope of Operations, October 1, 1943, File No. 601, 13th Naval District, Coast Guard Historic Subject Files, Box 7, RG

26, NARA, Seattle, WA; Sutherland, "The War Dog Beach Patrol of Bayocean"; Estate of Dora L. E. Poulsen, Deed Record 87, 338-344; Reeder and MacDonald, *Bayocean Memories Beneath the Sand*, 51; "Paul C. Bates Funeral Set," *Oregonian* , February 6, 1943, 6; Jesse Vance Mason Jr. to Bert Webber, January 18, 1974, Webber Research Archives.

33. Donny Meyers, February 9, 2016; Jesse Vance Mason Jr., in discussion with the author, January 30, 2016; Joann (Dolan) Steffey, in discussion with the author, August 19, 2015; Deed Record 87, 271. Since other Jesses appear in my book and Mason often referred to himself as Vance, I will do the same.
34. Bayocean Patrol Logs; Bishop, *Prints in the Sand*, 56; Vance Mason, January 30, 2016.
35. Bay Ocean Patrol Logs; Garibaldi Scope of Operations, October 1, 1943; "Barracks Being Erected," *Tillamook Headlight-Herald*, October 7, 1942, 1; Vance Mason, January 30, 2016; "Cape Meares WWII Radar Site," http://fortwiki.com/Cape_Meares_WWII_Radar_Site. The Bayocean Coast Guard station borrowed a truck from the Army because they had none, so they owed them a favor.
36. Bishop, *Prints in the Sand.*, 73; Bay Ocean Patrol Logs; Deed Record 91, 295; Deed Record 87, 344-345; "Buys Bay Ocean Property," *Tillamook Headlight-Herald*, April 13, 1944, 1; Deed Record 91, 295.
37. Reeder and MacDonald, *Bayocean Memories Beneath the Sand*, 51; Geological Society of the Oregon Country newsletter, January 1947, 1; Jerry Sutherland, "The Hicks House," https://www.bayocean.net/2015/06/the-hicks-house.html; Buck Sherwood to Bert Webber, April 15, 1989, Webber Research Archives.
38. "Bayocean Land Washes to Sea," *Oregon Journal*, March 15, 1945, 9; Births, Local and Personal, *Tillamook Headlight-Herald*, October 5, 1944, 5.
39. "Bayocean Land Washes to Sea," *Oregon Journal*, March 15, 1945, 9; Bayocean News, *Tillamook Headlight-Herald*, March 22, 1945, 6; Corinth L. Crook letter (n.d.) to Senator Wayne Morse, Box A126, Wayne L. Morse papers, Coll 001, SCUA.
40. "Congressman Mott Inspects Conditions of Bayocean Coast," *Tillamook Headlight-Herald*, April 12, 1945; Cape Meares News, *Tillamook Headlight-Herald*, April 29, 1948; Deed Record 90, 193-194; Deed Record 78, 514-515.
41. Jerry Sutherland, "Four Currin Cabins," https://www.bayocean.net/2016/10/four-currin-cabins.html; Ruth Currin Spaniol, "Over the Die or Do: A Story of a Marriage," (1992), 83, 85. The cabins were on Lots 23 and 24 in Block 30: 1951 Assessment Roll, Vol. 3, 52.
42. "Bayocean Land Washes to Sea," *Oregon Journal*, March 15, 1945, 9; "Bayocean Home Torn Down," *Tillamook Headlight-Herald*, March 15, 1945, 1; "Roberts House at Bayocean Slides into The Sea," *Tillamook Headlight-Herald*, March 22, 1945; "Tides Carries in Debris and Causes Resort Damage,"

Tillamook Headlight-Herald, March 29, 1945, 1; "High Tides Wash Out Garage," *Tillamook Headlight-Herald*, February 5, 1948, 1; Mrs. R. W. Watkins, Bayocean Community Club, Letter to the Editor, "Bayocean Not All Gone," *Oregonian,* March 21, 1945, 4.

43. "Blimp 'Slapped Down' In Bay; Crew Escapes," *Tillamook Headlight-Herald*, March 22, 1945, 1; Bayocean News, *Tillamook Headlight-Herald*, March 22, 1945, 6.
44. Reeder and MacDonald, *Bayocean Memories Beneath the Sand*, 55-56; Meyers, October 24, 2020; Vance Mason, January 30, 2016.
45. Jesse Vance Mason Jr., in discussion with the author, August 19, 1915; Reeder and MacDonald, *Bayocean Memories Beneath the Sand*, 47-48. Drale later told Brian Trimmer the same story about dropping date requests to a boy at Bayocean. Vance had picked the right pilot, because the lieutenant had also landed his blimp on a beach in Southern Oregon so crewmen could gather phone numbers from a group of girls: Brian Trimmer, in discussion with the author, February 7, 2016; Trimmer, "Defenders of the West: The History of Naval Air Station Tillamook", 67-68.
46. Deed Record 92, 77; Mason to Webber, January 18, 1974. The Lockeses' house was on Lot 4 in Block 55.
47. Deed Record 92, 314; Deed Record 98, 135-136; "Mrs. Swan Hawkinson," *Tillamook Headlight-Herald*, August 23, 1956, 8; Swan Hawkinson, Oregon Death Index, 1903-1998, OSA.
48. "New Store Planned for Bayocean," *Tillamook Headlight-Herald*, August 30, 1945; Cape Meares News, *Tillamook Headlight-Herald*, March 30,1950, sec. 2, 3.
49. "U.S. Engineers Investigating Bay Improvement," *Tillamook Headlight-Herald*, January 10, 1946, 1; "U.S. Engineers Hear Report on Needs of Tillamook Bay, Bayocean," *Tillamook Headlight-Herald*, September 13, 1945, 1.
50. Bayocean News, *Tillamook Headlight-Herald*, February 14, 1946, 12; "Bayocean Road Has New Store," *Tillamook Headlight-Herald*, February 28, 1946, sec. 2, 1.
51. "Improvement of Bay and Bar Question Delayed," *Tillamook Headlight-Herald*, July 18, 1946, 1; "Erosion Facts Stressed Before Army Engineers," *Tillamook Headlight-Herald*, September 26, Bay City Clam-Mor.
52. "Norblad, Back Home, Describes Congress," *Tillamook Headlight-Herald*, October 3, 1946, 1; Bayocean News, *Tillamook Headlight-Herald*, January 31, 1946, 11; *Tillamook and Vicinity Telephone Directory* (Tillamook: Pacific Telephone and Telegraph Co, 1945), TCPM. The Watkinses are listed in many of the extant Tillamook phone books whereas the Mitchells are not.
53. Latourette had been promoted to Portland City Attorney in February 1938: "Death Takes Ex-Attorney," *Oregonian*, August 16, 1963, 27.
54. "Bayocean Cottages To Open May 1st," *Tillamook Headlight-Herald*, April 4, 1946, 11; Bayocean News, *Tillamook Headlight-Herald*, August 17, 1939, 7;

Webber and Webber, *Bayocean*, 58, 95, 30; NARA M841, Roll 106; Harold Bennett, September 28, 2021. Latourette must have sold to the Hoovers on contract because no deed was recorded.

55. Webber and Webber, *Bayocean*, 95-96, 102. Russell Hoover had made the bungalows rectangular by filling the corner where the bathroom stuck out with a closet.
56. Tillamook County Court Journal R, 507-509; 1951 Assessment Roll, Vol. 3, 51; Deed Record 102, 226-227; Deed Record 104; Deed Record 109, 409. Rinehart's house was on Lot 3 in Block 57.
57. Cape Meares News, *Tillamook Headlight-Herald*, December 19, 1946, 8; Bayocean News, *Tillamook Headlight-Herald*, January 31, 1946, 11; "Cape Meares Boasts Spring Flowers, *Tillamook Headlight-Herald*, December 5, 1946, 4.
58. Barr, "The Bagleys of Bayocean"; Deed Record 119, 95-96; Webber and Webber, *Bayocean*, 30; "Obituary: Electrical Engineer's Ritest Set," *Oregon Journal*, July 13, 1970, 5; "Harold Bennett, September 28, 2021; Deed Record 105, 552-553; Deed Record 65: 343; The Rainbow Girls House was on Lot 27 in Block 57. The Thomases' house was on Lot 39 in Block 50. They must have been purchasing it on a contract from Ray's sister, Myrtle Handley, who owned the oyster beds, because they were never granted a deed: 1951 Assessment Roll, Vol. 3, 55; Deed Record 110, 599-600. Perry Reeder helped build their house before his family moved to Rainier, Oregon on the first of February 1948: Perry Reeder Jr., November 11, 2021; *Tillamook Headlight-Herald*, February 5, 1948, sec. 2, 2.
59. Perry Reeder Jr., in discussions with the author, September 13, 2017, and October 26, 2020; Harold Bennett, September 28, 2021; multiple discussions, Bayocean reunion, August 19, 2015, Barbara Bennett Community Center, Cape Meares, Oregon. Francis Mitchell did not let his Missouri upbringing influence business decisions because (on August 31, 2021) Donny Meyers recalled a métis family living in The Mitchell during World War II. But he is the only surviving resident who recalled having a non-white neighbor. The 1940 Census (Bayocean Precinct, Tillamook County) lists a Filipino servant living with the Marcelluses, but they left before Donny arrived. The redlining of metropolitan subdivisions was common when Bayocean Park lots were popular, but to which resort would salesmen have redirected wealthy non-whites? Would any have had the means or interest? I could find no discussion of this, nor anything to suggest non-whites ever owned property on the spit. In the early 1920s, Tillamook's Ku Klux Klan Chapter 8 was notably successful, but Portland receivers were still selling lots under court supervision then. Tillamook-Bayocean Company principals appear in the chapter's archives (Collection Bx 046) at the University of Oregon's Special Collections and University Archives Library, but by the time they took control, Tillamook's Klan was in decline. Bayocean was not mentioned, and it is highly unlikely that Arthur Beals and his cohorts had the occasion to turn

away non-whites because their percentage of Tillamook County's population has always been tiny: Eckard V. Toy Jr., "The Ku Klux Klan in Tillamook, Oregon," *The Pacific Northwest Quarterly* 53, no. 2 (1962): 60-64.

60. 2015 Bayocean reunion; comment in the copyedited draft returned February 6, 2023, by Lisa Jensen, who had interviewed Phyllis (Locke) Anderson and Susan (Bagley) Barr while gathering material for a novel about Bayocean.

Chapter 8

1. "Engineer OKs Bay Dredging," *Oregonian,* April 3, 1947, 12; "Tillamook Bay and Bar, Oregon," Letter from the Secretary of the Army, House of Representatives Document No. 650, 80th Congress, 2nd Session (1948); Dicken, Johannessen, and Hanneson, *Some Recent Physical Changes of the Oregon Coast*, 58.
2. Tillamook County Court Journal R, 198-200, 269, 479, 526; "Engineers Seek Better Bay Protection," *Tillamook Headlight-Herald*, December 10, 1953, 1; Donny Meyers, February 9, 2016; For Rent, *Tillamook Headlight-Herald*, November 3, 1949, 7; Del Gilkison to Senator Wayne Morse, June 2, 1949, Wayne L. Morse papers, Coll 001, Box A126, SCUA. Kaaren Ann Kottages was on Lots 4, 5, 6, and 9 in Block 51. No one recalls the number of units, but two chimneys and two doors appear in photos.
3. Donny Meyers, February 9, 2016; Bayocean News, October 2, 1947, sec. 2, 2; "Pair Married Half Century," November 23, 1947, 19.
4. Bayocean News, *Tillamook Headlight-Herald*, October 2, 1947, sec. 2, 2; Deed Record 108, 33; 1920 Census, Precinct 199, Portland, Oregon; Deed Record 45, 611; Deed Record 59, 517; Deed Record 65, 366; Deed Record 66, 25; Deed Record 106, 47-48; Deed Record 107, 390-391; Deed Record 114, 22-23; 1949 Assessment Roll, Vol. 3, 49. Hance's cabin was on Lot 30 in Block 44. The Strowger rental was on Lot 9 in Block 46.
5. Bayocean News, *Tillamook Headlight-Herald*, September 4, 1947, 2.
6. Deed Record 105, 115-116; Deed Record 107, 540-541; Deed Record 114, 542-543; "Engineer OKs Bay Dredging," *Oregonian,* April 3, 1947, 12; Deed Record 110, 39-46; "New Tract Land at Cape Meares Called 'Hauxhurst'," *Tillamook Headlight-Herald*, May 19, 1949, 8; Mike Watkins, e-mail to author, April 29, 2016; Deed Record 184, 235-247; Deed Record 191, 245-250; "Arthur Glenn Beals Pioneer Dies After Long Illness," *Tillamook Headlight-Herald*, December 11, 1958, 1, 8. The Wenzel-Braune place was on Lot 36 in Block 44.
7. "Cape Meares Enjoys Holiday Pogie Fishing," *Tillamook Headlight-Herald*, December 4, 1947, 11; "High Tides Wash Out Garage," *Tillamook Headlight-Herald*, February 5, 1948, 1.
8. Cape Meares News, *Tillamook Headlight-Herald*, February 5, 1948, sec. 2, 2; Cape Meares News, *Tillamook Headlight-Herald*, April 15, 1948, sec. 2, 6; Bayocean News, *Tillamook Headlight-Herald*, January 31, 1946, 11; Cape Meares News, *Tillamook Headlight-Herald*, July 15, 1948, sec. 2, 2.

9. Levesque, "History of Port Districts," Appendix Map #1; "Election Carries for Bayocean Port," *Tillamook Headlight-Herald*, March 25, 1948, 4; Governor John H. Hall papers, Collection 93A-22, Box 2 Folder 13, OSA. I derived port dimensions from the number of sections on Levesque's map.
10. "Tillamook Bay and Bar, Oregon," Letter from the Secretary of the Army, House of Representatives Document No. 650, 80th Congress, 2nd Session. The Port of Bay City did not officially change its name to Port of Garibaldi in 1991, but commercial shipping and port operations had moved to the north end of the bay by the end of World War II: Levesque, "History of Port Districts," 65, 86.
11. Deed Book 114, 410.
12. Medcalf Diary; loose notes, Jack Medcalf Box; Bayocean News, *Tillamook Headlight-Herald*, September 4, 1947, 2; Deed Record 113, 263-264. Medcalf's cabin was on Lot 25 of Block 44: 1951 Assessment Roll, Vol. 3, 51.
13. Medcalf Diary; Barr, "The Bagleys of Bayocean," 9. Medcalf referred to adults by the first initial of their last name preceded by *Mrs.* or *Mr.* I used contextual information to figure out who they were.
14. Medcalf Diary.
15. Ibid.
16. Ibid.
17. Ibid; "High Wind, Big Waves Hit Coast," *Oregonian,* November 4, 1948, 1; Bayocean Water District Board to A. T. Dolan, September 28, 1942, Bayocean Social Register No. 3; Bayocean Water District Board to County Judge Harold Woods, September 28, 1942, Bayocean Social Register No. 3. The letters asked Dolan to stop excavating and Woods to force Dolan to stop if he did not do so on his own.
18. Medcalf Diary. Rock Crusher gap had not breached since early 1939, so it was "new" to residents who had not lived there then.
19. Ibid. At high tide, there were three islands: one between Dolan and Jackson Gaps, one between Jackson and Rock Crusher Gaps, and one between Rock Crusher and Natatorium Gaps. The latter remained dry at low tide.
20. Ibid.
21. "Citizens Stay on Bayocean," *Oregonian,* November 8, 1948, 1; *Tillamook and Vicinity Telephone Directory* (1948); Deed Record 107, 436; Hoover to Webber, March 2, 1973.
22. "Bayocean Road Again Severed; Repairs Menaced," *Oregon Journal*, November 16, 1948, 6. As said earlier, Medcalf did not type out the full names of those who left, but the only people with last names starting with *L.* and *M.* then living on the spit were the Lockes and the Meyers.
23. Cape Meares News, *Tillamook Headlight-Herald*, November 18, 1948.
24. Medcalf Diary.
25. Ibid.

26. Mel Baldwin, "Breaks in Peninsula Threaten Whole Bay," *Oregonian,* January 2, 1949, NW, 8.
27. Elizabeth S. Ryan, "A Queen Dies: Victim of Time and Tide," *Oregonian,* January 2, 1949, NW, 8. Tillamook County did not give Oregon the tract at Kincheloe Point, and no part of the spit has ever been a park.
28. Ibid. Ida was eighty years old when Medcalf saw her working at the gaps with Francis. Others recall it being quaint, but she may not have had a choice.
29. "Trespassing At Bay Ocean Is Serious Problem," *Tillamook Headlight-Herald,* January 13, 1949, 8.
30. "Engineers View Bayocean Loss," November 11, 1948, 16; "Bay Ocean Protection, Officers' Salaries Brought Before C. of C.," *Tillamook Headlight-Herald,* January 13, 1949, 1; transcription of two phone calls between R. E. Hickson (Portland District) and Mr. Dvoracheck (Washington, DC), April 4, 1949, Folder 72, Box 273, Civil Works Project Files, 1902-1968, POR-81, RG 77, NARA, Seattle, WA. A wood water pipe coupler is shown at Sutherland, "Bayocean Park Plumbing."
31. Charles Oluf Olsen, "'Coney Island' for Clams," *Oregon Journal,* May 8, 1949, Magazine, 1, 4, 5.
32. Kaaren Ann Kottages to Russ Sacket, Sunday Magazine Editor of the *Oregon Journal,* May 12, 1949, Bayocean Miscellaneous folder, TCPM.
33. Ibid. David Baker was the only person living on the spit when the Gilkisons arrived in 1947 who also lived on the spit in 1909. The stress of watching his dream of a new life in Bayocean Park slipping away must have triggered the paranoid state diagnosed later by Oregon State Hospital psychiatrists. Losing The Mitchell thirty-five years earlier might have also been the trigger.
34. Ibid.
35. Ibid.
36. Jerry Schlegel, in discussion with the author, November 25, 2015.
37. Gertrude L. Gates, Lena V. Brownell, and Lutie E. Cake Bill of Sale to Milton Schlegel, March (n.d.), 1949, Mike Watkins's collection; "Pagoda House Moved," *Tillamook Headlight-Herald,* April 7, 1949, 2; Jerry Schlegel, November 25, 2015.
38. Mike Watkins, June 19, 1915; "Moving Pagoda Proves Exciting, *Tillamook Headlight-Herald,* April 14, 1949, sec. 2, 5.
39. Jerry Schlegel, November 25, 2015; Deed Record 106, 185-186; "Minor Building Damage Noted," *Tillamook Headlight-Herald,* April 14, 1949, 1; Jerry Sutherland, "Three Other Houses Moved from Bayocean," https://www.bayocean.net/ 2015/06/three-other-houses-moved-from-bayocean.html.
40. Jerry Schlegel, November 25, 2015; Mike Watkins, June 19, 1915; "House Warming Party," *Tillamook Headlight-Herald,* August 11, 1949, sec. 2, 4.

41. "Vacationers Enjoy Bayocean Beaches, *Tillamook Headlight-Herald*, September 29, 1949; Webber and Webber, *Bayocean*, 30, 58; Russell E. Hoover Sr. letter to Bert Webber, February 24, 1973, Bayocean Advance Copies box, Webber Research Archives; NARA M841, Roll 106. Hugh Glenn either continued Hoover's contract or set up a new one with Lyman Latourette because no deed was recorded.
42. 1940 Census, Home Acres, Vallejo Township, Solano County, California; Bennett to Webber, March 1971, Webber Research Archives; NARA M841, Roll 106; Perry Reeder Jr., October 26, 2020. All the bungalows were still standing when Nellie Walton left in 1954: Walton to Adamschuck.
43. "Bay Road Reported in Bad Shape," *Tillamook Headlight-Herald*, November 10, 1949, 8.
44. "Breakers Strikes [*sic*] Visitor to Ground," *Tillamook Headlight-Herald*, November 24, 1949, 6; "Storm Leaves No Damage," *Tillamook Headlight-Herald*, December 1, 1949, 1; Lillian Thomas, "Saga of Bay Ocean," Bayocean Genl. box, Webber Research Archives, Tillamook County Library; "Bayocean Post Office Gives Up Name Following Transfer to Cape Meares," *Oregonian,* April 5, 1953, 22.
45. Joann (Dolan) Steffey, August 19, 2015; "Bay Ocean Fire Destroys Home; Two Men Burned," *Tillamook Headlight-Herald*, January 12, 1950, 1.
46. Record of Appointment of Postmasters; Perry Reeder Jr., November 11, 2021; "George Baker Dies in Burning Home," *Tillamook Headlight-Herald*, October 12, 1944, 1; Deed Record 93, 249-250; Bennett and Sherwood map, March 1971, Webber Research Archives. Cople Britton co-owned the house and lot with Bauman but was not known to locals. They bought part of Lot 4 in Block 59 for $40 from the county in 1949: Deed Record 118, 548-549.
47. Cape Meares News, *Tillamook Headlight-Herald*, September 29, 1950, sec. 2, 7; "Ocean Breaks Through Gap," *Tillamook Headlight-Herald*, October 12, 1950, 1; "C of C Surveys ay Navigation Channels," *Tillamook Headlight-Herald*, March 22, 1951, 1, 8.
48. Cape Meares News, *Tillamook Headlight-Herald*, March 29, 1951, sec. 2, 7; Cape Meares News, *Tillamook Headlight-Herald*, March 15, 1951, sec. 2, 6; Cape Meares News, *Tillamook Headlight-Herald*, March 8, 1951, sec. 2, 7; "Cape Meares Takes Land Clearing as Project," *Tillamook Headlight-Herald*, July 20, 1950, sec. 2, 7.
49. "Cape Meares Community Bldg. Progressing," *Tillamook Headlight-Herald*, April 5, 1951, 2; Cape Meares News, March 29, 1951; Jerry Schlegel, 2015 Bayocean reunion.
50. Betty Watkins, "Bay Ocean Post Office History Told," *Tillamook Headlight-Herald*, April 9, 1953, 1; "Bay Ocean Post Office Moved," *Tillamook Headlight-Herald*, November 1, 1951, 1.

51. "Tillamook Bay Area Storm Racked," *Tillamook Headlight-Herald*, December 6, 1951, 1, 4; "Storm Takes Wahl House at Bayocean," *Tillamook Headlight-Herald*, March 19, 1953, 5.
52. Cape Meares News, *Tillamook Headlight-Herald*, January 10, 1952, 8; "Ocean Reported on Rampage," *Tillamook Headlight-Herald*, January 17, 1952, 4.
53. Cape Meares News, *Tillamook Headlight-Herald*, February 7, 1952, sec. 2, 8; Deed Record 136, 288-289; Deed Record 139, 376-377; Harold Bennett, September 28, 2021; Cape Meares News, *Tillamook Headlight-Herald*, August 13, 1953, sec. 2, 7.
54. "Bayocean Desolation Shocks Area," *Tillamook Headlight-Herald*, February 14, 1952, 1; "Committees Appointed for Bay Ocean," *Tillamook Headlight-Herald*, February 21, 1952, 4; "Engineer to Investigate Bay Ocean Destruction," *Tillamook Headlight-Herald*, February 28, 1.
55. Barr, "The Bagleys of Bayocean"; Sutherland, "The Hicks House"; "Firm Moves Bayocean Homes," *Tillamook Headlight-Herald*, February 7, 1952, 1; Deed Record 119, 95-96; Deed Record 120, 40; "A Present Day Scene at Bayocean," *Tillamook Headlight-Herald*, February 21, 1952, sec. 2, 3; "Bayocean Geology Interesting to Student," *Tillamook Headlight-Herald*, March 27, 1952, sec. 2, 2. Morgan Burckard and George Burckhard were not related. Like Coates and Coats, misspellings by the press made it appear they might be.
56. Sutherland, "The Hicks House"; "Bayocean Geology Interesting to Student"; Barr, "The Bagleys of Bayocean."
57. Webber and Webber, *Bayocean*, 97, 93; "Hugh B. Glenn Killed in Accident," *Tillamook Headlight-Herald*, July 24, 1952, 1; "'Breakthrough' Viewed by Throng of Sightseers," *Tillamook Headlight-Herald*, November 20, 1952, 1; Russell Hoover to Bert Webber, November 1973, Bayocean Gov. Doc. box, Webber Research Archives. Newspapers referred to the last bungalow manager as "Mr. Sandy" or simply "Sandy." His first name and middle initial come from a note on the back of a photo posted by Patrick Andrus on March 4, 2020 on Old Tillamook Times: https://www.facebook.com/groups/242715339171621/ permalink/2651978571578607.
58. Webber and Webber, *Bayocean*, 97, 104-105; Deed Record 126, 175-176.
59. Webber and Webber, *Bayocean,* 104-105, 97.
60. Sherwood to Webber, April 15, 1989; Donny Meyers, October 24, 2020; Cape Meares News, *Tillamook Headlight-Herald*, June 8, 1950; 1950 Census, Bayocean Precinct, Tillamook, Oregon; Cape Meares News, *Tillamook Headlight-Herald*, August 13, 1953, sec. 2, 7.
61. "Ocean Closes Bay Ocean Road," *Tillamook Headlight-Herald*, November 6, 1952, 8.
62. Deed Record 35, 289-290; Deed Record 90, 576; Mike Watkins, in discussion with the author, July 27, 2020.
63. "Last House on the Road," *Tillamook Headlight-Herald*, December 25, 1952, 2.
64. Ibid.

65. Ibid; Mike Watkins, July 27, 2020; Sutherland, "Three Other Houses Moved from Bayocean."
66. Paul D. Komar and Thomas A. Terich, "Changes Due to Jetties at Tillamook Bay, Oregon" (paper presented at the 15th Annual Coastal Engineering Conference, Honolulu, Hawaii, July 11-17, 1976), 1807-1808; "Aid Offer Declined," *Oregonian,* November 16, 1952, 1.
67. "Bayocean Scene," *Tillamook Headlight-Herald*, December 18, 1952, 1; "Four Currin Cabins." The *Headlight-Herald* misspelled "Currin" as "Kern."
68. "Mrs. Asta Bugge," *Oregon Journal*, September 6, 1950, 5; "Crew to Tillamook."
69. William Lambert, "Mighty Sea Carves Bayocean Peninsula into Crumbling Isle," *Oregonian,* November 23, 1952, 32, 33; Barr, "The Bagleys of Bayocean."
70. "Mighty Sea Carves Bayocean Peninsula into Crumbling Isle."
71. Cape Meares News, *Tillamook Headlight-Herald*, December 4, 1952, 7; Franklin T. Andrew, Oregon Death Index, 1903-1998, OSA; Cape Meares News, December 11, 1952, sec. 3, 3; "Elks Take Gifts to Bayocean," *Tillamook Headlight-Herald*, January 1, 1953, 1; "Mighty Sea Carves Bayocean Peninsula into Crumbling Isle." Who might have drilled the well is a mystery.

Chapter 9

1. "Review Report on Tillamook Bay and Bar, Oregon" (Portland District, Army Corps of Engineers, 1953), 1.
2. "U.S. Engineers Send Surveying Crew to Bay Area," *Tillamook Headlight-Herald*, January 1, 1953, 1.
3. "Review Report," 5-6, 29, Appendix hydrographic chart TM-1-139.
4. Ibid., 3, 6-8, 19, 28, 29.
5. "County Gives Unofficial Report of Vote," *Tillamook Headlight-Herald*, November 6, 1952, 1; Deed Record 254, 136.
6. Cape Meares News, *Tillamook Headlight-Herald*, January 8, 1953, 8; "One Killed as Storms Rake Area," *Oregonian,* January 10, 1953, 1; Cape Meares News, *Tillamook Headlight-Herald*, January 15, 1953, 7.
7. "Bayocean Storms Strike Heavily At Coast," *Tillamook Headlight-Herald*, January 15, 1953, 1; "Rogue River Waters Fall, Highway Reopens in Area," *Oregonian*, January 20, 1953, 7; Cape Meares News, *Tillamook Headlight-Herald*, January 29, 1953, 3; Sutherland, "Four Currin Cabins"; "Storm Takes Wahl House at Bayocean," *Tillamook Headlight-Herald*, March 19, 1953, 5; Perry Reeder Jr., October 26, 2020; Perry Reeder Jr. noted *Mark Wald* on a photo of Strowger's rental house, November 8, 2021.
8. Betty Watkins, "Bay Ocean Post Office History Told," *Tillamook Headlight-Herald*, April 9, 1953, 1; "Cape Meares Post Office Record Challenged," *Tillamook Headlight-Herald*, February 11, 1954, sec. 2, 8.

9. "Engineers Believer Rock Dike in Tillamook Bay Might Save Sea-Battered Bayocean Peninsula," *Oregonian*, sec.2, 4; "Prospects for Bayocean Breakwater Improve," *Tillamook Headlight-Herald*, March 19, 1953, 1, 5; "Action in Support of Bay and Bar Contemplated," *Tillamook Headlight-Herald*, April 9, 1953, 1; "150 Years of Oyster Farming," *Tillamook Headlight-Herald*, July 14, 2009. The breakwater is often referred to as a dike (Dike Road, for example) or a jetty, but the structures are technically different.
10. "Hearing Before Engineers Justifies Bay Breakwater," *Tillamook Headlight-Herald*, April 16, 1953, 4; "Mitchells of Bayocean Welcomed in Town," *Tillamook Headlight-Herald*, April 23, 1953, sec. 2, 5; Cape Meares News, *Tillamook Headlight-Herald*, April 9, 1953, sec. 2, 2.
11. "Hearing Before Engineers Justifies Bay Breakwater," *Tillamook Headlight-Herald*, April 16, 1953, 4; Tillamook County Court Journal V, 410-411; "Levesque, "History of Port Districts," 62-65, Appendix Map #1.
12. Tillamook County Court Journal W, 31; "Tillamook Bay Administers Oath to Commissioners," *Tillamook Headlight-Herald*, January 6, 1955, 3. The Port of Tillamook had been dissolved, and the channel from Bay City to Tillamook abandoned, in 1919, leaving its name available: Levesque, "History of Port Districts," 40-41.
13. Margaret Coates to Howard V. Morgan, September 7, 1955, Irrigation Reclamation Projects, Tillamook Bay and Bar (Bayocean) 1955, Folder 6, Box 16, Richard Neuberger papers, Ax 078, SCUA. Coates referred to a "tradition of the Indians, that once the entrance to the Bay was at the south end." I found no other mention of that tradition, but there is geological evidence of a prehistoric south bay inlet: Sutherland, "Prehistoric Geomorphology of Bayocean Peninsula"; Sutherland, "Bayocean Spit Breached in 1700."
14. "Rescued," *Tillamook Headlight-Herald*, October 22, 1953.
15. "F. D. Mitchell of Bay Ocean Troubled," *Tillamook Headlight-Herald*, November 5, 1953; "F. D. Mitchell Placed in Custody," *Tillamook Headlight-Herald*, November 12, 1953, 1.
16. "F. D. Mitchell Placed in Custody"; "Action, *Tillamook Headlight-Herald*, November 12, 1953; Mitchell File, OSH.
17. Mitchell File, OSH.
18. Ibid.
19. "Paranoid Reactions," in *International Encyclopedia of the Social Sciences* (2020).; Mitchell File, OSH; Department of Human Services, Addictions and Mental Health Division Oregon State Hospital Administrative Overview, https://sos.oregon.gov/archives/ Documents/recordsmgmt/sched/overview-hospital.pdf.
20. Mitchell File, OSH.
21. Ibid.
22. Ibid.

23. Ibid.
24. "Mrs. F. D. Mitchell Passes Away," *Tillamook Headlight-Herald*, December 31, 1953; Mitchell File, OSH; Jerry Sutherland, "Crabapple Park," https://www.bayocean.net/2017/03/crabapple-park.html.
25. "Breakwater Rejected by U.S. Engineer Corp," *Tillamook Headlight-Herald*, November 26, 1; "Engineers Seek Better Bay Protection," *Tillamook Headlight-Herald*, December 10, 1953, 1.
26. "Review Report," 33, 51; "Wire Announces Bayocean Okay," *Tillamook Headlight-Herald*, January 21, 1954, 1.
27. "Millage of 2.3 Mills Required in Bay Protection," *Tillamook Headlight-Herald*, March 11, 1954, 1; "Voters Refuse Approval of Bay Bonds," *Tillamook Headlight-Herald*, May 27, 1954, 1; "Election Tally Shows Upsets; Bayocean Project Wins Favor," *Tillamook County News*, November 4, 1954, 1.
28. Senate Document 128, 83rd Congress, 2nd Session, September 3, 1954; "Congress Approves $200,000 Bay Project Emergency Funds," *Tillamook Headlight-Herald*, July 14, 1955, 1; "Bay Improvement Included in President's Budget," *Tillamook Headlight-Herald*, January 19, 1956, 1.
29. Cape Meares News, *Tillamook Headlight-Herald*, August 13, 1953, sec. 2, 7; "Review Report," Appendix Map TM-i-139; "Bayocean Cottages Moving to Garibaldi," Cape Meares News, *Tillamook Headlight-Herald*, April 15, 1954, sec2, 7; *Tillamook Headlight-Herald*, September 2, 1954, 1; Deed Record 160, 89; Perry Reeder Jr., October 26, 2020.
30. Cape Meares News, *Tillamook Headlight-Herald*, April 16, 1953, sec. 2, 8; "Likes the Quiet of Bayocean," *Tillamook Headlight-Herald*, February 11, 1954, 1; Deed Record 144, 346; Deed Record 144, 374-375; "Bayocean Cottages Moving to Garibaldi"; Walton to Adamschuck.
31. Cape Meares News, *Tillamook Headlight-Herald*, September 30, 1954, 6; "Stormy Pacific Attracts Visitors," *Tillamook Headlight-Herald*, November 18, 1954, 8; "Bayocean and The Storms," *Tillamook Headlight-Herald*, December 2, 1954, 8; 1937 Assessment Roll, Vol. 3, 98; "Burton Home New Victim at Bayocean," *Tillamook Headlight-Herald*, December 16, 1954, 1; Cape Meares News, *Tillamook Headlight-Herald*, January 27, 1955, sec. 2, 7; Cape Meares News, *Tillamook Headlight-Herald*, January 27, 1955, sec. 2, 7. Burton's house was on Lot 2 in Block 50. Houses did not fall precisely in sequence from south to north because the inlet's configuration shifted over time, and some of them were higher on the dune than others.
32. Mitchell File, OSH.
33. Reeder and MacDonald, *Bayocean Memories Beneath the Sand*, 59, 101.
34. James L. Henshaw, "Report on Construction of the Bayocean Breakwater, Tillamook Bay, Oregon" (Portland District, Army Corps of Engineers, 1956), 4; "Design Memorandum on Tillamook Bay and Bar" (Portland District, Army Corps of Engineers, 1955), 3, 7, 8, 12.

35. "Design Memorandum," 3-6, 15-18.
36. Ibid.
37. "Bay Improvement Included in President's Budget," *Tillamook Headlight-Herald*, January 19, 1956, 1; Deed Record 166, 579; Henshaw, "Report on Construction," 7, Annex V; Drawing No. O-38-13/1, NPP 150, Tillamook Bay Folder 6, Box 500, Civil Works Project Files, 1902-1968, POR-81, RG 77, NARA, Seattle; Deed Record 88, 63; Perry Reeder Jr., in discussion with author, November 11, 2021. Fifty-four easements were signed, covering 356.37 acres, 140.00 of which were owned by Tillamook County: Levesque, "History of Port Districts," 65. According to the Corps, the Bennetts' cabin was on Lot 33 or Lot 34 in Block 59, Stein's on a tract across from Lot 30 in block 70, Long's on a tract just north of Stein's, and Carey's on a tract across from Lot 5 in Block 55.
38. Sutherland, "William George Owned Mitchell's General Store"; Henshaw, "Report on Construction," 3; Civil Works Project Photographs, 1839-1988, Box 64, POR-81, RG 77, NARA, Seattle, WA.
39. Bayocean Peninsula folder 2, 1, Civil Works Project Files, 1902-1968, Box 463, NPP800.925, POR-81, RG 77, NARA, Seattle, WA; *Latourette v. United States*; Tillamook County v. Harriet Cook, et al., Tillamook County Circuit Court Case No. 11-526; "Death Takes Ex-Attorney," *Oregonian*, August 16, 1963, 27. Arthur Beals owned more property than Latourette within Bayocean Park but it was predominantly on Cape Meares and not lost.
40. Henshaw, "Report on Construction," 3-6; "Engineers Prepare for Rock Quarry Near Bay Project, *Tillamook Headlight-Herald*, April 12, 1956, 1.
41. Henshaw, "Report on Construction," 22.
42. Henshaw, "Report on Construction," 23, Annex VIII, 13, 29.
43. Henshaw, "Report on Construction," 6, 17-19.
44. Henshaw, "Report on Construction," cover, 25-27. Captain Henshaw's comments about north jetty causation explains why I had to fill out a Freedom of Information Act request to get a copy of his report: Request No. FP-16-010690, Portland District, Army Corps of Engineers, March 11, 2016. Because most of their employees are civilians, it is easy to forget that the Corps is a military organization, not inclined to share internal debate nor spend time reflecting on past mistakes.
45. "Ocean Building Wide Beach Along Bayocean Dike," *Tillamook Headlight-Herald*, January 17, 1957. To see how significantly the central part of the spit has changed, see: Jerry Sutherland, "Bayocean Then and Now," https://www.bayocean.net/2015/02/bayocean-then-and-now.html.
46. Terich, "Bayocean Spit," 96.
47. "Youngsters Frolic in New Cape Meares Lake," *Tillamook Headlight-Herald*, June 6, 1957, sec. 2, 1; "Mr. Mitchell Still Optimistic About Bayocean," *Tillamook Headlight-Herald*, January 2, 1958, 2.

48. Cape Meares News, *Tillamook Headlight-Herald*, April 24, 1958, 3; Cape Meares News, *Tillamook Headlight-Herald*, February 11, 1960, 2; Cape Meares News, *Tillamook Headlight-Herald*, July 12, 1951, sec. 2, 6; "Merciless Storm Batters Cape Meares Homes," *Tillamook Headlight-Herald*, November 20, 1958, 1; Photos taken by Buck Sherwood (that he left to his niece Bonnie Reddekopp Lawrence) depict the Hough house deteriorating, but none are dated. This is the only house on the Caper Meares section of Bayocean I know for certain to have been destroyed by the sea. Many were moved back, some more than once, because no western shore stopped them.
49. Culp 106 and Sherwood 4, Lorraine Eckhardt's collection; Harold Bennett, September 28, 2021; Webber and Webber, *Bayocean*, 111, 114. The Eckhardt photos provide a date range for demolition of the Rainbow Girls House because Culp 106 is the last one showing it and Sherwood 4 is the first of it missing. Fortunately, both were dated.
50. I agreed to not identify my source or name the miscreants.
51. Jerry Sutherland, "The Last House," https://www.bayocean.net/2015/10/the-last-house.html; "Burford Wilkerson," *Oregonian*, January 23, 1994; Albert Kenney, interview by Samuel N. Dicken, March 22, 1960, Bayocean Box 1, TCPM.
52. For a list of every house, its location, last names of each owner, and its fate, see: Jerry Sutherland, "Bayocean Homes and Their Fate," https://www.bayocean.net/2022/10/bayocean-homes-and-their-fate.html.
53. Webber and Webber, *Bayocean*, 111.
54. Dale Webber, in discussion with the author, June 23, 2015; Webber and Webber, *Bayocean*, 122, 70-71, 33.
55. Dicken, Johannessen, and Hanneson, *Some Recent Physical Changes of the Oregon Coast*, 1-2.
56. Ibid., 58.
57. Ibid., 57-62.
58. "Speech To Be Presented 3 October 1962 at the 44th Meeting of the Committee on Tidal Hydraulics, Seattle, Washington by G. C. Hoare, Rivers and Harbors Section, Portland District," T077-86-0047, Civil Works Project Files, 1902-1968, Box 38, POR-81, RG 77, NARA, Seattle, WA.
59. "Jetty Project Clears Last Hurdle," *Tillamook Headlight-Herald*, May 20, 1962, 3; "Jetty Restoration Completed on Bay," *Tillamook Headlight-Herald*, August 29, 1965, 1; "One More Step Taken in Jetty Authorization," *Tillamook Headlight-Herald*, August 8, 1965, 1. The Corps hired Umpqua to finish the job after another contractor used up all the stone available locally.
60. Mitchell File, OSH.
61. Ibid.
62. Ibid.
63. Ibid; Mason to Webber, January 18, 1974.

64. Mitchell File, OSH; Sutherland, "Crabapple Park"; "Francis D. Mitchell," *Tillamook Headlight-Herald*, August 1, 1965, 1.
65. "Committee Debates South Jetty Project," *Tillamook Headlight-Herald*, August 1, 1965, 1; "House OK's South Jetty," *Tillamook Headlight-Herald*, September 26, 1965, 1; Senate Document 43, 83rd Congress, 1st Session.
66. "Army Engineers Approve Jetty In Tillamook Bay," *Oregon Journal*, May 16, 1965, 26; "General Design Memorandum on Tillamook Bay and Bar" (Portland District, Army Corps of Engineers, 1968) v, 1. The Port of Bay City morphed into the Port of Garibaldi on February 21, 1990: Levesque, "History of Port Districts," 83.
67. "General Design Memorandum," v, Supplementary Report No. 2, April 11, 1977. For the definition of mean lower low water, which the Corps uses to measure shoreline ocean depth, see: "A Guide to National Shoreline Data and Terms, https://shoreline.noaa.gov/glossary.html.
68. Ibid., 8.
69. B. E. Wilcox, Chief of Engineering Portland Division to Elizabeth Ryan, September 22, 1966, POR-81, Civil Works Project Files, 1902-1968, T077-86-0047, Box 45.
70. Donald L. Ward, "Case Histories of Corps Breakwater and Jetty Structures," *Report 6 of the Coastal Engineering Research Center* (North Pacific Division, Army Corps of Engineers, 1988), 29; "Jetty Work Halted for Winter," *Tillamook Headlight-Herald*, October 20, 1969, 7; "General Design Memorandum," 14-164.
71. "Jetty Work Halted for Winter"; "Jetty Starts May 1; Dredging Work Bid at Garibaldi Site," *Tillamook Headlight-Herald*, April 12, 1978.
72. "South Jetty Dedication Ends 10 Years of Work on Project," *Tillamook Headlight-Herald*, October 24, 1979, 1, 6; Richenda Fairhurst, *Fishers Landing* (Charleston, SC: Arcadia Pub., 2008), 105; Jerry Sutherland, "South Jetty Commemorative Plaque," https://www.bayocean.net/2015/07/south-jetty-commemorative-plaque.html.
73. "Extension of Tillamook South Jetty, Tillamook Bay, Oregon: Final Environmental Impact Statement" (Portland District, Army Corps of Engineers, 1978), 2-10, R-1. The citation was to *Development and Erosion History of Bayocean Spit, Tillamook, Oregon,* published by OSU's School of Oceanography a month after Terich turned in his dissertation because it was more readily available. Other than the title and introduction, the documents are identical. Each are available online at https://ir.library.oregonstate.edu/concern/graduate_thesis_or_dissertations/41687k63x and https://ir.library.oregonstate.edu/concern/technical_reports/r781wh276.
74. Terich, "Bayocean Spit", Acknowledgements; Komar, *The Pacific Northwest Coast*, 92; Tom Terich, e-mail to author, November 7, 2020; John Byrne, in discussion with the author, December 7, 2020. Terich was Professor Komar's

first Sea Grant scholar; Jonathan Allan, cited later, was his last: Paul Komar, in discussion with the author, October 16, 2020. Bayocean's significance to Komar's career faded as he went on to "author or co-author over 100 peer-reviewed papers" and several books, some of which I have cited: "Paul D. Komar Biography," https://www.agci.org/redhen/contact/1291.

75. Ibid., 18-20, 124. Hoare and Dicken may have come to different conclusions because of offshore soundings taken at different times of the year.
76. Terich, "Bayocean Spit", Acknowledgements, 97, 20, 2. If the Corps engineers who placed bricks on Bayocean's shoreline on May 22, 1939, had repeated the test a few months later, they would have discovered them moving south instead of north.
77. Ibid., 93, 50-51.
78. Ibid., 111-118; Committee on Tidal Hydraulics, "Tillamook Bay, Oregon," (Vicksburg, MS: Army Corps of Engineers, 1970), 6.
79. Terich, "Bayocean Spit," 110-115.
80. Ibid., 96; Map TM-1-212/2, "Tillamook Bay and Bar, Oregon, Bayocean Peninsula, Shoreline Changes," POR-80, Civil Works Project Maps and Drawings, T 077-98-0022, 1861-1992, Tube 48, NARA, Seattle, WA.
81. Paul D. Komar, *The Pacific Northwest Coast: Living with the Shores of Oregon and Washington* (Durham, NC: Duke University Press, 1997), 86.
82. Map TM-1-212/2; "Tillamook Bay Task Force Report," Oregon State University Extension Service Special Report 462 (Corvallis: OSU, 1976), 13-15.
83. Lizarraga-Arciniega, "Shoreline Changes Due to Jetty Construction on the Oregon Coast"; Dave Hogan, "Town's death blamed on jetty," *Oregonian,* August 27, 1984, sec. B, 2; Jule Gilfillan, Oregon Field Guide, "The Lost City of Bayocean," Oregon Public Broadcasting, January 16, 2020, https://www.pbs.org/video/season-31-episode-3-hpadgz; Heidi Moritz (coastal engineer, Portland District, Army Corps of Engineers), e-mail to the author, December 10, 2021. Gilfillan's "The Lost City of Bayocean" graphically portrays what happened to Bayocean.
84. Keith Tillstrom, "Sand Case Decision Nears," *Oregon Journal*, November 23, 1971, 5; Komar, *The Pacific Northwest Coast*, 103.
85. For a concise explanation of shoreline processes of the Oregon Coast, written by later Sea Grant students of Professor Komar, see: Barbara A. Katz and Stephen R. Gabriel, "Oregon's Ever-changing Coastline," Oregon State University Extension Marine Advisory Program SG 35 (Corvallis: OSU, Revised November 1982).
86 "Portland District FY 21 Industry Day YouTube Online Event," October 20, 2020, https://youtu.be/ar8RGiZkbk8; "Tillamook North and South Jetties, Garibaldi, Oregon, Major Maintenance Report," (Portland District, Army Corps of Engineers, 2003), i, 8.1 – 8.2.

87. Heidi Moritz, "Building Strong at Tillamook Bay," December 10, 2021, https://www.nwp.usace.army.mil/Locations/Oregon-Coast/Tillamook-Bay; Portland District, Army Corps of Engineers Facebook post, May 25, 2022, https://www.facebook.com/PortlandCorps/posts/pfbid02PYPT1gabQwrJwbsbkodSt288QhLTRu9nas8bTarV1rtJKsQSzD7xLw5rzf1ZuTRil; "Major Funding From New Infrastructure Bill for Tillamook Bay–$62 Million," *Tillamook County Pioneer*, March 24, 2022, https:// www.tillamookcounty pioneer.net/major-funding-from-new-infrastructure-law-for-tillamook-bay-62-million-included-in-army-corps-plan-to-repair-south-jetty.
88. Paul D. Komar et al., *Physical Processes and Geologic Hazards on the Oregon Coast* (1979), 28; NANOOS Visualization System Beach and Shoreline Changes," http://nvs.nanoos.org/BeachMapping; Jerry Sutherland, "Changes in Bayocean Beaches Studied by Dogami," https://www.bayocean.net/2015/02/changes-in-bayocean-beaches-studied-by.html.
89. Komar, *The Pacific Northwest Coast*, 18-24, 153; Heather M. Baron et al., "Incorporating Climate Change and Morphological Uncertainty into Coastal Change Hazard Assessments," *Natural Hazards* 75, no. 3 (2015): 2084.
90. People on horses and bikes will need to dismount to get through the dense underbrush of Bayocean's hills: Sutherland, "Bayocean's Highest Point."
91. Webber and Webber, *Bayocean,* 120; Webber, June 23, 2015.
92. In the Matter of Establishing, Regulations on the Use of the Bayocean Peninsula," Commissioners, Ordinance No. 42, signed January 30, 1991; Neal Lemery (Tillamook County District Attorney and council to county commissioners in the 1980s), e-mail to author, October 3, 2020; Jerry Sutherland, "Bayocean Lots in the Pacific Ocean," https://www.bayocean.net/ 2015/02/bayocean-lots-in-pacific-ocean.html.
93. Lemery, October 3, 2020; Ordinance No. 42, https://www.co.tillamook.or.us/sites/default/files/fileattachments/ordinance/22693/ordinance42-bayoceanpeninsula.pdf; "Tillamook County Recreation/Day Use Facilities," https://www.co.tillamook.or.us/gov/Parks/RecreationArea.htm.
94. Reeder and MacDonald, *Bayocean Memories Beneath the Sand*, 72-77; "In the Matter of Creating the Tillamook County Bayocean Task Force and Appointing Members," Order No. 02-40, Tillamook County Board of Commissioners, signed April 10, 2002; Tillamook County Board of Commissioners Minutes, May 5, 2003. County Surveyor Mike Rice confirmed the sign location to made sure it did not encroach on any privately-owned lots.
95. Jerry Sutherland, "Bayocean Eco-Park Rejected by Tillamook County Planning Commission," https://www.bayocean.net/2015/01/bayocean-eco-park-rejected.html; Brad Mosher, Commissioners move forward with plan to

rezone Bayocean Spit," *Tillamook Headlight-Herald*, April 10, 2015; "Bayocean Rezoning Approved by Tillamook County Planning Commission," https://www.bayocean. net/2015/ 08/bayocean-rezoning-to-be-considered-by.html.

96. Reeder and MacDonald, *Bayocean Memories Beneath the Sand*, 14-17; Sutherland, "Crabapple Park"; Sarah McDonald, e-mail to author, August 9, 2019. Though buried now, a phone I took and posted in the article shows the sidewalk, curb, and pavement soon after the Reeders uncovered them.

Acknowledgements

1. Jerry Sutherland, "Grant McOmie Captures the Bayocean Story," https://www.bayocean.net/2015/06/grant-mcomie-captures-bayocean-story.html.
2. Ken's "Research in the Land Entry Files of the General Land Office" is still available at https://www.archives.gov/files/publications/ref-info-papers/rip114.pdf.
3. Jerry Sutherland, "OPB on Bayocean," https://www.bayocean.net/2020/01/opb.html.
4. Lewis also authors articles for *Quartux: Journal of Critical Indigenous Anthropology* at https://ndnhistoryresearch.com.

BIBLIOGRAPHY

Abbott, Carl. *The Great Extravaganza: Portland and the Lewis and Clark Exposition.* Portland: Oregon Historical Society Press, 2004.

Allen, Elmer. *Allen: Memories of Childhood Days in Tillamook, Oregon Around the Turn of the Twentieth Century*. Edited by Mikayla Ebel. Tillamook: TCPM Publishing, 2018.

Baron, Heather M., Peter Ruggiero, Nathan J. Wood, Erica L. Harris, Jonathan Allan, Paul D. Komar, and Patrick Corcoran. "Incorporating Climate Change and Morphological Uncertainty into Coastal Change Hazard Assessments." *Natural Hazards* 75, no. 3 (2015): 2,081-2,102.

Barr, Sue (Bagley). "The Bagleys of Bayocean." 2019, https://drive.google.com/file/d/1LHlj5JDznCBGopqOCeUMM2ISz4UlDGmO/view.

Bishop, Eleanor C. *Prints in the Sand: The U.S. Coast Guard Beach Patrol in World War II.* Missoula: Pictorial Histories Pub. Co., 1989.

Clock, Paul Michael. *The Saga of Pacific Railway & Navigation Co.: Punk Rotten & Nasty.* Portland: Corbett Press, 2000.

Colmer, Montagu, and Charles Erskine Scott Wood. *History of the Bench and Bar of Oregon.* Portland: Historical Publishing Company, 1910.

Cooper, William Skinner. "Coastal Sand Dunes of Oregon and Washington." *Memoir 72.* New York: Geological Society of America, 1958.

Dicken, Samuel Newton, Carl L. Johanessen, and Bill Hanneson. *Some Recent Physical Changes of the Oregon Coast.* Eugene: Reprinted by *Eugene Register-Guard* and the Lane County Geographical Society, 1976.

Dobbs, Caroline C. *Men of Champoeg: A Record of the Lives of the Pioneers Who Founded the Oregon Government.* Portland: Metropolitan Press, 1932.

Emmons, Arthur B., II. *The Profession of Medicine: A Collection of Letters from Graduates of the Harvard Medical School.* Harvard Medical School, 1915.

Failing, Patricia. "Absalom Barrett Hallock (C. 1822-1892)." The Oregon Encyclopedia, https://oregonencyclopedia.org/articles/hallock_ absalom.

Fairhurst, Richenda. *Fishers Landing.* Charleston: Arcadia Pub., 2008.

Foden-Vencil, Kristian, and Jule Gilfillan. "Bayocean: The Lost Resort Town That Oregon Forgot." Oregon Public Broadcasting, January 16, 2020, https://www.opb.org/news/article/oregon-bayocean-ghost-town-resort-tillamook-bay.

Hawkins, William John. "Absalom B. Hallock. Architect, Engineer, Surveyor (1826-1892)." *Portland Friends of Cast-Iron Architecture Newsletter* 18 (1981).

Henshaw, James L. "Report on Construction of the Bayocean Breakwater, Tillamook Bay, Oregon." Portland, OR: Portland District, US Army Corps of Engineers, 1956.

Gilfillan, Jule. Oregon Field Guide Season 31, Episode 3. "The Lost City of Bayocean." Oregon Public Broadcasting, 29:40. January 16, 2020, https://www.pbs.org/video/season-31-episode-3-hpadgz.

Katz, Barbara A., and Stephen R. Gabriel. "Oregon's Ever-changing Coastline." Oregon State University Extension Marine Advisory Program SG 35. Revised November 1982.

Komar, Paul D. *The Pacific Northwest Coast: Living with the Shores of Oregon and Washington.* Durham, NC: Duke University Press, 1997.

———. *Physical Processes and Geologic Hazards on the Oregon Coast.* Newport, OR: Oregon Coastal Zone Management Association, 1979.

Komar, Paul D., and Thomas A. Terich. "Changes Due to Jetties at Tillamook Bay, Oregon." 15th Annual Coastal Engineering Conference, Honolulu, Hawaii, July 11-17, 1976.

Levesque, Paul. "History of Port Districts on Tillamook Bay, Oregon." 2010. https://www.bayocean.net/2015/06/paul-levesque.html.

Lizarraga-Arciniega, Jose Roman. "Shoreline Changes Due to Jetty Construction on the Oregon Coast." Master's Thesis. Oregon State University, 1975.

McArthur, Lewis A., and Lewis L. McArthur. *Oregon Geographic Names.* 7th ed. Portland: Oregon Historical Society Press, 2003.

McCamish, Brian. "Port of Tillamook Bay Railroad." http://www.brian894x4.com/POTBrailroad.html.

Mills, Dorthea Hahn. "Bayocean." *Oregon Coast Magazine*, Nov/Dec 1994: 40.

Minshall, William E. *Guide to Historical Markers of Tillamook County*. Wilsonville Lazerquick: Tillamook County Historical Society, 2004.

Moore, C. R. "Report on Beach Erosion Studies, Tillamook Bay, Oregon: With Reference to Bay Ocean." Portland: US Army Corps of Engineers, 1940.

Morrison, Scott, and Paul Morin. "History of State Highways in Oregon." Salem: RW Engineering Group for Oregon Department of Transportation, 2017.

Meyer Brothers Druggist 26, no. 1, (1905).

Oregon Secretary of State. "Oregon Legislators and Staff Guide." http://sos.oregon.gov.

Oregon State University. *Annual Calendar and Catalogue of the State Agricultural College of Oregon.* 1888–1892.

Osmond, Gary. "Portland's 'Aquatic Pied Pinter'." *Oregon Historical Quarterly* 123, no. 2 (2022): 170-193.

"Paranoid Reactions." In *International Encyclopedia of the Social Sciences*, 2020.

"Railroad History of Portland, Or." Pacific Railroad Preservation Assoc., http://www.sps700.org/gallery/essays/portlandrailroadhistory.shtml

Reeder, Perry C., Jr., and Sarah (Reeder) MacDonald. *Bayocean Memories Beneath the Sand.* San Bernadino, CA: Xlibris, 2017.

Ruff, Lloyd L, Jr. "Preliminary Notes on the Geology of Bayocean Peninsula." Portland, OR: Army Corps of Engineers, 1939.

Spaniol, Ruth Currin. "Over the Die-or-Do: A Story of a Marriage." 1992.

"Station Tillamook Bay." US Coast Guard, https://www.pacificarea. uscg. mil/Portals/8/District_13/lib/doc/factsheet/station_tillamook_bay.pdf.

Sutherland, Jerry. Bayocean, Oregon: The Resort Town Destroyed by the Sea. www.bayocean.net.

Taylor, Joseph E. III. *Persistent Callings.* Corvallis: Oregon State University Press, 2019.

Terich, Thomas Anthony. "Bayocean Spit, Tillamook, Oregon; Early Economic Development and Erosion History." Doctoral Dissertation. Oregon State University, 1973.

"Tillamook Bay, Oregon." Vicksburg, MS: Committee on Tidal Hydraulics, U. S. Army Corps of Engineers, 1970.

Timmen, Fritz. *Blow for the Landing; A Hundred Years of Steam Navigation on the Waters of the West.* Caldwell, Idaho: Caxton Printers, 1973.

Toy, Eckard V., Jr. "The Ku Klux Klan in Tillamook, Oregon." *The Pacific Northwest Quarterly* 53, no. 2 (1962): 60-64.

Trimmer, Brian James. "Defenders of the West: The History of Naval Air Station Tillamook." Pepperdine University, 1997.

US Army Corps of Engineers. "Extension of Tillamook South Jetty, Tillamook Bay, Oregon: Final Environmental Impact Statement." Portland District, 1978.

US Department of Commerce. "Seagoing Vessels of the United States, Part VI." Washington, DC, 1924.

———. "Forty-Third Annual List of Merchant Vessels of the United States, with Official Numbers and Signal Letters, and Lists of Vessels Belonging to the United States Government, with Distinguishing Signals, for the Year Ended June 30, 1911." Washington, DC, 1911.

Ward, Donald L. "Case Histories of Corps Breakwater and Jetty Structures." Coastal Engineering Research Center: Report 6. North Pacific Division, US Army Corps of Engineers, 1988.

Webber, Bert, and Margie. *Bayocean: The Oregon Town That Fell into the Sea.* Medford, OR: Webb Research Group, 1989.

———. *Maimed by the Sea: Erosion Along the Coasts of Oregon & Washington.* Fairfield, WA: Ye Galleon Press, 1983.

Wells, Gail. *The Tillamook: A Created Forest Comes of Age.* Corvallis: Oregon State University Press, 2003.

INDEX

Pages emboldened, including those at either end of a range, contain images related to the subject. Endnote pages are followed by *n* and the applicable number. Two given names following a single surname are married unless noted otherwise. All uncapitalized facilities, locations, and services were on Bayocean. Only the beginning and the ending of Potter-Chapin Realty Company and T. B. Potter Realty Company of Oregon are indexed because they dominate the early chapters.

INDEX

INDEX

INDEX

www.ingramcontent.com/pod-product-compliance
Lightning Source LLC
Chambersburg PA
CBHW071143130626
46553CB00004B/1507

* 9 7 9 8 9 8 7 3 4 6 3 0 3 *